AGAINST ALL ODDS. Copyright © 1993 by Yukiyasu Togo. All rights reserved.
Printed in the United States of America. No part of this book may be used or
reproduced in any manner whatsoever without written permission except in the case
of brief quotations embodied in critical articles or reviews. For information, address
St. Martin's Press, 175 Fifth Avenue, New York, N.Y. 10010.

Design by Michael Mendelsohn of MM Design 2000, Inc.

Library of Congress Cataloging-in-Publication Data

Togo, Yukiyasu
    Against all odds : the story of the Toyota Motor Corporation and
the family that created it / Yukiyasu Togo and William Wartman.
        p.   cm.
    ISBN 0-312-09733-6
    1. Toyota Jidosha Kogyo Kabushiki Kaisha—History. 2. Automobile
industry and trade—Japan—History. I. Wartman, William.
II. Title.
HD9710.J34T6738   1993
338.7'6292'0952—dc20

First Edition: November 1993

10 9 8 7 6 5 4 3 2 1

AGAINST
ALL
ODDS

**THE STORY OF THE TOYOTA MOTOR
CORPORATION AND THE FAMILY
THAT CREATED IT**

YUKIYASU TOGO
AND
WILLIAM WARTMAN

ST. MARTIN'S PRESS
New York

CONTENTS

PROLOGUE

Eiji Toyoda barely heard the proposal when it was first put on the table. He was presiding over a critical board meeting of the Toyota Motor Corporation in Japan, but his thoughts were five thousand miles away. It was December of 1983, and the company Eiji headed was trying to conclude tedious negotiations with the United Automobile Workers of America (UAW). Toyota, under heavy political pressure to begin assembling cars in the United States, was scheduled to open a joint-venture plant with General Motors in Fremont, California, in twelve months. At the moment, however, many labor issues were still unresolved.

What troubled Eiji most was the stubbornness of some UAW members. Toyota's renowned production system had catapulted the company from bankruptcy to record profits in three decades, while American auto manufacturers had lost market share and respect. Yet the UAW, with 28 percent of its membership unemployed, was resisting the installation of this highly efficient production system at the Fremont site, and Eiji couldn't understand why.

Toyota, the automobile company founded by Eiji's cousin, Kiichiro, prized efficiency above everything, and that was reflected in its history and products. Kiichiro's father, Sakichi, had earned the capital to enter the automobile business by improving the efficiency of Japanese looms at the turn of the century. Sakichi was the son of a humble farming family—the name Toyoda means "abundant rice fields"—and his values were imprinted on the company. Toyota had survived after the war by never wasting anything. Now it produced cars more economically than any other manufacturer in the world, and its careful attention to quality ensured that those cars were nearly defect free.

It was well enough, Eiji thought, for the Americans, with their boundless land and wealth, to be profligate. But he would not be part of any enterprise that had the wasteful Western mass-production system at its heart. Eiji was distressed by the lack of respect that traditional values received these days, and all the more so because this outlook was beginning to appear in Japan.

Toyota had been the top auto manufacturer in Japan for years. But because it was located in the country's industrial midlands and its cars were seldom flamboyant, it was thought to be stodgy. Nissan almost always sold fewer cars, but it was headquartered in cosmopolitan Tokyo, so it was held to be innovative. Nissan for technology, the Japanese saying went, but Toyota for sales.

Eiji Toyoda had gotten so tired of hearing those words that, several years earlier, he had ordered his engineers to develop a line of the most advanced engines in Japan. When cars with those engines were introduced amid a sweeping advertising campaign, Toyota's sales climbed to almost 50 percent of the Japanese market. What fascinated Eiji most was that even the sales of models with the old-design engines increased.

Eiji knew perceptions were as important as reality, and he was confident the misperceptions the UAW members had about Toyota's production system would vanish once they were exposed to it. Or, given the state of the negotiations, *if* they were ever exposed to it. As Eiji broke his musings and looked up, he was startled to discover his colleagues talking heatedly about the United States.

The board was discussing the car that was to succeed the Cressida, Toyota's top model in the American market in 1983. The director of the product planning section was arguing that, rather than just doing a facelift on the Cressida, Toyota should create a new and more opulent luxury car. He wanted a car that was truly luxurious, so Toyota's customers wouldn't leave the company as they became more affluent.

The proposal created a ripple of murmurs around the room, as company executives fell into debate. Japanese corporations are governed equally by philosophies and bylaws, and this was especially true at Toyota. The third of Toyota's five guiding precepts was "Be practical and avoid frivolity," and the luxury-car proposal stood in stark opposition to it. A number of Toyota executives argued that the company had been created to make honest cars for working people, not to serve the rich.

But as the debate raged, Eiji quietly reminded himself that the world was indeed changing, and perhaps it was time for Toyota to change with it. The company's near-obsession with total quality control had produced cars that represented tremendous value, yet it was still thought of as a maker of inexpensive, rather than great, automobiles. It was the European luxury-car manufacturers who were said to be prestigious, yet Eiji believed that component for component, Toyota's engineering was their equal.

Eiji knew Toyota's staff in America had been pleading for just such an upscale car for several years. They talked endlessly about the baby boom moving toward middle age. The thirty-something set was settling down, raising families, and approaching their peak earning years. But they were doing all of these predictable things with their own idiosyncratic style. American newspaper feature sections were replete with stories about the new breed of consumer, the yuppie. They were young, affluent people who had the best and who enjoyed displaying that through their purchases.

With the largest demographic group in the United States approaching prosperity, Toyota had no upscale cars to sell them. To make matters worse, it wasn't only immediate sales that would be lost. Car buyers were often surprisingly brand loyal. Once motorists bought from a different manufacturer, they often didn't return.

New-model development had gotten bogged down at Toyota in the late 1970s, when the company was distracted by the need to bring its cars into compliance with Japan's stringent emission control laws. Since then, the U.S. market had gotten the front-wheel-drive subcompact Tercel, the sporty Supra, and a large compact called the Camry. But at the top of the line there was only the Cressida, and while it was a good car, it wasn't the first vehicle the American staff thought of when they heard the word *cachet*.

The Cressida was a successful upmarket car in Japan, and that was its greatest liability in the States. Japan contained half the population of the United States in a land mass the size of California, and cars bigger than compact-sized were taxed at 23 percent of their wholesale price. Japanese luxury cars were small vehicles with lavish appointments, designed for the muted tastes of the older people who could afford them. Age is respected in Japan, and wealthy younger buyers would purchase cars intended for the tastes of their elders. But in America, everybody wanted to be young, and it was the rare younger person who would buy a grandfather's car.

Most luxury cars in Japan were driven by personal or corporate chauffeurs, and the vehicles' focal point was the left rear seat. The cars were designed to give a pleasant ride to the passengers, and the driving experience was not of concern. Some cars even had a hole in the back of the usually unoccupied front passenger's seat so that the owner in the rear seat could stick his feet through and stretch out.

Toyota's American staff had only to look at BMW's strong U.S. sales to know that many Americans, and particularly young ones, bought luxury cars for the driving experience. BMW's advertising slogan was "The ultimate driving machine," but all upmarket European cars were known for their performance and handling. Even Cadillacs and Lincolns, which were disdained by car enthusiasts for their wallowing ride characteristics, always had a massive V-8 that could tip the driver back into the velour front seat under hard acceleration.

The American staff was forecasting continued modest sales for the Cressida in the United States, but what they really wanted was a car designed specifically for their market—something Toyota had never produced before. They didn't know whether their dealers could sell more than twenty to thirty thousand copies a year of a car with a 1984 price of twenty thousand dollars. But they wanted to try. It wasn't a lot of volume, yet they hoped Toyota would build the car to get its foot in the door at a critical time. The luxury-car market was expected to approach 1.5 million vehicles annually by 1995, and there was unprecedented opportunity in that segment at the moment.

Most Americans who bought domestic luxury cars were over fifty-five, and their future new-car purchases were limited. Yet Ford and General Motors were selling a lot of high-profit vehicles to these people, and the auto makers couldn't alienate them by slanting their products toward younger buyers. It takes strong customer loyalty to survive in the automobile business, and the cost of winning conquest sales far exceeded the price of keeping current owners loyal. Given their customer base—and past business strategies—Ford and GM were unlikely to produce a radically new luxury vehicle until after they began losing market share to a competitor.

This approach had left the younger—and the more sophisticated older—luxury-car buyers to the Europeans. In 1984, the Europeans sold 412,000 upmarket cars in the United States, or 4 percent of the total market. The most profitable of those sales were made by BMW and Mercedes, whose cars offered prestige as well as quality—but not a lot of American-style creature comforts. The cars were admired and selling well, but they were becoming very expensive.

Wage and benefit costs in German auto factories were the highest in the world, while productivity was exceptionally low. The Germans, who essentially competed only against themselves, responded with frequent prices increases. Soon, the bulk of their models would pass the forty-thousand-dollar threshold. The manufacturers believed that discerning, affluent buyers would pay any price for a car with German engineering. But many people in the automobile business thought that Mercedes-Benz and BMW were leaving themselves astoundingly vulnerable in this, the most lucrative market segment in the industry.

Eiji Toyoda was thinking about the difficulties and opportunities the luxury-car project would present as his colleagues on the board continued their discussions. Eiji had been heartened by Toyota's recent success with the new engines, and although he was seventy years old, the daunting challenge of launching a luxury car in the autumn of his career excited him. He relished the idea of taking on the best in the world at their own game, and then seeing what the critics had to say. He was certain of one thing. If Toyota were to move on the project, it would not fail from lack of trying.

Eiji allowed the deliberations to continue for a time, then guided the group to a consensus. Eiji said he wanted to demonstrate Toyota's engineering prowess to the world by creating a new category of automobile—a Japanese luxury car built to international standards. The board, with Eiji's encouragement, endorsed the formation of a luxury-car project team as the first phase of the undertaking. In that moment, Toyota initiated a venture fraught with enormous risk.

It was an uncharacteristically daring move by the conservative company. A resounding success could reshape Toyota's image overnight. But if Toyota were to boldly announce its intentions and then produce the next Edsel, it would be the laughingstock of the automotive world. There could be tremendous financial repercussions for the multinational Toyota franchise—and incalculable loss of face for the Toyoda family in Japan.

John Koenig was unaware that planners at Toyota's headquarters had already begun the earliest stages of the luxury-car project when he flew to Japan in September of 1984. This was a high-jeopardy, long-term project that had to have the utmost security, lest a competitor learn of it and gain an edge, and the project had not yet been disclosed to the American staff.

Koenig was the head of Toyota's product-planning department in the United States, and he was making the trip to Japan on this occasion as the point man for the U.S. staff. Koenig, a member of the front edge of the baby boom himself, was going to make a formal pitch for a luxury car for the American market, and he was nervous. He was convinced, intuitively, that the market was there for this car, that Toyota could build it, and that his dealers could sell it. But he wasn't overly confident of winning approval. Most of all, he, like all of Toyota's American employees who traveled to Japan to make proposals, wasn't looking forward to the dreaded "five why's."

The "five why's" were Toyota's method for reducing all problems to their most elementary form in order to ensure that a worker truly understood the root cause of a situation, and wasn't being misled by surface symptoms of a more basic difficulty. Like a Zen master leading a student through a series of *koans*, or questions, in search of enlightenment, the supervisor encouraged the worker to discover the answer within himself, rather than rely on an external authority.

After he made his presentation to Toyota executives, Koenig, having done ample preparation, moved easily through his questioning. Why, he was asked, did he think the car he was proposing would sell in the United States?

Koenig explained about the advancing age and income level of the baby boomers.

Why did he think the automotive needs of this group wouldn't be served by cars already on the market?

Koenig described how young buyers didn't like domestic luxury cars, and how the Germans seemed to be pricing themselves out of the reach of many buyers.

Why did he think Toyota should be interested in this market?

Koenig talked about Toyota's orientation towards producing high-quality products, which luxury buyers appreciated.

Why did he think a Japanese manufacturer should follow this path?

Koenig recounted how Japanese camera and electronics manufacturers had successfully made the transition from producing inexpensive goods to making top-of-the-line products.

And why did he think there were similarities between the experiences of camera makers and automobile companies?

Koenig discussed how members of the baby boom, unlike their parents, had grown up surrounded by imported products and often believed them to be superior to domestic goods.

Just as he was ready to breathe a sigh of relief and sit down, Koenig was hit with a sixth question—an unanswerable "how."

How could he be certain U.S. consumers would be willing to spend so much money on a Japanese luxury car—no example of which existed in the American market—even though market research showed that vehicle prestige was the prime attribute required of cars in this category?

Koenig was forced to admit that he, like everyone else in the room, could offer no such reassurance. This was the great unknown—and unknowable—of a project that could cost the company a billion dollars. Consumers worldwide had demonstrated their willingness to purchase inexpensive, fuel-efficient, high-quality Japanese automobiles to drive to work or to the mall. But, would the requisite number of American doctors and dentists and lawyers risk social ostracism by driving an *expensive* Japanese car down the long, sweeping driveways of their country clubs, hop out and, tempting painfully blank stares, brag to their foursome on the first tee about the great new Japanese luxury car they had just purchased?

Shoji Jimbo, the chief engineer of the project team, who had carefully scrutinized Koenig's presentation, nodded for him to sit down. Jimbo didn't volunteer that a project team had been formed for a luxury car, nor did he offer any encouragement. Koenig left Japan as uncertain about the project as when he had arrived.

Koenig didn't hear much more until, in the spring of 1985, he learned the American office would be receiving twenty visitors from Japan. They were the top engineers and designers from headquarters staff who had been assigned to the luxury-car venture. They would be coming to the United States for an extended stay to perform the most vital task of the entire project.

They wouldn't be doing engineering studies or testing prototypes. Instead, they would be spending weeks eating, drinking, working, and sleeping amid the sumptuous, yet distinctly alien, world of upper-middle-class America. If they met their objectives, the Japanese visitors would leave knowing more about the lives and desires of their potential customers than the customers did themselves.

1
THE
CHALLENGE

When Commodore Matthew Perry sailed into Uraga Channel, near the mouth of Tokyo Bay, in July of 1853, his stated purpose was deceptively simple. He was there to deliver a letter from U.S. President Millard Fillmore to the Emperor of Japan, one requesting that Japan open its ports to trade with the United States. Although this was ostensibly a friendly mission, Perry understood that he was transporting a document the Japanese were not eager to receive.

Japanese law prohibited foreigners from entering Japan—let alone from engaging in trade there—and trespassers had been beheaded. So Perry had come equipped to change the minds of the Japanese. His entourage included 4 iron ships, 967 men, and 61 large-caliber guns. Perry's charge was defined, and his resolve was firm. Despite any contingency, Perry had promised his president, Japan would be opened.

As Perry's massive black ships moved into the channel, he ordered his men to discharge the ships' guns, blasting the rust from their barrels while also displaying their might. The ships were anchored, and Perry told his crew to stand fast and prepare for combat, while watching for signs of an impending Japanese assault. When no gunfire was heard from shore, Perry retired to his cabin to implement the next stage of his strategy. He would wait.

Perry knew his expedition was occurring at a critical time in U.S. history. The major Western nations were at the peak of their imperialistic ventures into Asia, and the United States had ambitions to become a world power. The United States had doubled its land holdings with its victory over Mexico in 1848, and expansion into the Pacific was considered its Manifest Destiny. But first, the United States had to become a more formidable force on the seas.

Less than a century after the Revolutionary War, the American navy was only the fifth largest in the world, but American commercial shipping was challenging the British for domination of foreign trade. China was one of the most important, albeit distant, trading markets in the world, and American financiers wanted to control it. They had invested huge sums of money in a weapon they believed would allow them to capture the bulk of the China trade—steamships.

There was one impediment blocking the United States from surpassing Britain in the battle for the China trade. Steamships required coal, and a ship that carried a sufficient supply of it to reach the Asian mainland from the United States had to sacrifice precious cargo space. The Americans needed a Japanese port as an intermediary refueling stop on the way to China, and the U.S. government had decided that that port would be obtained by force if necessary.

Perry was the man who had been sent to institute this policy, and now the commodore rested in his stateroom as his ship bobbed in the water off the coast of Japan. Perry was giving the Japanese time to peer out at the alien black ships that had violated their territorial waters. Perry had ordered the ships' boilers kept at full steam to be prepared for rapid movement, but he doubted that would be required. The Japanese had never seen steam-powered iron ships before, and it was Perry's bet they would be terrified.

Japanese sailors on junks in Uraga Channel stared in horror as they saw the arresting black ships entering their waterway. The vessels were moving briskly, pushing dense plumes of smoke into the morning sky. The Japanese were puzzled that the ships moved without sails, and they imagined the smoke meant the ships were afire. The one thing they were certain of was the harrowing truth. The ships contained foreigners, whom the Japanese took to be the devil incarnate. The sailors hurried to shore to sound a dire warning.

The villagers near the naval station were the first to learn of the arrival of the barbarians, but word spread rapidly from town to town. People ran through the streets in confusion. Local officials pushed through the crowds in the streets, ordering people to go about their business and forbidding them to discuss the ships. The shogun government exercised firm control over the Japanese people, keeping records on everything from family membership and land holdings to the types of livestock raised and crops cultivated. Until recently, they had maintained checkpoints on major highways to monitor the comings and goings of the population.

As the people in the coastal towns scrambled for cover, they could only hope that, yet again, the gods would protect their blessed land. Over the course of their two-thousand-year history, the Japanese had come to believe that theirs was a divine nation. Native legend held that the sun rose on Japan and that the primordial energy of the world originated there.

Only twenty-five years before Perry's arrival, a Japanese scholar had written, "Ours is a splendid and blessed country, the Land of the Gods beyond doubt, and we down to the most humble man and woman are the descendants of gods. Japanese differ completely from and are superior to the peoples of China, India, Russia, Holland, Siam, Cambodia and all other countries in the world, and for us to have called our country the Land of the Gods was not mere vain-glory."

The Japanese had only to look at their fabled history to be reinforced in this belief. The first Western account of this fanciful land was written by Marco Polo, who contributed heavily to the mythology about Japan after his thirteenth-century visit. Japan, Polo reported, was the new Eden, "far out to sea to the eastward, some fifteen hundred miles from the mainland. The people are fair-complexioned, good-looking, and well-mannered. They are idolaters, wholly independent and exercising no authority over any nation but themselves. They have gold in great abundance, because it is found there in measurable quantities."

Word of Japan's fictitious mountains of gold soon had plunderers at its shores. The first was Kublai Kahn, who came to make Japan a vassal state of the vast Mongolian empire in 1274. The shogun government of Japan refused to subjugate itself to Kublai, and Kublai sent an army of nine hundred ships and twenty-five thousand soldiers to enforce his will.

The war-hardened Mongols battered the small Japanese army during their first day of engagement, then returned to their ships to prepare for the next day's battle. The defeat and enslavement of the Japanese was a foregone conclusion. The people of Japan could only huddle in their homes and await the inevitable, while the Mongols recuperated in what they had every reason to believe was a safe harbor.

But then, as if by magic or divine intervention, a massive storm swept the coast of Japan during the night. The wind howled and the seas swelled, tossing the ships about in uncontrolled fury. By light of morning, the Japanese discovered that hundreds of ships had been sunk or destroyed by the storm and that the Mongolian army was in ruins. Stunned by the swift and unfathomable nature of their losses, the surviving Mongols retreated.

The lore of limitless gold remained palpable, however, and Kublai Khan returned in 1280 with a force that was increased fivefold—4,500 ships and 140,000 soldiers. Again the Mongols battered the Japanese army for a day and returned to their ships to rest. The Japanese emperor prayed to the sun goddess that evening to spare his country. This time an even larger storm appeared during the night to pound the ships.

In the morning, with the sea calm and the sky showing no threat of another storm, the Japanese discovered that 80 percent of the Mongolian military force had been destroyed. The surviving Mongols raised their sails in flight, never to attempt another invasion of Japan.

Having had nature twice repel a nation hundreds of times its size, the Japanese drew a single conclusion. Japan was indeed a hallowed nation that, although encircled by brutes, was under the express protection of divine forces. When Commodore Perry brought another squad of huns to their shores five and a half centuries later, the Japanese trusted that a storm would drive his ships to the bottom of the sea as well.

The officers of the Japanese military forces, however, were not so naive. At the first report of Perry's ships, they had dispatched a messenger boat to the national capital at Tokyo, then called Edo. Then they launched a squad of sailors in rowboats to confront the invaders in the strait. Their small boats were quick and nimble, but they looked minuscule as they approached Perry's sleek ships.

The Japanese attempted to tie lines to the American ships and to climb the ships' anchor chains, but they were rebuffed. Finally, a boat commander called out to an interpreter on Perry's flagship: What was their country of origin and purpose? Did they realize they were violating Japanese territorial waters and laws?

A Japanese officer was permitted to board the flagship, but the Americans held to their plan. They said that Perry intended to deliver a letter to the emperor. The Japanese officer declared this quite impossible. He insisted Japan was closed to foreigners, saying that any message they wished to deliver could be accepted only at Nagasaki.

The Americans knew all about Nagasaki, a city in Japan's southwest that was far from Tokyo. It was the outside world's keyhole on Japan. Japan was sorely lacking in natural resources, and some foreign trade was required. But it was limited to the Dutch and the Chinese and was restricted to Nagasaki. The shogun's troops reacted fiercely whenever Westerners broached their shores elsewhere, and adventurers, missionaries, or shipwrecked sailors who arrived were imprisoned or killed to prevent them from infecting the native population with foreign notions. Japan wrapped itself in the hermetic seal of a feudal island nation.

The urgency the Japanese felt about their isolationism only increased in the late 1830s when reports of the Opium War in China filtered into Japan through Nagasaki. The British fondness for Chinese tea had led to a trade imbalance between the two nations, and the British had responded by exporting opium to China. In short order, even government officials and military men became addicted, and Chinese society began to decay.

China banned the drug to halt this decline, but the British dispatched their troops to China, invading and occupying portions of the border. The Chinese were defeated quickly by the sophisticated British forces. The British compelled the Chinese to repeal the opium ban and then resumed supplying opium to Chinese citizens. For an extra measure of reparation, the British claimed Hong Kong Island as a new colony of the British Empire.

The seizure of Hong Kong Island was taken in Japan as yet more evidence of the essentially barbarous nature of the Western soul. Just as the shogun had always known in his heart, the Westerners claimed to seek trade, but occupation and conquest was their ultimate goal. The Westerners had to be kept from Japan, he resolved, or Japan would be colonized.

The weight of this history intensified the insistence of the Japanese guard-boat commander as he stood on the deck of Perry's flagship. He repeated the immutable policy of Japan: Any interchange with foreigners must take place through Nagasaki.

No, Perry's representative insisted, while escorting the Japanese officer from the ship, they would not go to Nagasaki. They would stay right where they were until arrangements were made for delivery of the letter to the emperor—or until their patience ran out and they unleashed their guns.

*   *   *

While the peasants in the coastal town near Perry's anchorage were shocked by his arrival, the leaders of the shogun's government, called the Bakufu, were not. The Dutch had warned the Japanese about the impending American voyage far in advance of Perry's arrival, even specifying the number of vessels Perry would command and their armaments.

Most members of the Bakufu had chosen either to dismiss the warning as false or to discount its implications for Japan. Bakufu officers were the most elite and sequestered people in Japan, and many of them continued to hold that the country was unassailable. Those few who believed Japan needed to strengthen its defenses against invasion were left to their own devices and given only meager resources.

The Bakufu had brought Japan its first period of internal peace in the modern era, ending centuries of internecine warfare among regional samurai and their subjects. The samurai of the Tokugawa family had united the country and formed a highly organized and sophisticated government. The country's capital, Tokyo, had grown to encompass a population of one million, making it the largest city in the world. By the time of Perry's arrival in 1853, however, the Bakufu had degenerated into a vast and swollen bureaucracy.

Corruption was widespread, famine and rebellion were becoming commonplace among the peasants, and the lesser samurai were lost in self-indulgence. The government was constantly on the verge of bankruptcy and that, in turn, had left Japan nearly defenseless. It had only ancient cannons to pit against modern, high-powered Western guns, and its coastal forts, the last line of defense against an invasion, were constructed out of clay. It was the military of a nation that, adrift in mythology and isolation, was an anachronism in the middle of the nineteenth century.

Confronted by Perry, Bakufu officials knew that military resistance would be suicidal. Instead, they tried to concoct a bluff that would send Perry away. They sent word to Perry that a representative would accept his letter, but the Japanese would reply only through Nagasaki. When Perry rejected this plan, the officials proposed that the Americans take part of the trade going to the Dutch, but at some unspecified time in the future. After each refusal, Perry raised the stakes by sending ships from his flotilla on exploratory missions that took them ever closer to Tokyo. Finally, there was no alternative for the Japanese but to make concessions.

Perry delivered his letter to a representative of the Japanese government during a reception held on July 14, 1853, seven days after he had arrived. Although Perry yielded on a number of points—it was not the emperor who received the document—Perry knew victory was his. He informed the Japanese that the materials he was leaving included a treaty agreement that required the emperor's signature. Perry said he would return in the spring, with an even larger fleet, to retrieve the endorsed agreements.

It was a momentous occasion for Japan when Perry's ships steamed out of Uraga Channel on July 17. The barbarians from the outer lands had not had their ships destroyed by a storm of mystical origins, but neither had the Americans made any attempt to occupy Japanese territory. To the Japanese, everything seemed as it had been before Perry's arrival. Yet nothing was.

Confidence in the Bakufu government continued its fatal slide. The Bakufu had controlled every aspect of feudal life in Japan, but the coming of foreign trade ripped the economy from their control. Merchants in large trading ports began to acquire wealth, and the entire Japanese economy became subject to the vagaries of world markets. Fits of inflation hit, and the peasants in the rural villages became progressively poorer. The social classes became more stratified, and peasant uprisings became more frequent. Finally, the Tokugawa shogun was forced from power in 1867.

A new government, called Meiji, was formed. The emperor, who had been a figurehead under the shoguns, was restored to godlike status. A new hierarchy was created, one giving great power to civilian government ministries while diminishing the role of the samurai. Although these were changes that Perry had neither anticipated nor sought, he precipitated all of them. Perry would never live to see it, but his intrusion into Japanese life would change Japan forever.

Ikichi Toyoda's first son, Sakichi, was born on the cusp of two worlds, on February 14, 1867. It was eight months before the start of the Meiji Restoration, but a decade before the full aftershock of that change reached the remote feudal village where the Toyoda family lived. The farming town of Yamaguchi was only several hundred miles from Tokyo, but it was a universe removed from the radical transformation of Japanese society that was unfolding in the capital.

Ikichi Toyoda lived on the same land his family had occupied for generations. It was a small plot situated in a narrow ravine and enclosed on three sides by small mountains and towering bamboo groves. Ikichi had built his family a simple six-room house on that site. It faced west, so the sun came in during the late afternoons, except during the winter when it was dark and cold inside. The only warmth available was whatever heat radiated from a small stove. In the rainy season each spring, the land around the house became saturated with water, and thousands of mosquitoes incubated in the bamboo groves. At the first hint of summer, they would fill the air.

Ikichi and his neighbors were closely attuned to these rhythms of the seasons, for their survival depended upon carefully monitoring them. Rural Japan was agrarian, with little industrialization, and each village was a world unto itself. The villagers had to provide for their own sustenance or their families starved. In this constant battle for survival, the elements in Japan usually worked against the villagers.

Japan has a mountainous landscape and a capricious climate that is ill-suited for agriculture. Nonetheless, 85 percent of the population produced crops in the third quarter of the nineteenth century. The bulk of the nourishment in the Japanese diet was derived from rice, but in contrast to more southern countries in Asia, where rice could be planted three times a year, rice could be cultivated in Japan only once annually. The seedlings had to be planted in the fields around each house before the rainy season in early summer, and the rice harvested before the typhoons in the fall, or the staple crop would be lost for the year.

The Toyodas and their neighbors labored assiduously at the same tasks, and all came to understand that they were united in a communal struggle for subsistence. Careful planning, discipline, frugality, and cooperation were givens in life. Extravagance was unthinkable, as the future was always uncertain. People joined in the thatching of one anothers' roofs, they consoled each other after a death, and they completed their own planting and harvesting quickly, for they were obliged to aid their neighbors in their farming tasks. Strict customs regulated the flow of irrigation water to insure that no one prospered at the expense of his neighbors.

Families lived on the same plot of land, which they often leased from feudal landlords, for hundreds of years, passing on their small parcels from generation to generation. But as the families grew, they had to cultivate new land to increase their acreage. They persistently cut away at the mountains, irrigating the land and creating new rice paddies and fields. Where they couldn't flatten the mountains, they built terraces and plowed to the tops of the hills.

Like all of his neighbors, Ikichi Toyoda provided his new son, Sakichi, with a home whose organization mirrored that of the town of Yamaguchi. The house was as austere as the Japanese landscape and as communal as the farmers who labored in its fields. The basic family group Sakichi was born to was the *ie*, or household. It encompassed the extended family and their ancestral home, with multiple generations often sharing the same shelter.

Each *ie* was headed by the *kacho*, or eldest male, to whom the national constitution granted the final word on all matters of familial importance. No property could change hands, and no family member could be married, without his approval. The powerful rights of the *kacho* were customarily passed on to the eldest son. It was the essential duty of the *kacho* to rear his first son to be strong and righteous, so that the son could lead the *ie* into the next generation with prosperity and security.

So it was that when Sakichi Toyoda was born, the heavy responsibilities of the first son passed to him. The fortunes of each family's eldest son were clearly defined by centuries of unimpeachable tradition. A first son was meant to carry forward the work of his father. Social mobility was limited, and no son had any expectation of rising above his father's rank. A son was compelled to do the best job possible at whatever it was that he had been born to.

After Sakichi completed elementary school, he began his apprenticeship. He found himself, at the age of eleven, heading out of the house with the dawn each morning, carrying his father's toolbox and learning his father's trade. He was becoming a carpenter.

Ikichi Toyoda was a stubborn, temperamental man, and the obligations of his role as *kacho* dictated firmness in his dealings with his first son. In addition, under the Confucian traditions of Japan, a father expected unquestioned respect from his children. Unfortunately, Ikichi's oldest son was not a model apprentice as a carpenter. Sakichi had little interest in carpentry, and he was given to daydreaming and distractedness while working. Ikichi did not respond well to his son's listlessness. He frequently grew impatient with Sakichi, hollering and telling him to pay more attention to his work. Sakichi would answer with a grunt and a short burst of attentiveness.

Under normal circumstances, it would be expected that a young boy like Sakichi would overcome his impetuousness and meld himself to the desires of his *kacho*, his *ie*, and his community. There was an inevitability to village life that ultimately fostered conformity. Sakichi only had to walk to the edge of the ravine where his father had built the Toyoda house and peer out. His entire world was within the range of his vision.

There was no concept that a person's life was his own in Yama-guchi. Rather, there was only obligation and the flow of history that passed through the village with two thousand years of force. The Jap-anese language didn't have a word to describe the pursuit of individual goals in opposition to the wishes of a larger group. People who refused to adjust were regarded as outcasts, and, in severe cases, they would be isolated and shunned by their neighbors.

Sakichi's distractedness was partially a product of his nature. But another component of it was the changes that were being imposed on Yamaguchi. While Ikichi Toyoda and his contemporaries fervently em-braced their regimented lives, members of the younger generation were being told that village life had to be transformed in Japan. The new Meiji government was instituting radical changes that were altering the very foundations and traditions of Japanese society.

After the opening of Japan to foreign trade, the government had sent representatives abroad to assess Japan's development relative to Western nations. The reports these men delivered upon their return were far grimmer than anyone had expected. Japanese military men who visited France and Prussia found modern national armies, while the Jap-anese had only small regional armies that were remnants of the shogun era. Officials who studied Western economies witnessed the industrial revolution in full bloom; in contrast, the bulk of the Japanese economy was composed of agriculture and cottage industries.

The leaders of the Meiji government concluded that if Japan was to retain its sovereignty, it had to become a modern nation. They re-solved to adapt whatever Western technology and institutions were necessary to transform the Land of the Gods into a rich and powerful country like those in the West. The first and most fundamental change they enacted was the creation of a highly centralized bureaucratic re-gime to replace the far-flung lords and aristocrats of the shogun's gov-ernment. Hundreds of regional lords, called *daimyo*, had played a critical role in ending internal warfare in Japan, but their relative autonomy was now an obstacle to the unification effort that would be required to bring Japan into a new era.

In 1871, the Meiji government abolished the domains of the *daimyo* and disbanded their regional armies, replacing them with a system of prefectures that were ruled from Tokyo. A national army was created and then staffed by conscription, while elementary-school education was made compulsory. To unite the country behind the national government, school texts stressed that the Japanese people were like a great family, extending from the father figure of the emperor down to the common man. Citizens were still seen as having obligations to their neighbors, but now everyone had a larger responsibility to sacrifice for the national good.

The conservative people of the villages were resentful of these changes, for they had a profound effect on daily life. The size of the family work force shrank when children were taken out of the fields to attend school or serve in the army. The familiar lunar calendar and its corresponding holidays, which had been observed for centuries, were summarily abandoned and replaced by the Western solar calendar. Then, in 1873, the government enacted a new land tax that was based on the value of a plot rather than the size of its harvest, and the tax was payable in money instead of rice. Villagers now had a fixed expense that failed to allow for the elements and the havoc they could wreak on rice paddies.

As village people watched local control disappear from government, they also found that Meiji officials seemed to be dismantling their culture. A wholesale endorsement of foreign practices was underway, with people in the cities embracing them as though they were emblematic of a higher form of life. Western clothing, food, fashions, and architecture began pouring into the country. A Tokyo office was established to translate and distribute Western books. And a Japanese book that provided encyclopedic descriptions of Western life, from table manners to medical care, sold over 150,000 copies.

But most insidiously, the people of Yamaguchi also saw their livelihoods being threatened. Weaving was one of the most primitive crafts in Japan, with much of it being accomplished by farmers' wives in their spare time. Although almost every family in Yamaguchi farmed, every home also had a simple, hand-operated loom that required a day's labor to produce a single yard of coarse cloth. Most of this fabric would be

used for family clothing, but the women also sold surplus cloth to provide extra income for the family.

Now, smooth cotton fabrics that were unlike anything produced in
Japan were among the inexpensive, high-quality Western goods that
began appearing in Yamaguchi. Once this cloth arrived, the Japanese
merchants who had purchased fabric from village families stopped calling on them. This loss of income was a new and more intractable element in the difficult life of Yamaguchi. The villagers could grapple with
the unpredictable weather and the lack of fertile soil, but they were
powerless to defend themselves against products from nations whose
sophistication was eons beyond anything they could even conceive of.

Cities throughout Japan were overwhelmed with commodities that
were less expensive and of higher quality than domestic goods. In addition, Japan had relatively little to offer the world in return to balance
its international trade. Rampant inflation and the devaluation of the yen
followed, at a time when the country needed capital for industrialization. Japan might have increased its import tariffs to stem the flow of
foreign goods, but foreign trade treaties prohibited this.

Civilian officials in the Meiji government began to take the first
small steps in combating this Western economic invasion. Just as the
West had sent missionaries to Asia to spread Christianity, the Meiji
government sent teachers into the agrarian villages to spread the principles of the industrial revolution.

Sakichi Toyoda and a group of young men from Yamaguchi found
themselves seated in the presence of one of these teachers from Tokyo
one evening in 1885. The teacher told the young men that they had
to learn from the West without being overrun by it, and reminded them
that the new foreign threat was not one that could be vanquished by
the samurai. Rather, he said, it could be controlled only if the entire
population of Japan worked to understand new ways.

On this particular evening, the teacher used the example of the
patent laws that had recently been enacted by the government. The
teacher told the men that it wasn't enough for everyone to be farmers
anymore, contributing to the well-being of their village. Now, he said,
young men had to consider how they could contribute to the well-
being of their country.

Eighteen-year-old Sakichi Toyoda, the reluctant carpenter, listened
carefully as the teacher explained that intellectual properties and inven-

tions would now be registered and protected by the government. The leader said that Japan needed to develop new machinery if it were to compete with the products of highly developed foreign industries, and that this law was intended to foster that.

Sakichi decided that evening to become an inventor and improve life for his countrymen. That he had neither the resources nor the education to undertake such a task did not trouble him. Nor did the fact that no one at hand in Yamaguchi was qualified to offer a young man guidance on such matters.

In the months that followed, Sakichi read a book entitled *Self-Help*, written by the British author Samuel Smiles. This book had become a best-seller in its Japanese translation, and it seemed to speak directly to young men like Sakichi at that stage of Japan's history. It described individuals who endured and overcame hardship to achieve great success, and it attributed their accomplishments to Puritan values, such as the building of one's character through self-denial.

Hardships that had to be overcome were abundant in Japan, and there were strong similarities between the precepts of discipline and dedication in Puritanism and the stringent samurai codes of Japan's heritage. Sakichi took the message of the book to heart.

He began his research in the only place accessible to him, the world as it existed around his village. Sakichi searched for a machine he could improve and found one right in his home: the ever-present and highly inefficient loom, where women labored long and hard for minimal output that was now of little value in the outside world.

Sakichi knew how pitiful Japanese cloth was in comparison with that produced in the West, and he recognized that Japanese looms were responsible for this. He began watching very carefully whenever he came upon a neighborhood woman working one of the machines, and he thought about how the devices could be made more efficient.

As a carpenter, Sakichi could easily understand the physical construction of the wooden looms, but the ideas and principles incorporated into their design were not self-evident. Still, he stubbornly refused to ask others for help or information in his work, and he had neither the training nor inclination to study mathematics or physics. Rather, he observed the operation of the machines and tried to divine the principles involved in what he saw. Then he built models, improving them on a trial-and-error basis.

Sakichi accomplished this work in his spare time in secluded places. Although the Meiji government had recognized the need for inventors to advance the nation, Sakichi's father was of another era, and he had not volunteered his son for this job. In Ikichi Toyoda's mind, Sakichi's fate had already been decided. He was to be a carpenter and the next *kacho* of the Toyoda *ie*.

2
KAIZEN

Sakichi Toyoda spent five years attempting to improve on primitive Japanese looms in his spare time. It was a halting and tedious process made even more difficult by Sakichi's isolation. While the smooth fabrics produced by Western looms made their way to Yamaguchi, the looms themselves did not. Sakichi could only examine the foreign cloth and guess at how the fabric had been created. Given Japan's lack of technology and Sakichi's limited education, he may as well have been reading tea leaves.

Officials in the Meiji government knew it was counterproductive for men like Sakichi to be reinventing the wheel when so much technical knowledge already existed overseas, and they were developing programs to expose the Japanese to Western machinery. One such effort was the National Industrial Exhibition that was held in Tokyo in 1890. To be displayed there were seventeen hundred of the latest foreign products and machines, many of which had been shown at an exhibition in Paris the previous year.

As soon as Sakichi learned of the program, he resolved to attend, an announcement that was received badly at home. Nonetheless, Sakichi journeyed to Tokyo by train and, where the railroad ended, by foot, to attend the exhibition. The huge collection of machinery was staggering, and Sakichi spent every day at the hall for the two-week run of the show. In his drab, country-boy clothes and with his quiet demeanor, Sakichi looked out of place in Tokyo. He kept to himself as he sat on the floor of the exhibition building, silently studying the foreign machines and carefully sketching their construction on a pad. After seeing the intricacies of the looms, Sakichi decided he had to observe them in operation, so he visited textile factories in Tokyo and

15

the nearby city of Yokohama, where Western machines had been installed.

The Meiji government was sponsoring a number of industrial pilot projects, buying entire factories abroad and importing foreigners to get them started. Once Japanese workers learned the operations, the foreigners were released and the trained Japanese workers were sent around the country to train others. The government financed the construction of factories that produced cotton, silk, bricks, and military hardware and then sold the plants for nominal prices to Japanese citizens.

Sakichi came to recognize that with his lack of capital and training there was no hope he could compete directly with the Westernized factories. On the other hand, the Westernized factories were large-scale, heavily capitalized mills, and these facilities were not yet widespread in Japan. Looked at in the right way, Sakichi decided, the challenge of the Western machines could also be seen as creating an opportunity.

Japanese looms were too inefficient to make the cloth of small Japanese weavers competitive on the open market but, at the same time, Western looms were far too expensive for small-scale Japanese weavers. Sakichi reasoned that if he were able to make a more efficient loom for the small weaver, and keep its price well below that of Western machines, he would be creating a product that had no competition.

Continuing to work in his spare time, Sakichi completed his first fully operational loom that autumn. It was only a wooden, manual loom, but Sakichi believed it to be a significant improvement on the existing Japanese machines. He persuaded a weaver in Yamaguchi to try it. The weaver found the quality of her cloth greatly improved, and her productivity increased by 50 percent. Overjoyed, Sakichi applied for a Japanese patent for his machine. Several months later, he received it.

With the validity the patent gave his work, Sakichi's image underwent a radical transformation in Yamaguchi. His father, who was now beginning to suffer from the infirmities of old age, accepted that Sakichi would never become a carpenter. Ikichi gave his blessing to his son's new occupation, and several people in the village offered Sakichi small sums to help him start a business. Sakichi built four or five of his new looms and then moved to Tokyo to become an entrepreneur.

Sakichi's plan was to hire weavers to operate his machines while he sold the cloth they produced. He also hoped to sell copies of his looms to other weavers while continuing to work on more advanced machines.

Although the cloth his company made was well received, Sakichi faced the same problems that afflicted other weavers in Japan. His company had no economies of scale, and the profits from his fabric sales were small. More ominously, the looms themselves were not selling as well as Sakichi had expected.

Even with the improved productivity of Sakichi's looms, small weavers didn't make enough profit to be able to afford them. Their cloth was in competition with the products of commercial weavers who used imported power looms. While these machines cost three hundred yen or more, operators with the necessary capital soon earned back their investment because of the large output of the machines.

Sakichi faced constant disappointments, stress, and financial pressure as he attempted to keep his company alive. He was a young man from a small town who was gradually coming to understand the enormous odds stacked against him. Amid this chaos, Sakichi returned home to his village one day to learn that his family had decided it was time for him to marry and had already selected his bride. Sakichi protested that the timing for the proposed marriage was not good, but his mother insisted he needed someone to take care of him. Recognizing he had already ignored his father's wishes about his career, and not wanting to cause his family further grief, Sakichi agreed to the marriage.

Sakichi returned to Tokyo after the ceremony with his new wife, but the marriage did not succeed any more readily than the business did. Sakichi was always busy taking orders, purchasing yarn, supervising the loom operators, and trying to design new machines whenever he could find the time. Even at home, he spent all his time working. Sakichi was consumed with his business, but in spite of his best efforts it failed. He was forced to close the operation, and, filled with disappointment, he returned to Yamaguchi with his wife, just three years after he had left.

Sakichi was restless and agitated at the Toyoda family home in Yamaguchi. Having obtained his first patent and started his first business, he found it more difficult than ever for him to resign himself to pursuing carpentry. Yet as a result of his shop's failure, his funds were gone. Then one day in 1894, one of Sakichi's uncles sent word that he wanted Sakichi to help him with a new project.

The uncle was a man of some wealth who had contributed funds for Sakichi's research from time to time. Like Sakichi, he was a man who wanted to participate in the industrialization of Japan, and he was always looking for opportunities. He thought he had found one in the government's plan to improve train service in Japan. The railroads were undertaking a massive expansion, and Sakichi's uncle wanted to win the contract to supply railroad ties. The uncle's plan was to create a new tie made of ceramic material.

Sakichi accepted his uncle's offer immediately and quickly relocated to his town, leaving his now pregnant wife behind in Yamaguchi. Since Sakichi's only expertise was in the textile business, he wasn't much help to his uncle with the ceramics. Recognizing this, Sakichi convinced his uncle to let him contribute to the project by inventing another textile machine that could be sold to raise funds for ceramics research. The uncle agreed, and Sakichi turned his attention to the yarn-reeling machine, a device for producing yarn for weaving.

Small reeling machines in Japan were as inefficient as looms, requiring the operator to use both hands to wind yarn onto a single reel. Following the same path that led to his first patent, Sakichi started with an existing machine and experimented to improve it. Again, he aimed to position his new product between the inexpensive but inefficient local machines and the expensive but productive imported ones.

Six months later, Sakichi completed a reeling machine that used a foot pedal to help feed the yarn, thus freeing one of the operator's hands and allowing multiple reels to be wound at the same time. Again, both the efficiency of the machine and the quality of its work were improved simultaneously.

Sakichi quickly got a patent for the machine, found a company that agreed to build it, and set off selling the machine door-to-door. This time sales of the machine were brisk, and Sakichi delivered the research funds he had promised to his uncle. Unfortunately, ceramics proved to be an unsuitable material for railroad ties, and the research Sakichi's uncle was conducting proved to be for naught.

While Sakichi was immersed in the development and sale of the new spinning machine, he seemed to lose track of the fact that he had a wife waiting for him at the Toyoda family home, and that his wife had given birth to his first son, who was named Kiichiro. Oblivious to the outside world, Sakichi seldom visited home and proved to be no more dedicated as a new father than he had been as a new husband.

The family of Sakichi's wife, learning how their daughter was being neglected, demanded that she return home and that the marriage be

Sakichi continued as before, dividing his time between overseeing business operations and conducting research. Sakichi's machines were acquiring a reputation for quality, and the new company, called Toyoda Shokai, did well.

Sakichi was continuing his development work on a broad-width steel loom when he was approached by a representative of Kanebo, one of Japan's most important spinning companies, in 1905. Until that time, Kanebo had used only foreign broad-width looms in its factories. Kanebo had heard about Sakichi's progress, and now the company asked if he would build some prototype broad-width steel looms for them.

Sakichi protested that he was unable to do that yet, as this machine was still under development. He also pointed out that in Nagoya, the closest large town, there were no steel foundries that were able to fabricate the steel parts he needed.

Kanebo countered by asking Sakichi to lend them his patent rights to the machine so Kanebo could have some Toyoda steel looms fabricated by a steel company in a larger city, Osaka. Sakichi was flattered by the interest of such a large company, and against his better judgment he consented.

When the machines were completed, Kanebo installed them alongside the British and American looms in their factory and conducted comparative performance tests. One year later, the results showed unequivocally that the looms of a British firm, Platt Brothers & Company Ltd., were noticeably more efficient than the Toyoda machines, and produced higher-quality cloth as well.

By 1906, Toyoda Shokai was producing 106 looms a month, and Japan was selling more cloth in China than U.S. companies. In fact, Japan was closing in on the English export volume in China as well. Business was booming, but Sakichi, still smarting from his defeat by the Platt Brothers machine, was more determined than ever to continue his research on the broad-width steel loom. That was why, even though Sakichi had broken off his previous venture with Mitsui Trading Company in disgust, swearing that he would support his own research in the future, Sakichi listened when Mitsui came calling a second time to try to lure him back into its fold.

What Mitsui proposed was a new loom-manufacturing company capitalized at one million yen, an amount equal to the total capitali-

ended. The two families decided that young Kiichiro would remain with Sakichi's parents, it not being unusual for children to be raised by someone other than their parents at the time in Japan.

Sakichi hardly seemed to notice this new arrangement, as his new reeling machine was proving to be a great success. He joined with his uncle and a third partner to open a store in Nagoya, the nearest large city, where the machines were sold to the public. The third partner operated the store, where sales flourished, while Sakichi concentrated on research for the machine that was his greatest passion—a power loom that would compete directly with the products of the huge foreign manufacturers.

It was the first time in Sakichi's life that he had both the time and the money to pursue his work unfettered by other concerns, but this idyllic era was short-lived. A year after the store opened, Sakichi's uncle noted financial irregularities with the business. An investigation revealed that although sales were excellent, payments to many suppliers were overdue. The third partner in the firm, who had disappeared, had embezzled a large portion of the company's receipts.

Sakichi moved into the store and took over its operation, hiring a lawyer to fight off the creditors who wanted to foreclose the business. He managed to keep the store open, but the company had accumulated large debts. Sakichi abandoned research on the power loom and became a full-time businessman, struggling to keep his company alive.

Sakichi restored financial stability to his reeling business within the course of a year. Had Sakichi been a businessman at heart, he could have relaxed and enjoyed a life of relative prosperity as a merchant. He was barely thirty years old, and already he had achieved success that was far beyond anything his neighbors would have imagined possible. But Sakichi had a larger purpose. He wanted to prove that the Japanese could make machines that were competitive with those from the West.

As soon as the business was profitable, Sakichi returned to his research. He hired additional employees and married a woman who took an active role in the business. Sakichi had his first power loom in operation by 1897. The cloth the machine produced was much improved, and because the loom was machine powered, it was far more efficient than manually operated machines.

Sakichi was pleased by this breakthrough, but he knew this machine suffered from two shortcomings. The machine was constructed almost entirely of wood, making it less durable than the foreign machines, which were constructed of steel, and it produced cloth of only the traditional Japanese width, 16½ inches, while most of the world demand was for 36-inch cloth.

Word of Sakichi's success with the power loom spread quickly, and soon he received a visit from a representative of Mitsui, one of the largest trading companies in Japan. The Meiji government was encouraging the concentration of economic power in Japan because, it believed, the large-scale adoption of Western technology could be financed only by large concerns. Japan also felt overwhelmed by the prowess of its Western competitors, and the government didn't want Japanese companies weakened by internal competition. By developing a few strong companies in selected fields, the government hoped to become competitive in the export market more quickly.

The Mitsui family had been the money brokers for the shogun government during the Tokugawa period, and they fulfilled the same role for the Meiji government after the Restoration. Mitsui had since evolved into a trading company with tremendous assets. The company was duly impressed with Sakichi Toyoda's achievements, and recognizing that he would require capital for expansion, they had a proposal for him.

Mitsui believed there was a large market for Japanese cloth and looms in China and wanted to establish a company with Sakichi to produce and sell his machines for export. In return for exclusive rights to sell the looms, Mitsui would finance the building of the plant and name Sakichi as its chief engineer. Better yet, Mitsui would oversee the management and operation of the company, called Igeta Shokai, leaving Sakichi free to do his research, for which Mitsui would provide complete financing. To Sakichi, it seemed like a dream come true.

Sakichi's next major goal was the production of a steel power loom that, while not fully automatic, would make the broad-width cloth that was the international standard. Sakichi resumed his research at Igeta Shokai just as Japan entered a severe recession near the turn of the century. The textiles industry was particularly hard hit, and the Japanese market for textile machines, which had been expanding rapidly, suddenly went flat. Then political developments in China, where the government had been unstable, caused disruptions in the Chinese market for Japanese textiles and machines.

As the income of Igeta Shokai dropped in the wake of these oc-

currences, Mitsui ordered a reduction in expenditures. The company cut Sakichi Toyoda's research budget, the availability of which had been Sakichi's primary reason for consenting to the formation of the company. Igeta Shokai became just another textile company, turning out products without facilities to improve their quality.

When Sakichi first began developing textile machines, he had no choice but to work continually to improve them. Japanese companies could not produce machines equivalent to those from the West. Sakichi recognized that the industry had to advance in small steps while striving to devise machines that met niche market needs not being filled by Western companies. As Sakichi progressed in his work, however, he came to recognize the importance of constantly improving the machines regardless of what his competition was doing. This policy of *kaizen*, or continuous improvement, became part of his basic philosophy. No machine or process, Sakichi believed, ever reached the point where it could not be improved, and he dedicated his research to this never-ending search for perfection.

While doing his research at Igeta Shokai, Sakichi had created a number of devices to make textile machines self-monitoring during their operation. One device maintained constant tension of the weft of a loom and produced greater standardization in its cloth. A second enabled a loom to automatically replenish the weft while it continued to weave cloth, increasing the productivity of the machine. These developments, which grew out of the drive for *kaizen*, had important long-term implications for Toyoda companies.

Sakichi knew the automated and self-monitoring features were reducing the amount of unskilled labor needed to produce a given amount of yarn or fabric. But he also realized the machines were adding additional economic value to the materials they produced. Since Japan had to import all of its raw materials, the profit from an export sale was its export price minus the cost of raw materials and labor. If additional value was added during production, more profit remained in Japan and the country's balance of trade improved.

With his research activities halted at Igeta Shokai, Sakichi resigned in outrage in 1902. He returned to the reeling-machine company he had founded with his uncle, which family members had continued to operate, and installed 138 of his power looms at the business. From that point forward, Sakichi vowed, he would never rely on a large corporation again. He would support his research with his own earnings.

zation of Mitsui itself at that time. Mitsui again promised Sakichi full access to research funds—but at a heavy price. Sakichi would have to provide his Japanese patent rights and all the assets of his company, Toyoda Shokai, as his contribution to the capitalization of the venture. Sakichi, anxious to get on with his research, reluctantly agreed. He dissolved his company and became a partner in the new firm, Toyoda Loom Works.

Sakichi resumed work on the broad-width loom, but the initial prosperity of Toyoda Loom Works came to a halt. The Japanese stock market crashed in 1907, and the economy went into deep depression. Orders at Toyoda Loom Works diminished to a trickle, and the company's board, looking to trim costs, began examining Sakichi's large research budget.

As financial pressure on the company mounted, conflicts between Sakichi and the board heightened, but Sakichi refused to compromise. Finally, seeing no other solution, he resigned from Toyoda Loom Works under duress in 1910. His contract provided a one-third stake in the future profits of Toyoda Loom Works, but he lost the rights to his machines, as well as the factory and all its employees. And the Toyoda name continued to be applied to all of the machines made in his absence.

Sakichi was devastated by his loss. Twenty years of work was gone, and he would be forced to find a new way to make a living. He fell into a depression and began considering leaving his country, since Toyota Loom Works controlled his patent rights only in Japan. Sakichi left on a trip to the United States in May of 1910, the first time he had been outside his native country. Although he didn't tell anyone, he planned to remain in the U.S. once he arrived.

He sailed to Seattle and then traveled across America by train, amazed at the massive scale everything took in comparison with his congested native land. For the first time he truly realized the incredible disadvantage the Japanese were at in competing with the Americans.

Although the Model T had come on the market only two years earlier, automobiles seemed to be everywhere. American manufacturers were already producing over one hundred thousand automobiles a year. One occasionally saw an automobile in the streets of Nagoya, but Sakichi noted how rapidly automobiles were becoming an everyday means of transportation in the United States. He realized he was looking at the future, and he was reassured that some mechanisms of the automobile seemed to be similar to those of the loom.

He was even more heartened when he visited Draper Loom Company, the top American loom manufacturer, which was located near New York. The plant foreman had never heard of Sakichi or the Toyota Loom Works, but he happily gave the foreign visitor a tour of his operation. As Sakichi walked the aisles and carefully examined the machinery, he silently reached an inescapable conclusion. Some aspects of Toyoda's most advanced looms were more efficient than Draper's. Barely able to contain his glee, Sakichi thanked his host and left.

Sakichi knew he couldn't consider setting up an operation in the United States without the advice of someone who knew the country well. He was aware that the Japanese population in the States had tripled in the last decade, to seventy-two thousand, and that anti-Japanese sentiments were building. So, the next day he visited Dr. Jokichi Takamine, a renowned Japanese chemist, and the discoverer of adrenaline, at his residence on the Hudson River. Takamine had a laboratory in New York, and he was a prominent figure in the Japanese-American community. He was also the man who was responsible for the Japanese government's gift of cherry trees to Washington, D.C.

When they were seated in the Japanese garden Takamine had installed at his home, Sakichi explained his dilemma. He felt he had been tricked out of his patents in Japan, and he wanted to relocate to the United States.

Takamine thought for a moment, then pointed to the red and white plum blossoms in his garden. "I brought those trees here from Japan," he said, "and it took two years of cultivation before they started to bloom. In order for those trees, which flower so beautifully in Japan, to bloom here, it takes that much more work."

Sakichi protested that he wasn't afraid of work, and that he felt he had been betrayed by his countrymen.

"Mr. Toyoda," Takamine said, "the United States is the most prosperous country in the world. If a brilliant inventor like you is truly troubled, then I am sure that this country will gladly welcome you. However, what will ever become of Japan if everyone who is troubled reacts the same way? In order for Japan to prosper like the United States, you must let your flower bloom in Japan."

Takamine's words caused Sakichi to remember that he had first dedicated himself to being an inventor to help his country compete against the West, and he recognized the wisdom of Takamine's counsel. He would return to Japan, and being unable to re-enter the loom manufacturing business, he would support his research by building a weaving mill and selling the cloth it manufactured. He moved his family into the new factory upon his return, and began work on the fully automatic loom, while turning the weaving mill into a profitable enterprise.

As was so often the case in the early years of Japan's industrial development, however, Sakichi soon found himself dissatisfied with the quality of his suppliers' materials. In this case the deficiency was in the yarn that was woven on his machines. The Japanese spinning industry was producing primarily coarse, low-thread-count yarn that was inferior to the high-thread-count yarn other nations were producing.

Sakichi decided that to achieve the level of quality he demanded, he would have to start his own spinning mill. For a spinning mill to be profitable at that time, however, it needed at least twenty thousand spindles in operation, and that required capital beyond the new company's means. After much agonizing, Sakichi realized that in a country as small as Japan, a businessman could not hold grudges if he was going to succeed. Sakichi then signed a deal with the Nagoya office of Mitsui, under which Mitsui provided a three-year note for the import of six thousand spindles.

World War I broke out shortly after Sakichi's spinning business got underway, and the Japanese economy blossomed once again as Western companies shifted their production to war materials and away from textiles. The Toyoda spinning mill was overrun with orders, and it was transformed quickly into a significant operation.

By 1918, the business, called Toyoda Spinning & Weaving Company, had developed into a mid-sized industrial company. Two years later, after China began increasing tariffs on imported textiles, Sakichi turned the operation of the company over to other family members, moved to Shanghai, and began construction of a spinning and weaving factory that would house eighteen thousand spindles and thirteen hundred looms.

Sakichi Toyoda, the son who refused to follow tradition, was fifty-three years old, a certified inventor and a man of financial means. Far from easing into an early retirement, however, he was busily taking on additional tasks. He had established yet another base of operation—and another location to carry forward his research. He had still not perfected a fully automatic loom that would outperform the machines from the West, and he told himself he would not rest until he had.

3
TREMORS

Although Sakichi Toyoda's son, Kiichiro, spent the first years of his life separated from his father, he passed those years in the ancestral Toyoda home in Yamaguchi, where his father had grown up. The villagers still planted their rice seedlings before the rains each summer and harvested the plants before the fierce typhoons of the fall. Everyone contributed to the eternal campaign against the fate of too many people with too few resources and too little land.

With this communal aura in the village, it shouldn't have become an issue with Kiichiro that his father was off devoting his attention to the nurturing of his machines and his country's development rather than to his young son, but somehow it did. Or maybe it was that Kiichiro would become too much like his father—someone who chooses his own path and has a steely determination to follow it.

Kiichiro went to live with his father after Sakichi took a woman named Asako as his second wife and fathered a daughter with her named Aiko. Sakichi retrieved Kiichiro from Yamaguchi then and united his family under the same roof. The Toyoda household was located within the factory property of Toyoda Shoten, the reeling-machine business that grew out of Sakichi's joint venture with his uncle. Sakichi was deeply involved in his research, and he relied upon his wife to manage both the business operations of the company and the Toyoda household. Asako was always busy, and Kiichiro and his half-sister, Aiko, were often left alone at the house. The two children became good friends, sharing breakfast and lunch, which Asako prepared for them before she went to work.

The Toyoda household was a place of high expectations, and Asako did not favor one child over the other. She gave them both a stern upbringing, as this was her way of teaching self-reliance and fortitude.

She scolded them equally when they misbehaved, and with all of the responsibilities she carried, she had little time to pamper either. Kiichiro became a melancholic and quiet boy in this atmosphere, while his sister became gentle and good-natured. Despite these differences, the children became deeply attached to each other.

Kiichiro's performance in elementary school was disappointing to the family, and Asako scolded him constantly to do better. Kiichiro would bristle at his stepmother's rebukes and turn sullen and remote after receiving one. Sakichi was too distracted to notice his son's discontent, and Kiichiro became resentful toward his father. Sakichi Toyoda, who had been a contrary son, learned what it was to have a contrary son himself.

When Kiichiro was old enough to attend middle school, Asako told Sakichi that, despite Kiichiro's poor performance in elementary school, she wanted the boy to continue his education. Six years of elementary school was all that was required of children in Japanese schools of the time. Few students attended middle school, and only a small number of college-bound students attended four years of high school, where admission was competitive.

Sakichi had little use for formal education, and he argued that it was pointless for Kiichiro to continue. Asako prevailed, however, and Kiichiro found himself back in the classroom. Kiichiro did no better in his middle-school studies, and when there was a financial emergency at the company and Sakichi had to scramble to find research money, Kiichiro's school tuition sometimes went unpaid for weeks.

Sakichi and Asako disagreed again when it was time for Kiichiro to attend high school. As a self-made man whose finances were still precarious, Sakichi saw little value in this expenditure. After a lengthy dispute, Sakichi gave in with a wave of his hand and returned to his research, while Kiichiro left home to become a boarding student at Japan's illustrious Number Two High School.

The Number Two High School was the domain of children of the elite of Japanese society, and Kiichiro was only one generation removed from an isolated farming village in the hinterlands. It mattered little that the Toyoda family was becoming prominent in Japan, for the families of the other students were already well-established in Japanese society, most often in the more cosmopolitan cities. To these students, Kiichiro was a country bumpkin.

Kiichiro was a quiet and withdrawn young man at high school, one who did not join in socializing with the other students. Mirroring the first of many traits he would come to share with his father, he became more interested in machinery and engineering than in going to parties. The government was encouraging technical education, and Kiichiro took to this material readily. He spent much of his free time sketching designs for machinery, and like his father he sometimes became so absorbed in his drawings that those around thought he was consumed by them.

Sakichi Toyoda paid off his 1914 loan from the Mitsui Trading Company for his spinning and weaving company as quickly as possible. Even with the enormous changes in his life, Sakichi never forgot the lesson he had learned about frugality in Yamaguchi. Having left two joint enterprises with Mitsui in disgust, he was uncomfortable being indebted to the company. Nonetheless, Sakichi knew he would be forced to have ongoing business ties with Mitsui, and he developed a rapport with Ichizo Kodama, the manager of Mitsui's Nagoya office. Kodama had gone out of his way to help Sakichi get the financing for his mill, and the men became friends.

Sakichi told Kodama one day that the Toyoda textile mill was growing too large for his wife to manage alone and that he was tired of overseeing the business operation himself. Sakichi's business acumen had allowed him to save his various enterprises from bankruptcy more than once, but his heart wasn't in administration. He felt he needed someone to assume responsibility so he could return to his inventing.

Kodama asked Sakichi why he didn't assign his son, Kiichiro, to this role. No, Sakichi said, sometimes it seemed that Kiichiro was going to continue his education forever. Sakichi wanted to take someone into the family to manage his affairs. As this was the type of situation that was often resolved through an arranged marriage in Japan, Sakichi was thinking of a husband for his daughter, Aiko, who was now of marriageable age. Kodama, as it turned out, was looking for a wife for his younger brother, Risaburo.

Risaburo Kodama was then the thirty-one-year-old manager of the Philippines branch of C. Itoh & Company, one of Japan's foremost raw-cotton trading companies. Risaburo was successful in his career, and his brother believed he might be just the man Sakichi needed. The Toyodas were becoming a formidable family in Japan, and Ichizo Kodama, with his family connections to Mitsui, concluded that this marriage could be beneficial for both families.

Learning Risaburo was qualified to manage the company, Sakichi sought to eliminate what he saw as the only obstacle to the marriage. Sakichi had seen his businesses fail, and his research funds evaporate, when strangers were running his enterprises. He had developed a strong aversion to having outsiders involved with his companies. Sakichi said he would agree to the marriage but stipulated that instead of becoming just his son-in-law, Risaburo had to take the Toyoda name and become his adopted son—a relatively common practice in Japan. Risaburo could then assume a leadership role in the business as a true family member.

While this arrangement offered many advantages, it also had its liabilities for Sakichi's son, Kiichiro. Since Risaburo was older than Kiichiro, his adoption into the Toyoda family meant that Risaburo would become Sakichi's first-born son by proxy, and all of the inheritance rights of the *kacho* would be transferred to Risaburo under Japan's civil code. Although Kiichiro sent his father a letter of protest when he learned of this arrangement, the *kachos* of both families consented to the marriage, and Risaburo became Risaburo Toyoda after his marriage to Aiko in October of 1915.

Risaburo proved himself to be as adept at running the rapidly expanding family business as Sakichi had hoped, and Sakichi appointed Risaburo managing director when Toyoda Spinning & Weaving Company was incorporated in 1918. Risaburo's adeptness at administration allowed Sakichi to devote more time to his still unfulfilled hope of creating a fully automatic loom. It also permitted Sakichi to pay more attention to the company's future. Thus freed from mundane concerns, Sakichi soon established his factory in China, leaving Risaburo in command of operations in Japan.

Kiichiro Toyoda was greatly distressed when Aiko married Risaburo. Part of that was simple jealousy. Kiichiro didn't want to share his sister's affections with another man. But Kiichiro's highly complex feelings towards his father also came into play and, when Sakichi arranged a marriage that displaced Kiichiro in the family, Kiichiro began to feel rage towards Sakichi.

Sakichi Toyoda was attracting attention in Japan at this time as his accomplishments became known, and people were constantly telling Kiichiro what a great man his father was. That only made Kiichiro angrier, and he tried to diminish the importance of his father's work when he spoke of Sakichi to his friends at school. Anyone who worked by trial and error, he would insist, could not be a great inventor.

While trying to contain all of these emotions, Kiichiro went on to become a mechanical engineering student at Tokyo University, the most prestigious college in Japan. In following this academic path, Kiichiro was fulfilling his stepmother's wishes. But in studying mechanical engineering at such a renowned institution, he was also establishing a means to spite his father.

Sakichi prided himself on what he had been able to achieve without benefit of education or family influence. He believed that a man didn't need education in the theories and principles of science and that he could learn all he needed to know by working on machines with his own hands. Now Kiichiro was obtaining the finest training a young man could get in Japan—and in his father's field. Kiichiro, in the matter of a few years, would learn all the scientific precepts his father had spent a lifetime assimilating through experience. Kiichiro was confident he would emerge from Tokyo University with all the tools he needed to surpass his father's accomplishments in short order.

It was a foregone conclusion that Kiichiro would join his father's company after college, but it was also inevitable that Kiichiro's arrival, after he graduated in 1920, would be unsettling. Kiichiro would be the young upstart, bristling with resentment towards his father, and over-flowing now with all the book learning for which his father had so little respect. And the managing director of the company would be Risaburo, the man who had stolen his sister's heart from Kiichiro—and who had replaced Kiichiro as his father's first son.

Kiichiro and Risaburo were men of vastly different temperaments, which only exacerbated matters. Kiichiro was reticent and introverted, the classic engineer who cared for his machines above all else. Risaburo, who was ten years older than Kiichiro and a seasoned business executive, was aggressive and authoritarian, a man who administered rather than constructed and who was used to getting his way.

Sakichi Toyoda anticipated the inescapable clash between his two sons and tried to smooth their relationship by sending Risaburo, Aiko, and Kiichiro on a tour of American textile mills shortly after Kiichiro graduated. But a relationship this intricate was immune to facile antidotes. Kiichiro reported to work at Toyoda Spinning & Weaving Company feeling he had something he wanted to prove. He attempted to do that by immediately setting to work on the machine his father had yet to perfect—the fully automatic loom.

Kiichiro was received warmly by the technicians in his father's factory, many of whom had been trained by Sakichi, and a quick mutual respect grew between Kiichiro and the men. Kiichiro was young and headstrong, but he soon recognized the value of the workers' practical experience with machines. The workers, in turn, appreciated the swiftness and reliability with which Kiichiro could make a decision or reach a conclusion, since his education allowed him to act on the basis of proven principles rather than trial and error.

With Sakichi spending most of his time in Shanghai, one of Kiichiro's first accomplishments was to design an improvement on an automatic shuttle-changing device his father had invented in 1903. Then he developed a new mechanism for feeding the warp of a loom and another that automatically halted a loom when a thread broke. By 1923 Kiichiro had made enough progress toward a fully automatic loom that the company won numerous patents.

Kiichiro seemed to have found his calling, and Sakichi, who became a *kacho* much different from the one his own father had envisioned, had two productive sons. His company was financially sound, and the completion of the first fully automatic Toyoda loom appeared to be close at hand.

The success Sakichi was achieving paralleled Japan's economic advancement. Agricultural yields, exports, and personal income were increasing annually, as was the size of the population. Japan, although still underdeveloped according to Western standards, was making steady progress in its industrialization. Yet for all of its advancement in selected areas, Japan remained especially far behind in one area of technology that was making an indelible impression on the rest of the world. It took a calamitous event like Commodore Perry's arrival in 1853, to bring this to the attention of the Japanese government.

On September 1, 1923, a momentous earthquake with a magnitude of 7.9 struck Japan at 11:58 A.M. The epicenter of the earthquake was in the Tokyo-Yokohama region, but the destruction it caused was far-reaching. Houses in densely populated urban districts collapsed, and many of those left standing caught fire. Because the quake struck at noon, people in homes and shops were preparing meals, and their stoves ignited gas and charcoal fires that quickly consumed the wood and paper building materials in traditional Japanese houses. Train rails buckled and utility wires fell, bringing transportation and communications within the country to a halt. By the time it was over, more than a million people had lost their lives, and the country was paralyzed with shock.

As Japan began to rebuild in the aftermath of the earthquake, it became apparent that with public transportation badly disrupted and not likely to be rebuilt for many months, a large number of motor vehicles were needed quickly in Tokyo. Buses and trucks were requisitioned from throughout the country, but the number available was minuscule.

Motor vehicles were still rare in Japan, with only thirteen thousand registered in the entire country in 1923. The vast majority of these vehicles were imported from the United States or Europe, and few of them were privately owned, as the cost of owning an automobile was far beyond the means of the ordinary Japanese family. Most were taxis, buses, or cars owned by companies for business use.

To obtain an emergency supply of vehicles, the Japanese government halved the import duties on automobiles, which stood at 35 percent on assembled cars and 25 percent on component parts, and authorized the import of eight hundred Ford truck chassis from the United States. The chassis were fitted with rudimentary bodies to transport people and materials during the massive reconstruction effort. Once the Japanese witnessed the practicality of motor vehicles, automobiles were destined to become an integral part of Japanese life.

The Japanese military recognized the strategic importance of motor vehicles in combat, and they had made several attempts to encourage domestic automobile production. The military's first effort occurred after the Russo-Japanese War, when the army conducted trial manufacturing of trucks in the army ordnance department in 1907. A few small manufacturers observed this operation and attempted to begin production, but the capital requirements were so high and the level of Japanese technology so low that the vehicles were essentially hand built. All of the manufacturers soon went out of business. As World War I began, the British army had twenty thousand vehicles, the American army had fifteen thousand, and the Japanese army had only ten.

The Japanese army made another attempt to foster domestic manufacturing after seeing the vital role motorized vehicles played in World War I. Troop-transport vehicles, tanks, portable artillery, and airplanes had been decisive in Europe, and the Japanese military recognized that motorized vehicles had become as important as bullets in modern warfare. The army drew up a set of specifications for a standard military truck in 1918, but since it didn't have sufficient funds to maintain the fleet it needed, it decided to offer the private sector incentives for producing and buying motor vehicles. The Military Subsidization Act of 1918 provided subsidies for both manufacturers and purchasers of vehicles that met military requirements. Under the plan, the military would then procure the vehicles from their owners during time of war.

Tokyo Gas & Electric Industry Company, Tokyo Ishikawajima Shipyard Company, and Kaishinsha Company were authorized to produce military-specification trucks under the law, but there were few buyers for their products. The subsidies being offered were sizable, but the specifications were so stringent the resulting vehicles, which were intended for military conditions, had little appeal to consumers. At the time of the 1923 earthquake, barely one hundred military-specification vehicles had been produced, and for all intents and purposes the Japanese motor vehicle industry was nonexistent.

When the 1923 earthquake both increased the demand for motor vehicles and spurred a reduction of automotive import duties, American manufacturers began thinking about establishing manufacturing bases in Japan. Initially, Henry Ford was hesitant, fearing he would lose his investment to another earthquake. But after a Ford staff member who was Japanese visited his native country and observed the progress being made in rebuilding and the receptiveness of the market to automobiles, Ford decided to proceed. Ford of Japan was established in December 1924 with an initial capitalization of four million yen. Ford built an assembly plant in Yokohama, where cars were constructed from components shipped from the United States—collections of parts known as knockdown sets.

General Motors followed Ford into Japan in 1925, sending a representative to the Imperial Hotel in Tokyo who announced that GM was seeking assistance from a local town for the construction of a knockdown plant. GM was flooded with offers and accepted one from the city of Osaka, which promised to exempt GM from city taxes for four years. GM, wishing to outdo Ford, capitalized its Japanese operation at eight million yen. Ford responded by immediately doubling its capitalization.

This initial competition between the two American giants continued once the plants were in operation and escalated into a price-slashing battle for market share once their cars were on the street. Since the few small Japanese manufacturers had nowhere near the economies of scale that Ford and GM had, their cars were priced out of the market, and most of the remaining few companies were driven out of business. So intimidating was the presence of Ford and GM that Japan's largest trading companies—Mitsui, Mitsubishi, and Sumitomo—all refused to enter the field, despite repeated requests from the army and the Ministry of Commerce and Industry to do so.

In 1924, Kiichiro Toyoda perfected the fully automatic loom his father had worked on for so many years. Sakichi was duly proud of his son and overjoyed with the performance of the machine, which he judged to exceed international standards. Nonetheless, given his experiences, Sakichi insisted the company proceed according to two of his most important precepts: Toyoda would perform all of its own fabrications, and the machine would be thoroughly tested before being put into mass production.

Toyoda Spinning & Weaving bought an iron works in Nagoya and used it to produce the metal for the looms, while preparing for large-scale testing. The company constructed a pilot plant with 320 looms, where the automatic looms were tested for a year. When the performance of the machines was judged to meet standards, Sakichi formed a new company, Toyoda Automatic Loom Works, and began full production in 1927.

Although the new loom cost 630 yen, compared with 200 yen for a conventional loom, one worker could oversee the operation of 25 looms simultaneously. The company estimated that the capital investment of a mill with 1,000 looms could be recovered in one year. By perfecting another design that maximized output while minimizing human labor, the company was following Sakichi's aim of creating machines that added high amounts of value to the raw materials they processed. For this accomplishment, and for the many other contributions he had made to Japanese industrial development, Sakichi Toyoda was awarded the Imperial Order of Merit, the nation's highest civilian honor, by the emperor in 1927.

The practice of adding large amounts of value to imported raw materials was not widespread in Japan at this time, however, and the Japanese economy was once again in a shambles. The deluge of orders that Japanese companies had received during and immediately after World War I disappeared as Western nations returned to peacetime production and superior, less expensive Western goods returned to the world market. The price of Japanese goods had become inflated during the wartime boom, and once again Japanese international competitiveness fell, causing a trade deficit.

Japanese exports dropped to half their wartime level, the prices of textiles and agricultural products fell, and unemployment became rampant. In March of 1927, rumors began to circulate in Japan that the banks were about to fail, causing a panic among depositors. The reports of impending bankruptcies were false, but the rumors fed on themselves, and soon there were runs on banks. Small and medium-sized banks, in particular, lacked the reserves to handle the withdrawals, and the rumors became self-fulfilling prophecies as banks were forced to close.

Toyoda Automatic Loom Works was spared the worst consequences of the collapse of the textile market in Japan because when Sakichi broke the company off from Toyoda Spinning & Weaving, he essentially created a machinery company rather than a textile company. Toyoda Automatic Loom Works prospered during the domestic market downturn by exporting its machines to India and China. Then, in 1929, Sakichi Toyoda received an unexpected inquiry. Mitsui Trading Company informed him that the British firm Platt Brothers & Company Ltd. had commissioned them to conduct a performance appraisal of the new Toyoda automatic loom.

Sakichi was stunned. Not only was Platt Brothers the largest manufacturer of textile machinery in the world, but it was also the same company whose machines had resoundingly outperformed Toyoda machines in a similar test held twenty-four years earlier. Sakichi, whose health was beginning to fail, eagerly agreed to the test. Sakichi was confident of the outcome and believed the test would provide official certification that, just as he had set out to do in 1892, he had beaten the masters at their own game.

The test proved what Sakichi had predicted, and officials of the British company were so impressed they paid Sakichi the highest compliment. A delegation from the company visited Toyoda Automatic Loom Works and offered to buy the patent rights to the Toyoda loom. The news was delivered to Sakichi at his Japanese home, where he was recuperating from a stroke suffered in Shanghai. Although negotiations were only at the preliminary stage, Sakichi suspected that world rights, exclusive of Japan, China, and the United States, would bring one million yen—a tremendous sum. Sakichi knew exactly how he thought the money should be used.

Sakichi had been carefully observing the tremendous success that Ford and General Motors were having in the Japanese market. The Japanese people had taken to the automobile as quickly as the inhabitants of Europe and the United States, and sales were high. In addition, by producing the components of the cars cheaply on mass-production lines in the United States, and then assembling the cars with inexpensive Japanese labor, Ford and GM were making huge profits on each car. Sakichi knew there was a future in automobiles, and he suspected that the automobile might provide him with a way to solve a personal problem.

Kiichiro Toyoda had proven to be a natural engineer when he went to work in his father's enterprises. He finished many of the designs his father had originated and devised others on his own. He was, in this and many other ways, his father's son. As time passed and Kiichiro gained the confidence of his own successes, he had matured, married, and started his own family. In the manner in which old wounds between father and son are often healed, time caused the past to be diminished in his mind.

Yet as Sakichi began to recognize the inevitable consequences of his advancing age, he realized that in placing his many business operations in the hands of Risaburo, his adopted son, he had denied Kiichiro the creative freedom that Sakichi had demanded for himself all his life. Risaburo was the president of Toyoda Automatic Loom Works, and technically Kiichiro reported to him. As long as Sakichi was alive, he could ensure Kiichiro was allowed to pursue work that interested him. After he was gone, however, Sakichi would no longer be able to exert this parental control, as Risaburo would inherit Sakichi's role as *kacho*.

Sakichi knew an enterprise as large as the Toyoda companies were becoming in the late 1920s required a man with Risaburo's business skills to administer it. This was not a job for Kiichiro. But Sakichi had devised a calling for Kiichiro, one that would provide him with the freedom he knew Kiichiro needed. Seeing the success of Ford and GM, Sakichi had quietly begun urging Kiichiro to think about entering the automobile business.

Kiichiro thought his father was crazy when he heard of this plan. To Sakichi, the self-educated trial-and-error engineer, it was enough that the United States had succeeded at making cars. As far as he was concerned, if the Americans could do it, the Japanese could do it. Sakichi needed only to look at the success of his loom business to find all the confirmation he needed.

Kiichiro, on the other hand, was a university-educated engineer. He knew that making automobiles, with their tens of thousands of parts, was infinitely more complex than making looms. Furthermore, he was acutely aware that although Japanese industrialization was advancing, the country still had a long way to go. The steel industry, in particular, was relatively primitive, and automobile production required advanced steels unavailable in Japan.

Kiichiro told Sakichi the idea of making a Japanese car to compete with Ford and General Motors was nonsense. If his father wanted conclusive proof of that, Kiichiro said, he only had to look at the refusal of the country's major trading companies, or *zaibatsu*, to enter the field, in spite of the government subsidies offered. Kiichiro told his father that after having completed work on the automatic loom, he was now working on further improvements for the yarn-spinning machine, and he was completely absorbed in that.

Sakichi understood patience, and he knew what it was to be a headstrong son, so he didn't press Kiichiro further until the time was right. As the Platt deal progressed and the one-million-yen purchase price was confirmed, Sakichi called his son to his side. He told Kiichiro that he was giving him the entire million yen from the Platt sale, but there was one condition attached. Kiichiro had to use the money for research on the production of automobiles. Kiichiro recognized this bequest from his *kacho* as being part command and part reward. He put aside his reservations—if not his doubts—and agreed to follow his father's wishes.

Sakichi told Kiichiro he should start work immediately by taking over the Platt negotiations scheduled in England. Kiichiro would have help with the legalities of the contract, but he should be sure to visit every automobile plant he could in the United States and England during the trip. Sakichi was instructing the next generation of the Toyoda *ie* to enter a new field in precisely the same way Sakichi had entered the loom business—by carefully studying the most successful and advanced machines and plants in the field.

When Kiichiro visited the automobile plants in the United States and England, he came with the words of his father's charge in his ears.

Suddenly the task of making cars didn't seem so intimidating, and Kiichiro concluded that although it would be difficult, it wouldn't be impossible. He also decided, as he looked around the massive Western plants, that Toyoda wouldn't have to form a cooperative venture with a foreign manufacturer or buy out an existing Japanese auto maker, neither of which Kiichiro wanted to do. Part of Sakichi's motivation for building automobiles was to help establish another industry that would compete with foreign companies, and Kiichiro thought a licensing agreement would be counterproductive to this end. Furthermore, there weren't any existing auto makers in Japan worth purchasing, even if Kiichiro could raise the funds.

As Kiichiro conducted his investigation, he learned that knowledge of automobile technology was disseminating throughout the world, and that there were professors at his alma mater, Tokyo University, who were studying the field. Kiichiro reasoned it would be possible to purchase foreign automobiles and disassemble them to study their parts. He could then write specifications to replicate the parts in Japan without violating patent laws.

With these specifications in hand, Kiichiro believed, he could assemble a skilled work force over time. By drawing on the metal-working knowledge that had been gained at Toyoda Automatic Loom Works and on the expertise available in the universities, Kiichiro thought it would be possible to begin production of a prototype in a few years.

Kiichiro also made a careful study of the assembly lines at the plants he visited in the United States and of the production equipment employed there. He recognized he would have to alter the mass production assembly methods Ford and General Motors used, since Japan had no hope of reaching their output level in the near future. The production machinery, too, presented a problem, since many of the machine tools were highly specialized. But Kiichiro knew it would be possible to purchase these machines in foreign countries, duplicate them in Japan, and adapt them to local market conditions.

When Kiichiro returned from his trip, he proceeded just as his father would have. He walled off a small area of the Toyoda Automatic Loom Works factory to provide the seclusion both men craved for their research, and he got to work. Kiichiro's first project was to disassemble and study a small engine from a motorbike. He worked in near-secrecy, telling no one of his mission save his research partner, a graduate of a technical high school. The number of university graduates in rural Japan was small at this time, and Sakichi, with his disdain for formal education, had preferred to hire uneducated men and train them himself. As Kiichiro and his partner went about their work, no one at the factory paid much attention to them.

Kjichiro decided the company first had to perfect the techniques of precision machining and become familiar with mass-production methods before advancing into auto production, and he began addressing this. He introduced a conveyor system into loom production at the plant, and he began ordering precision American and German machine tools, making the excuse that they were to improve loom production. He also installed an electric furnace in the foundry to provide high-grade castings and imported Japan's first molding machine. Meanwhile, he read Henry Ford's autobiography, *My Life and Work,* and urged the few coworkers who knew of his project to do the same.

Sakichi Toyoda seemed to be making slow progress on the road to recovery from his stroke as his son set to work on this ambitious project. But, at sixty-three, and with a lifetime of fighting constant battles to achieve his dreams behind him, Sakichi's strength was beginning to wane. In this weakened state, Sakichi caught a cold that worsened into acute pneumonia in October of 1930. This time Sakichi was unable to fight off his last opponent, and he died on October 30.

Over three thousand people attended Sakichi's funeral in Nagoya, a city not far from the village of Yamaguchi where Sakichi had begun his life. It was a remote and provincial area whose people had witnessed Sakichi's emergence in the closing days of the samurai era as an eccentric young man with wild ideas and larger-than-life dreams.

When the people of the Nagoya region laid Sakichi to rest, they honored him as a man who made his dreams a reality, who had embraced the challenges and opportunities of the Meiji Restoration, and who had helped lead his country into the modern world.

4
MACHINATIONS

The Japanese trade deficit continued to mount precipitously in the late 1920s, and the government realized it had to be reversed or the country's industrialization would halt. One of the first steps it took was forming the Committee to Promote Domestic Production. The committee included representatives of the military, government ministries, businesses, and universities, and its charge was to identify policies that would develop Japanese industries. The persistent influx of foreign automobiles was a key component in the trade problem, and the committee made this their main area of concern.

The statistics examined by the committee were glaring. Ford and General Motors assembled 29,338 automobiles in Japan in 1929, and another 5,018 completed vehicles were imported. In contrast, only 437 motor vehicles were produced by domestic manufacturers, with the majority being vehicles conforming to the military specifications developed in 1918. Given this ongoing imbalance, the committee concluded, a domestic automobile industry would never have a chance to develop.

Domestically produced vehicles were so scarce in Japan that a member of the committee, who had been sent on a speaking tour to encourage people to buy domestic vehicles, arrived at a meeting hall one evening in a Chevrolet taxi. When his reception committee pointed out this contradiction, the man resolved never to appear at a meeting again in a foreign vehicle. At many subsequent meetings, the man was forced to arrive in the only domestic vehicle available—a rickshaw.

The committee knew how formidable Ford and GM were, and it suggested in 1930 that domestic manufacturers avoid direct competition with them. The Americans were making full-sized cars as well as trucks with a one-ton load capacity. The committee advised Japanese manufacturers to build two-ton trucks and medium-sized cars. But even then,

the committee got little support from the populace. A group of businessmen who used foreign-made trucks and buses in their operations
sent a petition to the committee protesting their findings. They maintained the only action the committee should take was to revoke the
import taxes on foreign vehicles, so they could buy these superior products more cheaply.

There was no denying the domestic automobile industry had a long
way to go. All three of the Japanese manufacturers who remained in
business in 1930 assembled cars by hand, whereas Ford and General
Motors had three-thousand-foot assembly lines producing a car every
twenty-five minutes.

The situation with auto parts manufacturers was similar. Some companies were making parts for Ford and GM under contract, but the
majority of them were making imitation parts for the small replacement-
parts market. Ford and General Motors imported the bulk of their assembly parts from the United States.

As the committee continued with its studies, the Japanese military
became increasing impatient about establishing a domestic industry. After attempting to foster production for two decades, the military was
tired of having Japanese companies turn deaf ears to its requests. It
wanted to eliminate the biggest obstacle to Japanese manufacturing by
driving Ford and GM from the country—a move strongly resisted by
the civilian cabinet out of fear of protectionist retaliation from the
United States.

The broad differences between—and the separate but equal con-
stitutional powers of—the military and the cabinet had been a source
of friction for years. In the aftermath of World War I, the Japanese
government became a charter member of the League of Nations, embracing diplomacy as the accepted means of settling international disputes. The government began coordinating its foreign policies with
those of the Western powers, and sought to settle territorial disputes
through negotiation rather than force. Consequently, the scope of the
navy was diminished by treaty agreement, and the size of the army was
reduced to control budget deficits.

Many Japanese thought this posture towards the West was naive
and weak, especially after Japanese citizens were prohibited from im-
migrating to the United States by the Exclusion Act of 1924. The military and their supporters argued that Great Britain and the United
States were imperialists in Asia. On the other hand, neighboring Asian

countries were strategic to Japan's defense and security, and there was a shared cultural heritage, which they believed conferred upon the Japanese a right and a duty to maintain a stronger position in Asia than Westerners.

Japan had possession of Taiwan and Korea at this time, as well as special interests in Manchuria and northern China. Japan had seized Manchuria as a strategic barrier against Russia during the Russo-Japanese War, but it lost the northern half of the country to Russia in the final peace accord. In the two decades since, Japan had made substantial economic investments in Manchuria, making it the main source of Japanese coal, iron ore, and cotton fiber. These raw materials had become as vital to the military as Manchuria's strategic geographic position.

Against this backdrop, and with the debate about domestic auto production dragging out in the cabinet, the Japanese military was pushed to the brink by two events. China, after years of internal chaos, was moving toward unification, which threatened Japan's interest in Manchuria. Then the Japanese cabinet signed another treaty, against the advise of the naval general staff, further limiting naval expansion.

The military was guaranteed freedom from civilian influence by the constitution, but in January of 1930 the cabinet ignored this and signed a new naval arms-limitation agreement with Great Britain and the United States. Military leaders were furious, and they moved to regain some of their power by staging what became known as the Manchurian Incident in 1931. On September 18, the rails of the Manchurian Railway were blown up near a Japanese encampment. The Japanese army had set the explosion, but they denounced the act as the work of Chinese guerrillas.

The Japanese army then attacked the Chinese army headquarters in nearby Mukden, and the city fell to Japanese control. Japanese troops continued their attack in the following weeks and occupied most of southern Manchuria, eventually installing a deposed Chinese emperor as the titular ruler of the area, which the Japanese army then designated a newly independent state.

The civilian government in Japan was powerless to control the action of its army in China, and the attack raised an international furor. China protested the occupation to the League of Nations, which supported China and demanded the Japanese troops withdraw. The Japanese army refused to evacuate the area, however, and its defiance was supported by the press and public opinion at home.

Many Japanese thought their country had been unfairly stripped of the land conquered during the Russo-Japanese War, and they believed Japan had as much, or more, right to maintain Asian colonies as the West did. When the civilian government was unable to effect the removal of its army, Japan was forced to withdraw from the League of Nations.

The Japanese army utilized Ford and GM one-ton trucks in Manchuria, as well as two-ton domestic trucks developed in response to the endorsement by the Committee to Promote Domestic Production. The army found that the smaller foreign trucks, which it had requisitioned from private companies and citizens, were much more mobile and reliable than the larger domestic vehicles. Based on this experience, and eager to force a confrontation on the issue, the army announced it was supporting the construction of one-ton domestic trucks, which would put Japanese manufacturers in direct competition with the West. A showdown on the issue became inevitable.

Kiichiro Toyoda was keeping a close eye on political developments relating to auto manufacturing in Japan. The growing political strength of the military seemed to foretell increased support for the domestic auto industry, and Kiichiro paid frequent visits to two friends from Tokyo University who were closely involved with the government discussions. One was Kazuo Kumabe, now a professor of automotive engineering, who served on the Committee to Promote Domestic Production. The second was Kaoru Ban, the chief of administration for manufacturing industries at the Ministry of Commerce and Industry.

Kiichiro was never one for small talk, and he told these men directly what he had told few other people: he planned to honor his father's wishes and enter the automobile business. Kiichiro's friends were pleased with his decision, but they warned him not to put too much faith in the possibility of government support. Ban said that most high-ranking civilian employees of the government supported Japan's ties with the United States, and they feared that Japan would be drawn into a war with the U.S. if Ford and GM were forcibly ousted from Japan. Nonetheless, the men promised to keep Kiichiro informed about developments in the government, where new events seemed to be unfolding almost daily.

Around the same time as his visits to these men, Kiichiro was proceeding with the first small production project in his workshop.

He had completed an exhaustive study of a two-cylinder, 60-cc engine that Smith Motors manufactured for small vehicles in the United States. Kiichiro knew the details of the engine inside out, and he was preparing to produce facsimiles. These prototype engines would be tested and then installed on a few motorcycles to simulate production.

When Kiichiro wasn't working at the plant or holding strategy sessions, he brainstormed. He jotted down ideas as they came to him, constantly weighing one against another and against the technological capabilities of his equipment. Just as Sakichi had carefully calculated the market placement of his looms in the face of strong foreign competition, Kiichiro did as well. He realized that no matter how good his vehicles might be, they would be of little use if they were too expensive for Japanese people to buy and maintain.

Kiichiro knew that his cars, like his father's looms, would have to be cheaper than foreign models. And, increasingly, Kiichiro acknowledged the practical implications of that axiom. Since Kiichiro could never match the economies of scale of Ford and GM initially, he would have to sell his cars at a loss for a while. The goal of the company would be to increase production, while holding down costs, until production expenses fell below the selling price.

Kiichiro knew this formula would require that his automobile production be supported by the profits of Toyoda Automatic Loom Works for a number of years. He also recognized this would not sit well with Risaburo Toyoda, the crack administrator who was still the president of Toyoda Automatic Loom Works. Risaburo took his role as *kacho* of the Toyoda *ie* seriously, and he saw his first obligation as being the diligent protection of the now considerable family holdings. Risaburo was well aware Kiichiro was experimenting with a motorcycle engine, and that Sakichi had assigned Kiichiro funds for his research, but Risaburo regarded this enterprise with extreme wariness. Japan's largest *zaibatsu* had refused to enter the automobile business, and Risaburo knew these trading companies did not employ fools.

Risaburo's dread of the motor-vehicle business was based on more than hearsay evidence. While serving as the vice president of the Nagoya Chamber of Commerce, he had been involved in a failed attempt to produce buses. A number of businessmen in the Nagoya area had wanted to make the city the Detroit of the Orient, and they each had contributed money to produce a bus prototype. The project required far more expertise than the investors had available, however, and the project had failed, costing everyone his investment.

Although Risaburo was foresworn to protect the family's assets, he was also acutely aware he was the adopted member of the family who served as a manager. Kiichiro was the natural son, and the second-generation engineer. Sakichi had wisely left the business operations in Risaburo's hands, but Risaburo sometimes wondered if the ultimate value of his work wasn't secondary to Kiichiro's creative work. This caused Risaburo to be defensive and conflicted in his dealings with Kiichiro. He demanded that Kiichiro recognize his authority, while wondering if he actually deserved it. Risaburo's solution was to allow Kiichiro to indulge himself in his research, while resolving to tolerate it only up to a point.

Kiichiro brought his own misconceptions to his dealings with Risaburo. Kiichiro believed, incorrectly, that Risaburo had come from a privileged family and that he had been pampered as a child. This did not sit well with Kiichiro, whose difficult childhood was often spent close to poverty. Kiichiro thought that Risaburo hadn't suffered the way the Toyodas had, and Kiichiro's dealings with the president of Toyoda Automatic Looms Works were often overlaid with a veneer of contempt.

With all of their conflicts, Risaburo and Kiichiro tried to stay out of each other's way. Risaburo kept to his office, and Kiichiro remained in the shop. Yet whenever a mutual friend of the two men visited one of them, he would be quizzed incessantly about what the other was doing and saying. If Kiichiro learned in this way that Risaburo had spoken against him, he would fly into a rage about Risaburo at the man who had delivered the message. When Risaburo learned of something Kiichiro had said, he would react in the same manner. Ultimately, their friends learned never to speak of one Toyoda to the other.

But the flurry of activity taking place in Kiichiro's walled-off research area meant the day of reckoning was close at hand. It was becoming impossible for Kiichiro to insist he was simply conducting a research project, with only vague ideas about beginning automobile production some day. And Risaburo could only play dumb for so long.

Kiichiro finally went to Risaburo in September of 1933 and told him the prototype production of the motorbikes had been successful. The next step, Kiichiro said, was to expand the scope of his research. He hadn't been anxious to give this information to Risaburo, but he knew research on full-size automobiles was going to consume a lot more money. Kiichiro was careful to present this announcement as a statement of fact, rather than as a request for Risaburo's approval.

Risaburo reminded Kiichiro how difficult it was to build automobiles, how unsophisticated the related industries like rubber and steel were in Japan, and how many companies had already failed in their efforts to take on Ford and GM. Each time, Kiichiro told Risaburo with great assurance that it would be different this time. Hadn't Sakichi Toyoda succeeded in the face of his many nay-sayers? Ultimately, as both men knew it would, the discussion came down to the question of money.

Toyoda Automatic Loom Works was a medium-sized business in 1933, with capitalization of one million yen, and profits of 182,000 yen on sales of 1.96 million yen. Risaburo asked Kiichiro how much it would cost to get into the automobile business, beyond the one million yen Sakichi had left him. Kiichiro responded vaguely. He said it would probably cost about one or two million additional yen. He wouldn't be any more specific, and he was careful not to ask for any immediate disbursement of funds.

For his part, Risaburo said it might be possible to raise the money needed, but he didn't commit himself to a specific amount or a date when it would be available. Thus, each man left the encounter certain he had won his point. Kiichiro believed he had duly informed Risaburo of his intention to move the new automotive department of Toyoda Automatic Loom Works toward production, and Risaburo believed he had avoided making a firm commitment to a large and risky expenditure of funds.

Kiichiro's spirits brightened immediately, and he set about increasing the size of his small staff. Many of his new employees were colleagues from his university days who had studied auto technology. One of these men was an engineer named Takatoshi Kan, who had been chief engineer when the Nagoya businessmen undertook their bus project. Kan was working at Toyoda Loom Works, the company Sakichi Toyoda had disassociated himself from when his research funds were cut by Mitsui, and Kiichiro took particular delight in hiring this man away from his father's former enemy.

Another new employee was Seigo Ito, a high school and university classmate of Kiichiro's. Ito previously had been working for a manufacturer of three-wheeled vehicles in Kobe. That company had sent Ito to the United States to do research, after extracting a promise from him that he would remain with the company after his return. But Kiichiro, whose way of convincing people was to push without letup, was so effective in his courting of Ito that Ito agreed to join him.

Ito persuaded a physician to write a letter to his current employer saying he had to resign from his job to recover from tuberculosis. When the company, which didn't want to lose Ito, offered to pay for his convalescence, Ito had to tell them the truth. The company president was so caught up in the spirit of Japan's industrialization that he told Ito to go with his blessings because it was for the good of Japan.

Kiichiro sent some of his men to the United States to undertake additional studies of plant layouts, parts manufacturing, and materials. Others were assigned to do a detailed study of a 1933 Chevrolet that Kiichiro had purchased. The car was brought into the workshop and disassembled piece by piece. After a part was removed, a worker carefully measured it, then made a drawing of the part to exact scale. By the time all the drawings were completed, the disassembled parts of the car were laid out on the floor in the precise order in which they had been removed.

Kiichiro's friend Kan was assigned the task of designing a pilot manufacturing plant. Kiichiro's plan was for a 3,600-yard assembly and machine plant with a materials laboratory and an 1,800-square-yard warehouse. Kan made the drawings for the floor plan and consulted with Kiichiro on the type and placement of machines for the plant while others ordered what machines they could from catalogues. Often employees had to be dispatched to the United States or Europe to purchase machine tools.

Kiichiro and Kan also visited companies in Tokyo and Osaka that made imitation Ford and GM parts. The men asked questions and observed production in the plants, but neither was impressed with the expertise they found. The quality of the imitation parts was extremely low. The more Kiichiro saw, the more convinced he became that, at least initially, he would have to manufacture many of his components in-house or import them from overseas.

The list of components that he would have to manufacture himself swelled significantly when Kiichiro was unable to find a source for sheet metal in Japan. No steel foundry would invest in the equipment required for so uncertain a market, and all of Japan's steel-production capacity was being used by the military for shipbuilding and armaments and by the civilian government for railroads. Kiichiro had no choice but to build his own steel mill.

Kiichiro was so lost in this preproduction work that he barely had time to reflect on the enormity of his task or the measureless odds against success. It was a heady time of adventure and possibilities, but that mood changed abruptly when Kiichiro received a telephone call on December 26, 1933, from Kaoru Ban at the Ministry of Commerce and Industry. He told Kiichiro that another Japanese company had just upped the stakes considerably in the battle to get a domestic car into mass production.

The company, Nihon Sangyo, had acquired the manufacturing and sales rights to a little-known compact car called the Datsun. Several other companies had failed to make a go of the Datsun, but now Nihon Sangyo was going to make another bid through a new company called Jidosha Seizo. Jidosha Seizo, which would shortly be renamed the Nissan Motor Company, had a huge capitalization of ten million yen and expected to go into full-scale production within months.

The trading company behind Jidosha Seizo had planned to learn automobile production by cooperating with Ford and GM over an extended period. As a first step, their subsidiary companies began supplying Ford and GM with cast-metal and electrical parts as well as exterior paint. The company's scheme was to gain experience, draw closer to the Western manufacturers, and eventually form a joint venture with one of them. The company's plan, however, had been thwarted on every front.

Ford let it be known outright that it would not engage in a joint venture, and GM said it would consider one only if it retained majority ownership in the enterprise. Jidosha Seizo was ready to accept GM's position, but Japanese authorities were not. The Ministry of Commerce and Industry refused to permit majority ownership by a foreign company, and the Japanese military was opposed to any foreign participation in domestic automobile companies.

Realizing they had little hope of succeeding with their initial plan, Jidosha Seizo officials had decided to begin manufacturing on their own in a noncompetitive market. The compact Datsun was much smaller than any Ford or GM product, and because it had a tiny 750-cc engine, its operators were not even required to have a driver's license under Japanese law.

Jidosha Seizo may have wanted to avoid competing with Western products, but the company planned to swallow the Western mass-production approach whole. During their telephone conversation, Kaoru Ban told Kiichiro that the company intended to build the largest automobile plant in Asia—one that surpassed even Ford of Japan and GM in scale. It was to be Japan's first mass-production factory after the American model, with eighty-four thousand square yards of land, twenty-four thousand square yards of building space, and a seventy-eight-yard conveyor belt for the assembly line. The company was prepared to buy over sixteen-hundred machine tools in the United States and to hire a small cadre of American engineers as well. All of this was intended, Ban told Kiichiro, to enable the production of ten-thousand Datsuns a year.

Kiichiro was stunned. Jidosha Seizo was not merely unexpected competition; the factory the company was about to construct was eight times the size of the plant Kiichiro had on the drawing board. Kiichiro was still reeling when Ban gave him the second bit of bad news. As the military continued to gain power, the likelihood of protectionist automotive legislation was increasing. But if it were enacted, government assistance would be extended only to those companies that had proven their ability to mass-produce motor vehicles.

Kiichiro went directly to Risaburo's office after he got off the telephone. It was imperative, Kiichiro told Risaburo, that a meeting of the board of directors be held within a few days. Risaburo was not pleased, and he asked why a meeting was needed on such short notice. Kiichiro said events he was not at liberty to disclose made it imperative that automobile manufacturing be added to the company's articles of incorporation. It was also time, Kiichiro said, for the capitalization of the automobile department to be made official. Risaburo had no choice in the matter; he couldn't deny Sakichi's son a hearing before the board. He could only hope the company directors would be able to dissuade Kiichiro from his foolish obsession.

When the meeting of the board of directors was held on December 30, 1933, Kiichiro had to choose his words carefully. He could not reveal what he had learned about the growing likelihood the military would force Ford and GM from Japan, as that was highly confidential government information with international political consequences. Instead, he presented a carefully reasoned case for entering the automobile business, seasoned with a poignant reminder of the Sakichi Toyoda's legacy.

"It goes without saying that this company was built on looms," Kiichiro began, "but a company is a living thing. It shouldn't always stick to one product. May I remind you that Sakichi felt the same way?

"Even though this company at first only produced looms, from 1930 on, loom sales have dropped by half. Now we are sustained by our newer product, the spinning machine. Unfortunately, the international situation has steadily worsened since the Manchurian Incident, and in the first half of this fiscal year we posted disappointing exports. This does not foretell continued prosperity for the company."

Kiichiro knew he was making a good case, but when he started talking about automobile production—which was an enormous leap from the textile industry—he made the new project sound conditional enough to be less threatening.

"We are a machine manufacturing company," he said, "not a cosmetic or clothing company. And so I'm asking you to consider the automobile. If nothing else, we can revise our articles of incorporation to make research and trial manufacture of automobiles a possibility.

"Sakichi's courage and spirit have something to say to all of us about the development of automobiles. At present, the United States and Europe are going great guns making cars. Whenever you look at the industrialized Western world, cars are being made by human hands. Mitsui and Mitsubishi say we can't do it in Japan, but that's only because they're conservative aristocrats whose power lies in their money. And that's their shortcoming: they won't do anything risky.

"If someone does take the risk and succeeds, people will say anyone could have done it, just as I said anyone could have invented what Sakichi invented. What I'm saying is this: It's not a matter of whether or not it can be done, but of who will do it. You understand that, don't you? It is in the national interest to start an auto industry in Japan. That is why my father instructed me to enter this business."

At the conclusion of the meeting, the directors, having been duly moved by Kiichiro's presentation, voted to fund the automotive department through a two-million-yen increase in the capitalization of Toyoda Automatic Loom Works. And automobile manufacturing was added to the company's articles of incorporation. All the votes were affirmative on each question, including those cast by Risaburo Toyoda.

In January of 1934, Kiichiro dispatched Takatoshi Kan to the United States, where he would join another worker named Risaburo Oshima, who had been overseeing the Toyoda Automatic Loom Works contract with Platt Brothers in London. Kiichiro assigned these men to go on an intensive buying spree and study session at U.S. auto and auto-parts factories, as well as at the facilities of machine-tool manufacturers. In the period of a few months, and with limited funds, the two men were expected to purchase all of the remaining tooling needed to equip an automobile factory, while also acquiring a basic knowledge of how this equipment operated.

To insure that Japanese workers would be able to run these machines, the two men had to become familiar with countless work procedures. They had to learn how to heat, cast, machine, brake-press, and otherwise shape and form metal; how to mount glass; how to produce seats, dashboards, and other interior components; how to assemble, align, and paint or chrome-plate components; and how to monitor each production and assembly procedure for quality and efficiency. The men worked at a furious pace, stopping only to sleep and eat, while somehow getting each of the vendors to promise delivery of the machines in Japan by March.

The purchase of machine tools was an especially intricate task because of the way automobiles were produced in the United States. American automobile factories had large numbers of machines dedicated to performing a single task—stamping out a left door for a Model A or molding a steering wheel for a Chevrolet. These machines produced tens of thousands of identical parts in a never-ending flow from production line to warehouse, where the parts were stored until they were needed on the assembly line. As long as most of the parts produced were used, the cost of each individual part was held to a minimum.

Kiichiro Toyoda knew his fledgling operation would not be able to afford such an abundance of specialized machines, nor would he be able to utilize their enormous output. But even if he had been able to purchase them, Kiichiro wouldn't have. Just as Sakichi Toyoda had sought to produce looms for the Japanese market, Kiichiro wanted to produce automobiles for the Japanese market. To Kiichiro, American mass production, with its stockpiling of components and inherent waste, was an idiosyncratic American approach to manufacturing. It was a method developed in a land of vast open spaces and seemingly limitless natural resources, neither of which Japan had.

Kiichiro wanted to develop a Japanese production method that reflected the country's lack of space and resources, as well as the flexibility and versatility its people had developed under those restrictive conditions. He therefore instructed his men to buy general-purpose rather than specialized machines. Kiichiro planned to adapt each of these machines to multiple purposes when they were installed in his factory. He wasn't quite sure how he was going to do it, but he was confident he would be able to figure something out.

As Kan and Oshima made their rounds in the United States, Kiichiro sat down with his designers to specify the components of his first model. Kiichiro knew he could not get his enterprise off the ground under such a tight deadline without copying the designs of the huge Western auto manufacturers. Producing a car that was a facsimile of existing models also had a secondary benefit: it insured that replacement parts would already be on the market when his cars needed repairs.

After studying all of the Western cars he could, Kiichiro decided to model his engine and frame after Chevrolet components, his steering and drive train after Ford, and his body after the sleek DeSoto Airflow model. Kiichiro had his designers make drawings of each of these components. Hoping he wouldn't have to produce everything in-house, he sent other men out in largely futile efforts to find local manufacturers who could supply them. The basic layout of the pilot production plant in Toyoda Automatic Loom Works was completed in March of 1934, but the number of unexpected tasks that continued to crop up far outweighed the amount of work that had been accomplished. Nothing seemed to be going according to schedule, and everything was more difficult than anyone had anticipated.

One of the few specialized machines Kan and Oshima had purchased was an expensive gear-cutting machine that produced gears for the differential, or driving axle, of a car. When the machine was installed in the shop, no one could understand how to use it to produce the sophisticated involute gears with curved, spiral teeth that differentials required. Kiichiro called a friend at Tohoku University, but there was only one man at the school who had any information on these gears, and his knowledge was limited. Kiichiro was forced to send one of his engineers to the university for forty days until the engineer and the professor were able to resolve the problem.

Kiichiro received a call from his friend Kaoru Ban at the Ministry of Commerce and Industry in April. Ban said that Japan's relations with the United States and Europe were continuing to deteriorate in the face of ongoing Japanese military action in China. As a result, the Japanese military had stepped up its campaign to support domestic automobile production. The army was acutely aware that if relations continued to deteriorate and Western countries cut off auto exports to Japan, the army would be left without vehicles.

Ban said the Ministry of Commerce and Industry still wanted to permit auto imports, but the military people were pushing harder to prohibit foreign manufacturers from selling cars in Japan. There had even been talk about the military forming a nationalized automobile company. Something was sure to happen in the near future, and Toyoda had to move quickly. Ban added that it was important for Toyoda to inform the military of its production plans and said he would be happy to arrange such a meeting.

A few day later, Kiichiro met with Major Ito, who was responsible for the army's auto policy. Ito was very pleased to hear that Toyoda was going to make a car to compete with Ford and GM, and he asked Kiichiro for additional information. Kiichiro described the car he was working on and said that although he was only in prototype production, his company had already decided to buy land for a factory in the city of Koromo. He realized his company would not be profitable at first, but said he believed the loom works would be able to absorb a loss of one million yen a year for five years.

Major Ito said the army was in desperate need of companies to manufacture trucks for military use, and he almost begged Kiichiro to put a truck into production. Kiichiro would only say that he would think about it. He wanted to make cars, not trucks. Cars were where Ford and GM had made their reputations and their fortunes, and, like his father, he wanted to beat the Westerners at their own game. Nonetheless, Kiichiro left Ito's office thinking about manufacturing trucks— with their guaranteed market—as a means of gaining financial support and production experience for the automobile business.

Kiichiro's next contact with Kaoru Ban came in June, when Ban showed him a government report indicating that the domestic production issue was about to be resolved. As all the preliminary signs had indicated, there was to be some form of protectionist legislation, but its cover would be extended only to a few domestic companies, which would have to qualify for government certification. The relief offered would be enough to allow a company to escape from the shadow of Ford and GM, but the certified companies would have to prove they were capable of going into production. The terms of the legislation were to be finalized within weeks, and the bill would be introduced in the Diet by the end of 1934. Because under the Japanese political system any differences over legislation were resolved before a bill was introduced, passage was assured by spring of 1935 at the latest.

Another deadline was the last thing Kiichiro needed. The pilot plant had been constructed and the steel mill had been installed, but little else was working the way it was supposed to. Kiichiro had purchased a 1934 Chevrolet engine in May to use as the final model for his production engine, but there were serious problems with the engine.

The casting of iron for an automobile engine had turned out to have little in common with the casting of a loom. Whereas a textile machine was composed of an assortment of thin, flat metal components, an automobile engine was a thick block of iron that required holes for pistons, as well as passages for lubricating oil and coolant, all of which were required to withstand great heat and pressure. To produce those passages, an engine had to be cast around cores that occupied the space that would later be filled with pistons or fluids. These cores had to have special properties, and discovering the right combination of ingredients wasn't easy. It demanded the use of a process that Sakichi Toyoda had embraced, while his son disdained it: trial and error.

The metal-casting team began by using cores of river sand mixed with powdered coke, only to have the cores crumble and disintegrate when they were surrounded with molten iron. For weeks, the workers altered the mixture and tried again, but each attempt was a failure.

While this experimentation was going on, Takatoshi Kan returned from his trip to the United States and suggested the workers add a variety of oils to the sand, a process he had observed at a Ford foundry in the States. The casting workers were near despair, and they eagerly accepted the suggestion. But when the molten iron was poured over the oil and sand cores, the thousand-degree iron was suddenly expelled from the mold and spewed into the air, where it showered down upon the workers who were collected in the room.

The engine-casting problem was eventually solved, but it was soon replaced with another dilemma that also stymied everyone for hours or days. Kiichiro was at his wit's end. Almost a year had passed since he had first spoken to Risaburo about expanding his research, and when was it all going to end? Almost every day an expensive new production machine arrived, and the number of employees in the department was nearing a thousand. The initial capital of two million yen was long gone, and although he hadn't asked, Kiichiro suspected his expenditures were nearing five million yen—two-and-a-half times Toyoda Automatic Loom Works' 1933 profits.

Risaburo Toyoda could barely contain his rage as the bills poured into the company. "Toyoda is an awful place," he hollered at anyone who would listen. "Kiichiro does whatever he pleases! I never should have come to work here." The directors of Toyoda Automatic Loom Works, who, like Risaburo, had authorized this folly, were near mutiny. If this weren't enough, the Ministry of Commerce and Industry was pressuring Kiichiro to supply documentation to support Toyoda's motor-vehicle-production performance.

What the Ministry didn't realize, while everyone at Toyoda was acutely aware of it, was that the company's five-million-yen investment and one thousand employees had yet to produce a single vehicle.

5
FIRST SALES

Kiichiro and his staff completed their first prototype engine, called the type A, in September of 1934. The six-cylinder, 3,389-cc motor took some coaxing before it roared to life, but it ran and that was the important thing. Groups of workers in the shop crowded around in excitement after they heard the burst of unmuffled exhaust. The weary engineers were ready to celebrate, but Kiichiro reserved his judgment until the engine's output could be measured on a testing machine.

Sure enough, the engine was producing only thirty horsepower, while the Chevrolet engine it was modeled after produced sixty. Kiichiro grimaced and told his men to find the source of the power loss. Although this work would be urgent, it wouldn't hold up production, as the remainder of the car was months from completion.

The component now causing the most difficulty was the sheet metal for the body. Kiichiro had purchased large presses in the United States to stamp body parts out of sheet metal, and he had even imported the sheet metal itself when his staff couldn't produce the quality of steel the job required. But the dies for the stamping machines were proving to be a tremendous obstacle.

The dies went into the bottom of the presses, and when the ram on a press hammered a piece of sheet metal into a die, the metal would flow over the die and replicate the die's shape. Since the dies were unique to the car Kiichiro's staff had designed, they had to be made from scratch. Kiichiro discovered that no one on his staff had the skills and experience to make dies that would stand up to the tremendous pressures generated during stamping, and outside shops said it would take them over a year to fabricate what Kiichiro needed. Just to keep things moving, Kiichiro had sheet-metal workers hammer out body parts by hand. This was acceptable for a prototype, but the die problem would have to be resolved before production could begin.

At this point, with costs continuing to mount and the deadline for certification as a motor-vehicle producer looming in the near future, Kiichiro resigned himself to truck production. The guaranteed military market and the less rigorous body design of a truck made this an immediate solution that was too easy to pass up. Kiichiro was adamant about producing automobiles, however, so he refused to forsake cars for trucks. Instead he did something that would have been unthinkable to anyone else. Amid the incredible confusion and strain of trying to begin car manufacturing, Kiichiro decided he was going to make cars *and* trucks.

Kiichiro called Risaburo Oshima away from his design work one day and told him there had been a change of plans. Oshima was to stop working on the car project. After his months of fervent work, Oshima thought Kiichiro had either gone crazy or bankrupt. But Japanese customs would not allow a worker to say such a thing to his employer, so Oshima stood there with a look of horror creeping over his face.

Kiichiro could tell what Oshima was thinking, so he sought to reassure him. No, he said, we are not abandoning the automobile. We will still make cars, but first we are going to make trucks. Oshima relaxed for a moment until Kiichiro gave him a second piece of shocking information. The truck would have to be in production in less than a year.

Only Kiichiro knew this plan was not totally mad. Many of the components the workers had prepared for the car could be transferred to the truck, particularly the engine and drive train. In addition, Kiichiro had purposely selected a car frame that was longer than it needed to be. The extra frame length meant the engine could be moved forward on the frame to create room for a truck bed in the rear.

The employees in the auto department greeted the news of truck production with enthusiasm, even though it would greatly increase their workload. Their venture would have a greater chance for success with two products, and everyone redoubled their efforts. Takatoshi Kan, who had been working on the engine, immediately set to work to find the lost horsepower.

Kan suspected the intake manifold was the problem, and sure enough, he found a blockage that was restricting the flow of air-fuel mixture into the cylinders. But when the engine was tested again, the horsepower had increased only to fifty. Now he suspected the cylinder head. He thought the exhaust gases were not exiting from the cylinders properly. If spent gases remained in the cylinder, they would dilute the incoming gasoline mixture and decrease engine power. Kan cut one cylinder free from an engine and enclosed the sides with glass. He then blew cigarette smoke into his model and observed how the smoke moved during the piston cycle. The test confirmed there was an obstruction in the cylinder head, and after experimenting with modifications, Kan coaxed sixty-two horsepower out of the engine—two more than the original Chevrolet engine produced!

The first prototype car, called the A1, was completed in May of 1935. It was a sleek, black sedan with a prominent chrome grille that swept back onto the top of the hood in the style of the DeSoto Airflow it was modeled after. In actuality, all of the car's components except the engine block, cylinder head, transmission case and other housings, and a few accessories were adapted from existing Western models.

Nonetheless, Kiichiro and his men had done what most everyone in Japan said they couldn't do. They had produced a car that, at least in appearances and initial performance, rivaled the Western imports. Everyone, and especially Kiichiro, realized this was only one small victory in a long battle, but the automotive department of Toyoda Automatic Loom Works took a moment to mark the occasion.

A tent was erected in the courtyard of the pilot factory, where a ceremony was held. A *shimenawa*—a rope that is hung from the gates of Shinto shrines and tied around sacred objects—was attached to the car, while a Shinto priest blessed the car and prayed for the future success of the company. Kiichiro observed the proceedings from off to the side with a mixture of pride and sadness, for this visible symbol of his accomplishments provoked bittersweet memories of how he had come to arrive at this point.

Sakichi Toyoda had been in the final months of his life when he gave Kiichiro the charge to make automobiles, and Kiichiro could feel his father's presence at the factory now. All the bitterness Kiichiro had sometimes felt toward his father was gone. He realized part of the congratulations being offered this day belonged to Sakichi. Sakichi had been the first Toyoda to refuse to listen when people told him something couldn't be done. In that way, Kiichiro was simply carrying on his father's work.

When the festivities were over at the factory, Kiichiro got into the A1 prototype by himself and drove out to the cemetery where Sakichi's ashes were buried. Kiichiro was a stoic who didn't show emotions easily, and this was a difficult time for him. He pulled the first Toyoda automobile ever made over to the side of the road near the family grave. Then Kiichiro got out and told Sakichi he had done as his father had asked.

The automotive department produced a second and third prototype of the A1 in the following days, and then production was stopped. The engineers took the cars out on the streets around Nagoya and subjected them to endless road tests. The drivers were aware that their initial cars were not perfect, and they were not ashamed by this. Kiichiro had taught his men as his father had taught him. *Kaizen*, or continuous improvement, was an integral part of the production process. To men in the automotive department, they were not correcting mistakes, they were improving their product.

Kiichiro contributed to this process by driving the first A1 to Tokyo University to visit the professors who had contributed so much to the car's development. Kiichiro wanted to show off his new machine at his alma mater, but he also wanted the professors to tell him how it could be improved. The professors, too, had something to learn, for the A1 had served as a proving ground for all the engineering theories they had read about but had not tested.

When Kiichiro returned to the automotive department, all of the sentimentality he felt about his father quickly faded. Kiichiro knew he had to do something Sakichi never would have approved of. Kiichiro told his workers that everyone was to make an all-out assault on the truck prototype. It had to be finished by the end of summer, he said, and then it would immediately go into production.

The engineers were astounded at Kiichiro's instructions. It would be very difficult to finish the prototype that quickly, but it would be highly irregular to then put the truck into immediate production. No matter how much of the design was copied from Western trucks, all of the factory workers were novices at automobile production. And everyone was well aware that Sakichi had firmly established the ethic that no product should ever be offered to the public without sufficient testing and improvement.

Kiichiro didn't tell the men about the political developments he had been monitoring so closely or the tremendous costs that needed to be recouped. Instead, he rolled up his sleeves as he had every day and plunged into the middle of the factory work himself. When the truck prototype was progressing and the workers seemed focused on their new tasks, Kiichiro went to see Risaburo Toyoda about a final piece of business.

Kiichiro began by telling Risaburo he wanted to call a meeting of the board of directors. After Risaburo pressured him, Kiichiro told Risaburo why. In order to begin truck production within a few months, the automobile department needed *another* three million yen—a doubling of its current capitalization. Risaburo was incensed, and he accused Kiichiro of intending to bankrupt the family with his foolish nonsense. How could he think about further debt when he had yet to sell a single vehicle? Kiichiro refused to argue with Risaburo or to become angry. Rather, he simply restated his request for the meeting.

Risaburo, whose diligent oversight had kept the textile operations profitable while Kiichiro repeatedly plunged the company into debt, had had enough. Risaburo said that he would not call the meeting, nor would he authorize another cent in expenditures. Very well, Kiichiro said, then I will leave the company.

Risaburo was inconsolable for several days after the confrontation. He had been certain he would be able to rein Kiichiro in when the dabbling in the automotive business truly began to threaten the company. But now he knew he had been wrong. Risaburo no longer felt conflicted about dealing firmly with Kiichiro. He was convinced he had to stop him from bankrupting the company.

The person who had always been caught in the middle of Risaburo and Kiichiro's feuding was Aiko, Risaburo's wife and Kiichiro's half sister. Although she loved both men, she understood Kiichiro in a way that few other people could. They were both Sakichi's children, and she knew she had to support her brother in his efforts to carry forward their father's work. Ignoring Japanese custom of the time, which dictated that women not involve themselves in their husbands' business affairs, Aiko told Risaburo that, regardless of the financial consequences for the company, he had to find the money for Kiichiro.

Risaburo's fury was unleashed again when his own wife refused to support him, but he also came to realize that he had no options if he was to remain in the family. He had to secure the funds for Kiichiro.

Risaburo sought the advice of Tojiro Okamoto, a manager of Toyoda Spinning & Weaving Company who had been very close to Sakichi. Okamoto had left the Mitsui Trading Company to work for Sakichi in the early days of the textile business. He was younger than Sakichi, but the two men took an immediate liking to each other, and Okamoto became Sakichi's confidant. Okamoto had since become an arbitrator in the ongoing battles between Risaburo and Kiichiro. Now Okamoto was playing that role again as he listened to Risaburo and sympathized with him, while urging him to schedule the board meeting nonetheless.

Although many of the directors of Toyoda Automatic Loom Works were, like Risaburo, seriously alarmed about Kiichiro's continuing drain on the company's resources, there were also a number of executives in the company who had worked with Sakichi for many years. These men understood and respected Sakichi's drive to fulfill his own vision and his desire to improve the lot of his countrymen, regardless of the cost. This was the spirit that had created their company, and these men believed it remained vital to the company's long-term prosperity.

Tojiro Okamoto was a man who could see both sides of the question, and he recognized it was time for him to play a vital role. He would become a matchmaker between the two factions of the company and find a way to resolve the current crises. Okamoto reminded Risaburo that Toyoda's Shanghai operation had been very profitable in the fourteen years since Sakichi had established it.

Risaburo looked at Okamoto without saying a word. Risaburo was well aware of the profits that had been piling up in China. But he also knew that strict laws, with harsh criminal penalties, governed the transfer of large sums out of China. Such transactions required the permission of both the Chinese and Japanese governments, and with Japanese troops currently occupying Chinese territory, there was no chance such approval would be given. Okamoto held Risaburo's silent gaze for a long moment before quietly bowing and leaving the room for a trip to Shanghai.

In the following days, Okamoto quietly arranged for a social gathering to take place before the directors' meeting, inviting Kiichiro, Risaburo, and Akitsugu Nishikawa, the head of Toyoda's operations in Shanghai, whom Okamoto knew had fond memories of Sakichi. In inviting Nishikawa to the gathering, Okamoto explained the situation and asked if there might be something Nishikawa could do to resolve the impasse.

On the evening of the meeting, Risaburo and Kiichiro were startled and annoyed to find themselves seated at the same table with only the other two men as buffers. Okamoto had told neither Risaburo nor Kiichiro who would be attending, but Risaburo instantly understood why the head of the Shanghai operation was present.

Nishikawa quickly broke the tension as sake was served. He offered a toast and, then began speaking of his high regard for Sakichi. "During his stay in Shanghai," he said, "Sakichi spoke frequently of the role of the automobile in civilizing Asia. Yet he was very distressed to see that every automobile that arrived was made in either the United States or Europe. It was his feeling that Japan must devote its energies to developing an automobile industry to rival that of the United States.

"Now I hear the Toyoda concern has finally taken the lead in Japan by deciding to produce automobiles. I was overjoyed to learn that the first prototype has already been built and is in operation. Were he alive today, Sakichi would be very happy indeed."

Nishikawa continued to speak glowingly of Sakichi, and of the importance Sakichi placed on moving the company into automobile production. Then he got directly to the point of the evening. "I have heard from Mr. Okamoto that you are planning to increase your investment in the automobile department by three million yen," Nishikawa said. "If I do not offend, please let me contribute that amount from my end of the business."

Risaburo could hardly believe the deftness with which Okamoto had arranged the entire affair. Without saying anything more than the minimum necessary to each man involved, Okamoto had arrived at a solution that met everyone's needs. Kiichiro would be able to move forward with production. Everyone left the restaurant happy that evening, and the increase in capitalization was approved unanimously by the board of directors the next day.

News of the impending domestic-automobile-production law had been circulating through the expatriate community in Japan for several years, and Ford of Japan was taking a series of steps to try to strengthen its standing in the country. Ford had greatly increased its parts purchases from Japanese suppliers, and the company was also talking about producing a car with 100-percent Japanese content sometime in the future.

But Ford's main strategy was a plan to replace its knockdown assembly plant with a full-scale plant, one that included all of the equipment needed to manufacture cars from scratch. Ford's executives believed that if they bought real estate and built a large plant before the new law was enacted, it would be very difficult for Japan to exclude Ford from the Japanese market without provoking trade retaliation from the United States.

Ford attempted to purchase a large plot of reclaimed land from the city of Yokohama, an industrial town just south of Tokyo, in April of 1934. The city was anxious to make the sale, since the land was vacant and the Ford factory would increase its tax revenues. But the Japanese military, aware of Ford's strategy, was strongly opposed to it. In the middle of the land negotiations, a Japanese army officer met with the mayor of Yokohama and persuaded him to cancel the talks. Ford was stymied momentarily.

Then, in April of 1935, Ford located another plot of ground in Yokohama that was owned by a private corporation. Ford began negotiations with the owner, and again a military officer visited in an attempt to disrupt the sale. This time, however, the owner resisted the pressure from the military, and the sale was concluded. Ford began moving forward with its construction plans at a rapid pace.

Until this time, the Ministry of Commerce and Industry had resisted the army's wishes to exclude foreign manufacturers from the Japanese market. Ministry officials changed their minds, however, once they learned that Ford's expansion plans were about to become a reality. The officials believed that once Ford became a larger presence in Japan, the domestic manufacturers would never have a chance, and foreigners would dominate the local market for years to come. The possibility always existed, also, that in time of war Japan could be totally deprived of motor vehicles. Ministry officials contacted their military counterparts and said that they were now prepared to support the military's position. Everyone agreed they had to move quickly to prevent the Ford factory from becoming a *fait accompli*.

Drawing up the legislation required a degree of finesse, since the Japan–United States Commercial Treaty guaranteed reciprocal commercial rights to citizens of both countries. The solution the ministries of commerce and war arrived at was to declare motor vehicles an industry vital to national defense. No country allowed foreigners to operate its airplane factories, the officials reasoned, and Japan would restrict foreign ownership of its automobile factories for the same reason.

In August of 1935, the two ministries jointly presented the proposed

Law Concerning the Manufacture of Motor Vehicles to members of the cabinet. The proposal specified that any manufacturer producing more than three thousand cars annually had to be licensed by the government; that the majority ownership and voting rights of a licensed company had to be held by Japanese citizens or entities; that licenses would be restricted to only a few manufacturers; and that existing auto manufacturers that were not awarded licenses would be required to restrict their business activities to their current production levels.

The proposed bill also granted financial relief to licensed manufacturers, including a five-year exemption from national and local business taxes, as well as a similar exemption from import duties on machinery, equipment, and materials purchased abroad. Conversely, import duties were raised on completed vehicles and knockdown sets, and foreign exchange regulations were tightened for foreign companies doing business in Japan. As a final incentive for domestic companies, the commercial code was altered to facilitate raising capital, but the bill also awarded the government approval rights over the business plans of licensed manufacturers.

Kiichiro Toyoda judged the proposed bill to be a mixed blessing when he received a copy at the factory in August. The legislation provided the financial breathing room he knew a domestic manufacturer would need to avoid being crushed by Ford and GM, but the vehicle Kiichiro would be entering into the competition for a license was a truck rather than a car. As always, Kiichiro resolved he would return to the automobile one day, but in the meantime had to get back to work. He had to see his prototype truck, designated the G1, through the final days of its construction.

Kiichiro had barely left the factory since the car prototype was completed in May. He had brought bedding to the workshop, and when fatigue forced him to, he retired to it for a few hours a day. Every other hour of the day and night, seven days a week, he worked. There were designs to approve, technicians to urge on, suppliers to locate, and technical difficulties to troubleshoot. Always, there were more things to do than there was time to do them.

Kiichiro had still not resolved the difficulty with the stamping-press dies, and he was forced to subcontract out the sheet-metal work for the truck body. The solution the subcontractor devised was incredibly primitive. He had his workers dig holes in the ground, which they then used as dies. They placed pieces of sheet metal over the holes, and then hammered out body panels by hand.

Somehow, the first G1 prototype was completed on August 25, 1935. The truck was just under twenty feet in length, with a carrying capacity of 1.5 tons. The engine was the model A engine that had been produced for the car, and many of the components were again based on Western models, this time trucks rather than cars. The cab of the truck was in the style of the 1930s automobile—prominent chrome grille, freestanding headlight pods, and rounded fender lines—and the bed was formed with wooden planks. It was a sturdy-looking vehicle, built high off the road and with heavy-duty suspension to keep it from self-destructing on Japan's notoriously bad roads.

There was no time for a celebration on this occasion. Kiichiro was too acutely aware of the government license for which he would soon have to qualify. He knew there was no margin for error in the proposed law. Just a few companies—perhaps only one—would be licensed. Given the heavily restrictive provisions of the law, an unlicensed manufacturer would go bankrupt overnight. After all the months and years of toil, and all the millions of yen, Kiichiro could not even allow himself to think about the consequences of failing to get a license.

So, with one prototype vehicle completed, Kiichiro announced to his staff the date on which the G1 truck would be presented to the public. It would be November 18, the anniversary of the founding of Toyoda Automatic Loom Works—less than ninety days away. If that goal weren't enough of a reach, Kiichiro had already told the stockholders he would be producing 150 to 200 vehicles a month by January of 1936.

The date for the first Tokyo showing of the G1 had to be pushed back three days, until November 21, but five vehicles were completed by that time. Kiichiro went ahead to Tokyo by train with his newly hired marketing director, Shotaro Kamiya, and left it to his men to deliver the trucks.

In preparation for their Tokyo trip, the drivers filled the truck beds with spare parts and tools. Packing spare parts was not an act of bad faith, it was an acknowledgment of reality. The first G1 trucks had been road tested, and design alterations were made constantly while the trucks were in production, but everyone was aware there were many more improvements to be made. The automotive department at Toyoda was inexperienced, and motor vehicles were tremendously complex; so no one thought spare parts were anything but prudent.

The truck convoy left the Toyoda factory at 5 A.M. on the day before the exhibition, receiving a send-off from employees and from local reporters, who were on hand to record the historic event. There were several mountain passes between Nagoya and Tokyo, and a truck broke down before the convoy had cleared the first one. The truck's steering wheel locked, and an inspection revealed that a piece of the steering linkage had broken in half.

Some workers crawled under the truck to remove it, while others hunted through the spares for a replacement. Although no other major parts broke during the trip, the engines required adjustments every few hours. The trucks would pull to the side of the road, and mechanics, lacking gauges and instruments, would tune the engines by ear.

The trucks arrived in Tokyo at 4 A.M. the next morning, one hour short of a full day since they had left Nagoya—less than two hundred miles away—and only hours before the exhibition was scheduled to begin. The weary men who had made the journey hastily set to work washing and polishing the trucks, which were filthy from their passage over dirt roads. Kiichiro, who had been frantic that the trucks would not arrive in time, breathed easier as they were moved into position and the doors were opened to the public.

The exhibition was a huge success. Representatives from government bureaus, members of the military, and average citizens crowded into the hall. Kiichiro gave a speech in which he vowed to lead the way in establishing a domestic motor-vehicle industry, and everyone offered kind words of congratulations. It was a vital step forward for the company.

After months of hope and despair, a Toyoda motor vehicle was now a publicly acknowledged truth. Those in attendance were especially impressed with the price of the G1. It was selling for 2,900 yen, 200 yen less than Ford and GM trucks of a comparable class. The price was, however, far less than the actual cost of building the truck.

Kiichiro knew that although the Tokyo exhibition was important for public relations, the exhibit to be held in two weeks in Nagoya was ultimately more consequential. In Tokyo the G1 was showcased in a display hall for the purpose of exhibition. In Nagoya the trucks would be unveiled in a dealership—and they would be for sale. Kiichiro trusted that Shotaro Kamiya, his new marketing man, would make the Nagoya show as successful as Tokyo's had been.

Shotaro Kamiya had been the highest ranking Japanese national at GM of Japan before coming to work for Kiichiro one month before the Tokyo show. Kamiya left GM because he was concerned about the coming regulations on foreign auto manufacturers, but also because he had become disillusioned with GM's treatment of its Japanese dealers.

It was the custom in Japanese business dealings for each party to assist the other so that their enterprises would be mutually successful. GM, however, worked by American standards, and each party to a deal was interested only in his own success. GM terminated dealers who didn't produce, whereas Japanese manufacturers traditionally tried to help them improve their performance. Kamiya felt torn between two worlds, and no one at GM was interested in adopting local practices.

As Kamiya became increasingly dissatisfied, he went to visit an old friend, Tojiro Okamoto—the man who had helped arrange Kiichiro's funding through Toyoda's Shanghai office. Kamiya told Okamoto he was thinking of leaving GM, and Okamoto arranged a meeting between Kamiya and Kiichiro for that night.

Kamiya was intimidated about meeting the son of the famous Sakichi Toyoda, but Kiichiro's honesty put him at rest. Kiichiro spoke directly. He said he had excellent engineers in his employ, but no one, including himself, knew anything about selling motor vehicles. If Kamiya joined the company, he would be allowed to make all marketing decisions himself.

Kamiya was excited about the prospect of getting in on the launch of a new Japanese enterprise, and although everyone at GM of Japan told him he was crazy, he took the job immediately—so quickly that he forgot to inquire about his salary. His first paycheck came as a shock. Whereas he had been earning 600 yen a month at GM, he was paid 120 yen at Toyoda—the same salary that Toyoda's directors received.

Kamiya brought a number of Japanese GM employees with him when he left, and, even more importantly, some GM dealers switched over to Toyoda as well. The first GM dealer to defect was the owner of Hinode Motors of Nagoya. Since Hinode Motors was one of GM's leading dealers, as well Toyoda's first recruit, their showroom became the setting for the G1's initial offering to the public. But as with the Tokyo show, the first G1 truck almost didn't make it to the Nagoya opening.

The final trim work for the G1 was being farmed out to a subcontractor, and when Hinode's first truck was being delivered to the trim shop a day before the opening, the driver brushed a back wheel against a utility pole. Weak rear-axle welds being the Achilles' heel of the G1, the axle broke on contact. A replacement truck was rushed out from the factory, and its trim work was completed the morning of the Hinode Motors show. Risaburo Toyoda, having heard about the incident, arrived at the show and immediately asked the manager of Hinode, "Is our truck still running?"

The G1 received an enthusiastic response from the people in Nagoya, since it was not only a domestic truck but a locally produced one; however, many of the sales people at Hinode Motors were ill at ease. They wondered if the product's reliability was equal to the customers' enthusiasm. The company made a decision to proceed cautiously. They would restrict the first sales to people who were close to Toyoda, or those who were strongly motivated to buy a domestic vehicle. That is, they sold the first G1s only to people who would tolerate the inevitable breakdowns.

No one was pleased by the many defects in the first Toyoda trucks, but no one was suicidal about them either. Kamiya and the people on the sales staff constantly told their dealers that the company would stand fully behind the product. Repairs were made free, regardless of the cost, and sometimes trucks were replaced with new ones. On one occasion when a truck carrying a load of fish stopped running and the fish spoiled, the company compensated the owner for his loss. If a dealer didn't have enough service technicians to handle repairs, Toyoda mechanics were sent out. In the factory, Kiichiro and his men worked just as hard to eliminate the flaws from their trucks as they had worked to bring them into production.

Kiichiro made the elimination of defects his top priority. He often left the factory to call on dealers to discover what problems they were having with the trucks. He also asked officials of Hinode Motors to keep careful records of the problems they discovered, to help identify trends. When Kiichiro learned of a run of problems with a specific component, he would set his engineers to work to discover the cause of the flaw. If the defect was in a component from a supplier, Toyoda engineers would visit their factory to help them diagnose and eliminate it.

Kiichiro had so much confidence in his product and in his

ability to upgrade them through *kaizen* that, without saying much about it to anyone, he instructed a designer to begin working on sketches for a plant that would produce five hundred passenger cars and fifteen hundred trucks a month. This production figure was equal to the combined monthly output of Ford and GM in Japan—at a time when Toyoda was making barely fifty trucks a month. The designer hid his surprise for a moment, until Kiichiro gave him the second part of his instructions. Leave room for expansion, Kiichiro said, since we will be making ten thousand vehicles per month in the second stage, and twenty thousand in the third stage.

The automotive department was preparing to move out of its temporary quarters at Toyoda Automatic Loom Works and into a small-scale production plant nearby in early 1936. One by one, the defects were being eliminated from the truck, and things were beginning to go more smoothly. Kiichiro finally had some breathing room. But just as Sakichi had not rested on his laurels after his first success, neither did Kiichiro.

He added a bus to the product line, then returned to work on revising his first passenger car, the A1. Public response to the aerodynamic style of the A1 had been mixed, so Kiichiro developed a new model, called the AA. The AA had softer lines and a more upright grille, giving it a more formal appearance. Kiichiro had located a company that was able to produce stamping dies for the AA, and these critical components were nearing completion. For added measure, Kiichiro also had his staff design a convertible model of the car, called the AB Phaeton. As all of these elements came together, the car was eased back into prototype production.

During this relative lull in the normally frantic process of getting his automotive department into production, Kiichiro took the time to reflect on what he had learned over the past few years. The most salient conclusion he reached was that many of the problems he encountered were due to lack of expertise.

Kiichiro had received a fine education, as well as the assistance of Japan's top researchers, but yet that had not been enough. The difficulty was that Japan, eighty years after Commodore Perry had removed its veil, was still eons behind the West in understanding and using modern technology. Kiichiro had men pounding fenders out of sheet metal on the ground, while Henry Ford's workers had the world's most sophisticated steel mills at their disposal.

The knowledge gap meant that, too often, Kiichiro's men were working as Sakichi had—by trial and error. When the rear axle housings on G1 trucks continued to crack, it took Kiichiro's staff months to identify the cause. They discovered the origin only after comparing their axle housings with GM's. They learned that GM used electric welding—which actually fused the parts together—on their axle housings, while Toyoda was using gas welding, which merely tacked the parts. Had Kiichiro or his men had a more thorough grounding in metallurgy, they would have been able to anticipate this problem before the axle housing was put into production.

Kiichiro realized that if his company was ever going to make cars to compete with those from the West, let alone develop innovative products, he needed to organize a research and development department. He wanted the department to be free of everyday production concerns to encourage creativity, and that meant locating the research building away from the factory. The site Kiichiro chose was Tokyo.

Kiichiro's decision to open a small office in Tokyo came at a fortuitous time. The pressures of getting the G1 truck into production had not done much to improve relations between Kiichiro and Risaburo Toyoda, and the men continued to have heated disagreements. Their disputes strained operations at company headquarters, and they also produced tensions among family members away from the office. Kiichiro's wife had been urging him to avoid this situation by moving the family to Tokyo, and locating the research office there was the perfect justification for doing that.

The increasing government involvement with the automobile business also made it important for Toyoda to have an official business location in the nation's capital. Kiichiro had been commuting frequently from Nagoya to Tokyo, and he was forced to use the Tokyo office of his in-laws, who were in the department store business, to conduct his affairs. The Tokyo location would also allow him to keep in closer touch with the many contacts he was establishing in government circles.

Kiichiro learned firsthand what being in the middle of government developments meant shortly after he moved his family. The Manchurian Incident had brought an end to party rule in Japan, and political violence was constant. Radical young army officers, convinced that Japan was growing weak and vulnerable to the West, agitated for an overthrow of the civilian government. On February 26, 1936, more than 1,500 of these soldiers seized government offices in Tokyo, while roving bands of assassins attempted to kill the premier and key cabinet officers. Some senior military officers, sensing this might be an opportunity to seize power, allowed the coup d'etat attempt to play out. The rebellion ultimately collapsed, but disaffection within the military continued unabated.

When the situation in Tokyo cooled off, Kiichiro established his research lab and offices in a building that was used as a car hotel. Automobiles were strictly regulated in Japan in the 1930s, and because cars contained gasoline, they couldn't be parked on the street but had to be stored in fire-retardant structures. Only wealthy people owned private cars, and they were usually driven by chauffeurs. The chauffeurs had to return the cars to flame-resistant storage buildings at the end of the day, so parking garages were built where the cars could be stored. Kiichiro joined with several other companies to build one of these structures in Tokyo, then reserved part of the space for his offices.

Toyoda's first employee at the new location was Eiji Toyoda, Kiichiro's cousin, who had just graduated from college. Eiji boarded with the family in Tokyo and became an integral part of the household. He became something of an older brother to Kiichiro's oldest son, Shoichiro, who was then eleven. Eiji also became a young protégé to Kiichiro, with whom he shared many characteristics. Both Eiji and Kiichiro had spent their early years living adjacent to the textile mills their fathers owned, and both were quiet and reflective men who paid little attention to their appearance. Most importantly, Eiji and Kiichiro were both enthralled with machines.

Kiichiro wanted to do a wide range of research in his new lab, so he gave young Eiji an eclectic assortment of assignments. Kiichiro would show up at the office, tell Eiji to find out about machine tools, and then disappear for days. One day Kiichiro bought a small French airplane, had it transported to the lab and instructed Eiji to disassemble the engine and make sketches of its internal parts. Another time Eiji was dispatched to an army base to study a new military autogiro—a forerunner of the helicopter.

Kiichiro recruited a number of academics to work in the lab. He sometimes gave them specific assignments when there was a problem at the assembly plant, but that was infrequent. The men worked on rockets and alternative fuels and amphibious vehicles. Kiichiro's aim was to allow the researchers to work on whatever it was that interested them. He was a man who strongly believed in the ultimate worth of research, even though it seldom paid off in immediate production improvements or new products. Kiichiro realized it was the unexpected or even misunderstood discovery that would pay long-term rewards. He knew intuitively that the research lab would one day help him make the world-class automobiles he yearned to build.

The Law Concerning the Manufacture of Motor Vehicles was passed in May of 1936, and the government announced it would identify the companies to be licensed under the new law in September. Kiichiro was relieved that the law was official at last, but he tried not to think about the long wait for word on the licensing decision. The company was so heavily involved in motor-vehicle production at this point that it made no sense to worry about the license. Kiichiro had taken the automotive department well beyond the turn-back point. He had no option other than to work under the assumption that his application would be approved.

The company had enough prototype AA and AB cars off the assembly line to begin offering them to the public, so Shotaro Kamiya and his marketing people prepared for the launch. The passage of the automotive law was a great help in wooing GM and Ford dealers into the Toyoda fold, and once they had a dealer body, the marketing staff prepared to introduce their cars to the public. Advertising and publicity materials were created, and a traveling exhibition of the cars was planned for September.

An exhibition in Tokyo on September 14 displayed the full Toyoda line to the public for the first time—the model AA and the AB convertible, and an improved version of the truck, called the GA. It was a proud and happy moment for Kiichiro. Just as he had planned, he was a manufacturer of trucks *and* cars. A silent movie that Kiichiro had commissioned about auto manufacturing was playing at one end of the room, while an attractive young woman read the script out loud. It was a gala event, with all the men in suits and the hall decorated with potted trees.

To supply the day's final moment of drama, a government official stopped by to notify Kiichiro that Toyoda Automatic Loom Works had been awarded the first of only two auto-manufacturing licenses that were being issued. Kiichiro was overcome with the relief of a man who, after a long and arduous journey, has arrived home.

A final fortuitous event occurred later in September. Shotaro Kamiya and the marketing staff had suggested staging a contest to select a logo for the new car. Kamiya thought the contest would be a great way to attract publicity, and he was right. Twenty-seven thousand entries were received, and the winner was a logo that incorporated the name *Toyoda* written horizontally in Japanese script, surrounded by a circle.

Risaburo Toyoda, finally recognizing his brother-in-law's vision, became an enthusiastic supporter of the automotive department when it was licensed, and he seldom interfered in its workings. But when Risaburo saw the winning logo, he insisted on one change. He wanted the department name changed to *Toyota*, rather than *Toyoda*.

It took only eight brush strokes to write *Toyota*, and eight was a lucky number, since the Japanese character for eight suggested growth. *Toyoda* required ten strokes, and the character for ten was not fortuitous. After the company's miraculous escape from what Risaburo thought was certain bankruptcy, he saw no reason to tempt fate again.

6
OMENS

The automotive department of Toyoda Automatic Loom Works was becoming the tail that wagged the dog by early 1937. What Kiichiro had undertaken as a research project seven years earlier was now a sizable venture that was overshadowing the company from which it had sprung. Kiichiro had three thousand people on his payroll, offices in three cities, and a massive new plant on the drawing board. The Toyoda Automatic Loom Works had become an automobile company that also made textile machines. The next logical step was to break the automotive department off to form a new entity. The only problem was, the automotive department was still hemorrhaging money because Kiichiro's cars weren't selling.

The Toyota vehicles on the market were much improved over Kiichiro's first trucks, but problems persisted. One vehicle would break down or fail to start, and though the company would correct the problem, the owner told friends and neighbors of the trouble. The image of Toyotas as inferior vehicles became fixed in people's minds through word of mouth. A newspaper in Nagoya ran a cartoon depicting a Toyota truck stranded on the side of the road with a broken axle. The caption read, "Toyota truck in Zen meditation."

Despite the heroic efforts Kiichiro was making to constantly improve his products, the problem he was up against was larger than just getting the bugs out. The Japanese public was in awe of all Western products. They didn't believe any domestic company could make vehicles as good as those from the West. People who had connections with a domestic manufacturer or those who wanted to support Japanese industries would suspend this disbelief. But most others wouldn't. The Catch-22 for Kiichiro was that unless he sold enough of his cars to make a profit, the automotive department would go bankrupt before it could equal the quality of Western cars.

Whenever a Toyoda Automatic Loom Works director asked Kiichiro when the automotive department would stop losing money, he would reply that he couldn't say when, but he could explain why it would happen. Kiichiro would point out that in the United States there was already one car for every four people. Even given the relative poverty of Japan, he reasoned, the day had to be coming when there would be one car for every ten Japanese citizens. With a population of almost one hundred million in Japan at the time, that meant an automotive market of ten million vehicles. If cars were replaced only once every ten years, that represented one million sales a year.

These figures kept people at the loom works happy for a while. But with the automotive department dwarfing the textile operation—and capable of bankrupting it—Kiichiro knew he was going to have to come up with something more concrete, particularly since the company had to make a decision about constructing a new plant soon. Approving that expenditure was going to require enormous courage.

Kiichiro asked Risaburo to call another board meeting and then closeted himself off from the endless demands on his time for a few days. Kiichiro played with production figures and costs, balancing one against the other, before producing a report for the board entitled "Cost Accounting and Prospects for the Future." Sakichi Toyoda had been an entrepreneur as well as an inventor, and now Kiichiro was adding accounting to his engineering skills.

Kiichiro told the board that Ford and GM trucks were selling for 3,000 yen in 1937, meaning the manufacturers were probably charging their dealers 2,800 yen for the vehicles. Working backwards, the production cost of a truck was probably 2,400 yen. By making trucks at a cost of 2,400 yen, Ford and GM, as well as their dealers, were making good profits.

Kiichiro said that even with Ford and GM's future in Japan now uncertain, the company was going to have to undercut their prices. The U.S. companies had established a price reference point in Japan, and consumers wouldn't buy a Japanese vehicle that wasn't cheaper. To make a profit, Toyota's production cost would have to be lower than 2,400 yen. Kiichiro then revealed that Toyota's unit production costs in October had been 2,948 yen, but with a 33-percent boost in production in November, unit costs had fallen to 2,761 yen.

Kiichiro argued that the only path to follow was proceeding with the new production plant, where the monthly manufacturing quota would be 1,500 vehicles. With production at this level, he promised, unit costs would fall below 1,900 yen, and the automobile department would be profitable within a year and a half. Kiichiro could see his audience was impressed with the simple logic of his presentation. Then he dropped his bombshell. Construction of the plant would cost thirty million yen.

Surprisingly, there was little resistance to Kiichiro's proposal. The directors had gradually come to see the future for automobiles was bright, even if the present was uncertain, and the only question was how the company could raise the required funds. Toyoda Automatic Loom Works was a privately held company with a capitalization of six million yen. Kiichiro was asking for five times that amount for factory construction alone. There was little chance the company would be able to raise the money Kiichiro needed and remain privately held. The answer was to spin the automotive department off as a separate, stock-issuing company, then hope Japanese investors shared their optimism about the automobile business.

Toyota Motor Company, Ltd., was formally established that summer. The capitalization was twelve million yen, and a twenty-five-million-yen line of credit was arranged. The company sold 240,000 shares of stock to twenty-six stockholders, primarily family members, company directors, and the Mitsui Trading Company, which had been encouraged to make the investment by the Japanese government. Outside investors remained unenthralled with auto manufacturing.

In recognition of his role as *kacho*, Risaburo Toyoda was elected president of the new company, and Kiichiro was executive vice president. Thus, Toyota Motor Company came into the world, its ledgers awash with red ink and its parking lot filled with unsold cars and trucks.

Kiichiro believed that with the financing for the new plant and the legalities of incorporation under control, he could address the expansion of the company in a rational way. World events quickly altered those plans, however. The military situation in China took a turn for the worse in July of 1937, when Japanese and Chinese troops clashed near Peking. The Chinese government had been anxious to drive Japanese troops off the mainland of Asia, and they used the fighting at Peking as a rallying cry to launch a full-scale assault against Japanese troops in China. China and Japan were soon at war.

The fighting in China precipitated a huge demand for motor vehicles, and the unsold Toyotas were cleared out of Nagoya overnight. Toyota and Nissan Motor Company, the second licensed manufacturer in Japan, were each given orders for six thousand trucks, with instructions to manufacture them quickly. Military expenditures soared to over 50 percent of the national budget, and the government began taking control of the economy. In order to meet the demand for munitions, harsh measures were instituted, restricting the flow of staple goods and capital within the country. Life in Japan was altered radically, and Toyota's gamble began to look like it might pay off more quickly than anyone had expected.

The site Kiichiro selected for the new Toyota plant was in the city of Koromo, twenty miles east of Nagoya. The land was a stretch of virgin slopes and plains covered with red pine, but it was not suitable for agriculture. Sakichi Toyoda, remembering the constant struggle of the farmers in the village of Yamaguchi, had taught Kiichiro not to construct a factory on arable land. Kiichiro made that one of the guiding principles of his location search.

Large manufacturing plants were usually built near a port to facilitate transportation of materials and finished products. Kiichiro ignored that bit of conventional wisdom when he purchased a 472-acre inland plot in the town of Koromo, which was actually rather remote. There wasn't even a direct train line to the location from the Nagoya area, where most factory workers lived.

Kiichiro's plan for getting his men to the job was twofold. First, he didn't envisioned the plant as a free-standing factory. He was going to build a company town, like those constructed in the United States in the early twentieth century. The complex would encompass company housing—dormitories for the single men and apartments for those who were married—an education center, parks, a hospital, and a food store. The various Toyoda businesses around Nagoya had become known in Japan as rural enterprises, whose employees came from small towns, and Kiichiro wanted to maintain that rustic atmosphere even though he was building a modern plant.

The second part of Kiichiro's plan was more visionary. Kiichiro knew that not everyone would want to live in a company town and that these people would require transportation. The closest rail line was distant from the factory, but Kiichiro believed the day would come when his employees would drive to work in their automobiles. This notion was unimaginable to even the most optimistic person in Japan in the mid-1930s. The price of an automobile represented five years' wages for a factory worker. That may be true now, Kiichiro would tell those who scoffed at his idea, but it won't always be.

Even with his grand dreams and his backlog of truck orders from the military, Kiichiro recognized that making a go of a plant as large as the one he was designing for Koromo was a shaky proposition. The company had stockholders now who would be expecting dividends before long, and there were huge bank loans and interest to be satisfied first. Production costs were going to have to be minimized in every way possible. No savings could be overlooked as too small. The staff of Toyota Motor Company would have to be ruthless in finding ways to eliminate waste. This endless search to eradicate waste, which was second nature in a country with so few resources, would become a vital factor in the company's future.

Kiichiro began by designing the production methods that would be employed at the new plant. He studied the flow of components through the existing factory in the same manner that his father had scrutinized the manual looms in his neighbors' homes. Kiichiro walked around the shop and observed workers doing their jobs, looking for wasted motion and inefficient techniques. He had a reputation for delegating authority and for asking each employee to bring his intelligence to bear on his work. Now Kiichiro took to touring the factory to talk with his men about their work methods. How, he asked them, could they perform their tasks more quickly and efficiently? With the number of steps involved in the construction of an automobile, a few seconds of waste in each procedure resulted in tremendous cumulative inefficiency—waste that was easy to overlook because it occurred in such small increments.

The assembly workers at Toyota's first plant were paid on a piecework basis. Given the natural differences in people's abilities and motivations, some workers in the assembly process produced more finished components than others. When the variations in work speed were great enough, bottlenecks were created and components piled up in certain areas. This problem was compounded by the differing degrees of complexity each job entailed and the amount of precision involved. The result was a production process that didn't operate smoothly and, when components were damaged as they sat around waiting to be moved to the next station, a waste of resources.

Kiichiro lived in a culture that valued harmony and simplicity. The prospects of achieving these attributes in the early stages of automobile production had been nil. Everything had been chaos and complication then, as workers scrambled to somehow get things done. People were learning as they were doing, and this process was not conducive to order. It also generated tremendous amounts of waste, as piles of faulty components had to be scrapped.

But the automotive department's old ways were in the past now. Kiichiro was starting with a clean sheet of paper, and as he studied the production process and thought about the new plant, he was determined to make it the industrial equivalent of a Japanese garden—a place of balance and consonance.

Kiichiro knew that the Americans, with their vast resources, could afford to stockpile massive numbers of parts, but waste grated on Kiichiro. The sons of rural villages knew the importance of thrift. If his process could be perfected, Kiichiro reasoned, there would be no need to warehouse components, and the capital usually required to pay for warehoused parts would be freed for more productive use. Taken to its extreme, Kiichiro could imagine a day when no automobile component would be produced unless it was needed to assemble a car. If the car could be sold before payments to suppliers of the component parts came due, there would be no need for operating capital at all.

Kiichiro knew his master plan would take decades to enact, if it could be done at all, but in the meantime he carried forward the first parts of it. In his operating factory he hung a sign that read: JUST IN TIME. What he meant, he told the workers, was that no component for a car should be produced before it was needed. Components should be made, therefore, just in time.

To reinforce this, he had his foremen check the production schedule each morning and then issue slips of paper to their workers. The papers specified the number of components that were to be produced that day. If a worker finished his allotment early, he was free to leave. If a problem developed, the worker would have to work overtime to complete his assignment.

After talking to his workers and observing them perform their tasks, Kiichiro also began writing a set of standardized work procedures for every job in the plant. He was trying to develop an all-encompassing training manual for the new Koromo factory, where the work force would be increased to five thousand men. As an additional benefit,

Kiichiro acquired a keen understanding of production methods, which he used to create a meticulously detailed formula for locating production machinery in the new plant.

The directives Kiichiro sent to his designers were unequivocal: arrange the various buildings so their proximity will be conducive to the smooth flow of complete automobiles; place special-purpose machines so their location will be favorable to the flow of work from one station to the other; build machines that will be flexible enough to meet any requirements, bearing in mind that they would be used for twenty or thirty years.

Although Kiichiro was pragmatic enough to know he couldn't eliminate warehouses at this point, he directed that their size be kept to an absolute minimum. He was determined to never allow more than one day's supply of any part to sit idle beside the assembly line.

Kiichiro visited the construction site of the new factory constantly, and, as was his practice, he had bedding sent out so that he could sleep there when necessary. He was a familiar figure to the construction workers as he charged through the muddy fields, studying blueprints, barking orders, and taking notes. The only way Kiichiro knew how to manage a project was to plunge into the midst of it. People at the site who didn't know Kiichiro would never have guessed from his appearance and degree of involvement that he was the executive vice president of an important corporation.

Kiichiro brought his young cousin, Eiji, out from the research office in Tokyo and gave him oversight responsibility for the details of the construction. It was the summer of 1938, a very hot and humid time in the area, and the factory was being equipped with machines while it was still being built. Eiji identified machine locations from the floor plan and painted locating marks on the floor while construction workers were building the walls. Before lights were installed, the machine shipments often arrived at night, and everyone groped around in the darkness, working like miners in a shaft. The chaos of reality was brought to bear on Kiichiro's fastidious master plan.

With the military pressuring Toyota to move into full production promptly, the Koromo plant was in operation by November of 1938. The war in China was raging, and Toyota sold every truck it could make. The unrelenting demand for military vehicles proved Kiichiro wrong in his estimate of the plant's profitability. Kiichiro had made the then fanciful prediction that Toyota Motor Company would be profitable within a year and a half of opening Koromo. Instead, Toyota was profitable instantly.

The company recorded a net profit of 800,000 yen for its first full year of operation. As profits continued to increase, previously uninterested trading companies and institutional investors asked to become stockholders, and the company was able to draw on external capital for the first time.

Kiichiro was not satisfied with this financial success with trucks, and he returned to his experiments with automobiles every chance he got. When a friend traveled to Europe, Kiichiro asked him to buy any interesting cars he saw and ship them back to Japan. The man sent a German front-wheel-drive car with a wooden body. Kiichiro had the research lab study the car, and used their results to try his hand at front-wheel-drive prototype cars. He made several minicars with 600-cc engines that might be able to compete with the 750-cc Datsun being made by Nissan, and he refined the model AA into a new model AC. All of this effort was for naught, however, for the military was taking more control of industrial production every day, and the military was not interested in passenger cars.

The military began rationing gasoline for private automobiles in early 1938. As Western countries cut off shipments of raw materials to Japan because of the war in China, the military issued orders forbidding the manufacture of any automobiles except for military use. Kiichiro could argue that the cars he was working on had military applications, but steel was difficult to obtain, and when it was available he could not specify the grade he wanted. As controls on manufacturers continued to escalate, Toyota and Nissan were ordered to build truck assembly and service facilities on the war front in Manchuria.

Ford and GM continued with minimal operations in Japan at this time. With the restrictions placed on them by the Japanese government, and the likelihood of another world war increasing daily, the two American companies were looking to salvage whatever they could out of their Japanese businesses.

GM had approached Toyota in 1936 about a joint venture, but Kiichiro hadn't been interested. Kiichiro had said from the beginning that he was opposed to a joint venture, particularly with GM. GM didn't allow its foreign partners to export finished cars to the United States, or to manufacture their own engines and other major subassemblies.

Ford, however, permitted foreign partners to do both, so when Ford contacted Toyota in 1938, discussions were held.

The talks with Ford concerned only trucks, which were of secondary interest to Kiichiro, so he didn't object when Toyota and Ford reached a tentative agreement to produce full-sized trucks jointly. Ford had produced tens of millions of vehicles, and such an arrangement would give Kiichiro access to much more Western technology than was available to him at the time. At first the government couldn't decide whether to allow the deal to go through, and then the military insisted on withholding approval unless Nissan was also included.

More talks were held, and they progressed to the point where a three-way provisional agreement was signed. It gave 30-percent shares of the business each to Toyota and Nissan, with the remaining 40 percent going to Ford. Before any further action could be taken on the deal, war broke out in Europe and relations between the United States and Japan reached the breaking point over the Japanese military action in Asia. In December of 1939, Ford and GM halted their business operations in Japan.

In January of 1941, Kiichiro assumed the presidency of Toyota Motor Company, and Risaburo Toyoda retired to the position of chairman of the board. Kiichiro took full responsibility for the sizable company he had created but, with the military taking over more of the economy each day, the company was hardly his to run anymore. Conditions in Japan deteriorated rapidly after the country went to war with the United States in December. At the inception of the war, Japan's annual production of crude steel was equal to twenty days' production in the United States. Steel seemed to evaporate from the country after Pearl Harbor. There were massive shortages of materials in resource-poor Japan from the first day of the battle.

Toyota was supposed to be building vehicles, but most of the company's energy went into finding materials. The military told the company what could be built and when, but the bureaucratic controls were such that it was difficult to produce anything. One department of the army placed orders for vehicles, another allocated manufacturing materials, and a third controlled distribution of completed vehicles.

After working so hard to rationalize the production process at Koromo, Kiichiro could only bury his head in his hands. Rather than having the flow of the assembly line control the production of materials, the availability of materials was determining the flow of production. The just-in-time production system ceased to exist.

The one bright light in an otherwise dim situation was that Toyota was able to develop a more complete and competent network of suppliers. The Japanese automobile parts industry was disorganized and unsophisticated before the war, and Kiichiro had thus put only limited effort into developing suppliers. He knew he would have to establish a strong supplier network sometime to fully enact his just-in-time production system, but he hadn't had the time. With the beginning of the war, Japan was forced to impose order on the supplier network to insure the continuation of military production.

New government regulations specified that parts suppliers were to be regarded as branch plants of manufacturers, and the manufacturers became responsible for the performance of their suppliers. Business relationships between suppliers and manufacturers were to be regarded as permanent under the regulations, and the underpinnings of good alliances were put into place. Both parties were forced to find reciprocally beneficial solutions to their problems. Toyota suppliers formed their own mutual assistance and cooperation organization, where information and technology was shared among the members.

The regulations on suppliers were only a partial solution for Toyota, however, and the company was forced to manufacture 45 percent of its own component parts. This helped expand its areas of expertise and often led to the formation of new companies. A machine tool division that was created to equip the factory at Koromo also began selling its products to other companies, as did the electrical-parts manufacturing department, which became the Nippondenso company.

Kiichiro oversaw the operation of the factory and the maintenance of manufacturing standards during this time, and he strove to preserve the technology the company had acquired. But as he saw his company slip from his grasp and his country move toward defeat, Kiichiro fell into depression and resignation. He lost his enthusiasm for the business, and began spending little time at Koromo. Mitsui Trading Company, as a major Toyota shareholder, sent a vice president to the factory, and Kiichiro turned the operation over to him.

Kiichiro spent most of his time in Tokyo, doing research in preparation for the day when his company would be returned. He read extensively about the industrial recovery of Germany after World War I and developed plans for making another assault on the automobile business after the war. But he never lost his love for machines, and sometimes he participated in research assignments to create new military vehicles that interested him.

The company developed an amphibious four-wheel-drive vehicle that would run at full speed on water and manufactured 198 of them. It was a large, hulking vehicle that resembled a cross between an armored truck and a boat. With its slab sides and porthole windows, it looked nothing at all like the elegant and distinctive prewar vehicles the company had made. But utility was the order of the day, and at least the engineers could treat it as a technical challenge.

The company also built a kit truck with a body and frame that were constructed in sections. The vehicle was designed to be disassembled easily so soldiers could carry the components over steep mountain passes and reassemble the vehicle on the other side. Kiichiro had continued his research on aircraft, and in 1943 the army proposed that Toyota enter the business. So the company set up a joint venture with Kawasaki Aircraft to make powerful Benz V-12 aircraft engines.

But these creative experiments were the exception to the rules of military supervision and rote production of trucks. Toyota was officially designated a supplier company of military goods and placed under the direct authority of the Ministry of Munitions in 1944. The plant was being operated by a greatly reduced number of regular employees, complemented by thousands of people of all ages and backgrounds who had been conscripted into production work by the government. The workers Kiichiro had trained so carefully were replaced by soldiers, schoolchildren, and townspeople—even Buddhist priestesses, geishas, and convicted criminals.

By August of 1944, resources in Japan were almost fully depleted and the government began to improvise. The implications for the motor-vehicle business were tragicomic. After having firmly established the principle of constant improvement as the guiding light of the company, Toyota was directed to build trucks with one headlight, with only rear-wheel brakes, and with wooden cabs, running boards, and rear beds.

Kiichiro kept to his house in Tokyo as the war neared an end. When the house he was living in was destroyed during a bombing raid in May of 1945, Kiichiro moved his family to a house in the suburbs. He dug a pond in the back yard to occupy himself and to supply the dirt he needed under his fingernails to feel like he was alive. Then he used the pond as a fishing hole where he could forget about what was going on outside of his estate.

Kiichiro was at the house on August 14, when word came that B-29s had dropped a bomb on the casting shop of the Koromo factory. The workers had been warned off by the air-raid sirens, but 50 percent of the operation had been wiped out.

Toyota's workers returned to the plant on August 15 and began cleaning up debris. Word spread that Emperor Hirohito was going to make an important radio broadcast—the first ever for a member of the imperial family—and a radio speaker was installed outside on the grounds.

Everyone was stunned when they learned Japan was acknowledging defeat. Conditions at home made surrender inevitable, but people hadn't allow themselves to think it was possible. Unable to continue with their work, people drifted back to their homes or dormitories.

Most of the conscripted workers who had been relocated to the Koromo plant began searching for a means of transportation home in the following days. That was a formidable task. Railroad service was totally disrupted, and fewer than 50 percent of the trucks and 18 percent of the cars in Japan were still operable.

Millions of houses and up to a third of the nation's industrial capacity had been destroyed. Resources that were scarce naturally had become nonexistent. Food supplies were so short that there were serious concerns about mass starvation. After decades of progress in industrial development, Japan was, in many ways, back to the nineteenth century.

The weeks after August 15 were a time of enormous uncertainty for the Japanese. No one knew what life under the occupying forces would be like, and rumors were epidemic. After living in fear of foreign occupation for hundreds of years, the worst nightmare of the Japanese people was about to become a reality. Westerners were going to control their country. This prospect would have sent the population into panic a hundred years earlier, but now people were too tired and hungry to do anything but hope for the best.

Kiichiro Toyoda, who had gone into a malaise as the war dragged on and his machines were employed for purposes he had never intended, suddenly regained his old drive. The Koromo factory he had built was heavily damaged, and he had no idea whether he would be allowed to resume motor vehicle production, but he had thousands of employees who were depending on his company. A core of over three thousand employees had stuck it out at Toyota Motor Company through the worst of the war years, and they needed to feed their families and get on with their lives.

Showing the resourcefulness that had allowed him to manufacture cars with the most meager of resources, Kiichiro prepared to put his people back to work. He firmly believed that, somehow, Toyota would return to the automobile business soon, but he couldn't stake people's lives on a decision that would ultimately be out of his hands. Instead, Kiichiro began investigating and creating new enterprises.

He focused on needs he knew were beyond the control of the occupying forces: food, shelter, and clothing. With the company's textile operations already making cloth, Kiichiro invested in a sewing machine company. For shelter, he looked into starting a company that would manufacture fireproof homes from precast concrete. For food, he considered raising loaches—small, eel-like freshwater fish that were high in protein—and dispatched an employee to consult with an expert at Kyoto University. He sent his cousin, Eiji, to set up ties with a ceramics maker in a nearby town that was famous for glazed china. He planted crops on the grounds of the plant and built a flour mill, bakery, and charcoal plant. He sent his oldest son, Shoichiro, to the northern end of Japan to learn about the fish-sausage business.

Shoichiro Toyoda had graduated from high school in 1945 and was studying mechanical engineering at Nagoya University. Kiichiro told Shoichiro to interrupt his studies and travel to Wakkanai, located on Hokkaido, the northernmost Japanese island. A friend of Kiichiro's had bought a processed-fish-products company there, and Shoichiro's instructions to his son were to learn how to make *chikuwa*, or fish sausage.

Hokkaido was noted for its very harsh winters and its deep-water-fishing industry. Shoichiro spent six months there. He worked, ate, and slept in a plywood-planked attic with a handful of fellow workers. They bought fish from the local markets, processed it, then stuffed it into casings. Shoichiro used his engineering background to develop and repair the automatic machines that cooked the sausages on a conveyor belt over charcoal, and he waited for word from his father on when he could return home.

Kiichiro, with his plants all but idle, began manufacturing electric stoves and irons and making pots and pans out of materials originally intended for aircraft. He also invested in dry-cleaning businesses. But building cars remained close to his heart, and when Japanese military officers with technical skills returned to civilian life, Kiichiro hired two hundred of them, even though he didn't know whether he would be able to resume auto production. To occupy these men in the meantime, he told one of them—with all seriousness—to design an automobile that would also fly.

As soon as the staff of the General Headquarters of the Allied Forces (GHQ), the command office of the occupying army, established their outposts, they announced they would institute sweeping reforms in Japan. The aim of GHQ was to promote demilitarization and democratization of Japan's political, economic, and social environment. The constitution was to be revised, farmland was to be redistributed, militarists were to be expelled from public office, and the *zaibatsu* that were the nucleus of the economy were to be dissolved, with almost all important business leaders being purged.

Kiichiro was notified in September that Toyota could resume production of a limited number of trucks for use in the reconstruction effort. The intention of GHQ was to delay the manufacture of consumer goods until economic reforms were instituted, but the dearth of raw materials would have prevented this from happening anyway. Kiichiro manufactured the first postwar trucks using materials that were on hand, but in subsequent months things got far more complicated.

When Kiichiro attempted to obtain additional steel for production, steel mill officials told him they lacked the raw materials needed to fill the order, and that they had no idea when they would be able to obtain them. To get steel, Kiichiro had to dispatch men from his purchasing staff to the coal mines in southwestern Japan. The men would buy coal from the miners, arrange for trucks to transport the coal to the nearest port, and then ship the coal to the steel mills, where it would be used to fill Toyota's orders.

While his assembly workers were easing back into truck production, however minimal, Kiichiro had his designers and engineers working on a new car—one that would be radically different from past Toyotas. Kiichiro needed only to look out the factory windows to see the poverty that had gripped Japan. His automobile company had to grow crops to insure that its workers would have something to eat. Automobiles were being rigged to run on burning charcoal because of the lack of gasoline. An occupying army was preparing to totally dismantle Japan's economy. With things this bad, Kiichiro knew they weren't going to get better anytime soon. He decided it was time to rethink the Japanese automobile.

Kiichiro decided the passenger cars that would be appropriate to postwar Japan would not be imitations of large American-style cars. Conditions in Japan had always been significantly different from those in the United States, and that was especially true now. Japan was a small country with fewer resources than ever, and to Kiichiro that meant it was time for him to build small cars.

Other Japanese manufacturers had attempted to build small cars, but given Japan's lack of manufacturing experience, they had simply been not-especially-good cars that happened to be small. They suffered from cramped interiors, excessive weight, low horsepower, and severe vibrations. It was no wonder all of these cars had failed to find a market.

Kiichiro resolved to build a car that was designed to be small from the start—a car that was fuel efficient and inexpensive to build, but one that was also comfortable and had adequate power. Kiichiro knew the Germans had moved in this direction with the Volkswagen, and he told his people to start thinking about a similar car for the Japanese. A good small car would sell well in Japan, with its narrow roads and expensive imported gasoline. Kiichiro reasoned that if the car was reliable and a good value, it could probably also find a large export market around the world.

Using the Volkswagen as their model, Toyota's designers set about rethinking their approach to the car. The first change they decided on was to abandon the bulky steel frame that had given existing Toyotas their rigidity. Steel frames worked like beams in a building, but they also protruded into the passenger compartment and added substantial weight. The new car, dubbed the model SA, would have a monocoque, or unit-body, construction in which rigidity was derived from a one-piece body shell. Racing cars used this type of construction because of its strength relative to its weight, and perhaps the ultimate monocoque was the egg. Every aspect of the car would require new components, and Kiichiro assigned other men to create an engine, a suspension, and a drive train that would make the SA the most remarkable car Toyota had ever built.

7
AT THE PRECIPICE

General Douglas MacArthur, the supreme commander of the Allied Powers in Japan during the Occupation, was the twentieth-century equivalent of Commodore Matthew Perry. Perry's primary—if unstated—mission had been to secure a coal depot for U.S. steamers engaged in trade in the Orient. Perry knew, however, that if his visit was successful it would remove the veil from Japan and open the country further to the West. The ramifications of Perry's visit had ultimately been much more profound than anyone suspected. The shoguns lost their power, the emperor was restored to the throne, and a civilian legislative body was created.

Feudalism in Japan was supposed to have ended fourteen years after Perry left. But when Douglas MacArthur arrived in the country in 1945, he concluded that vestiges of it were still present. The structure of Japanese society was hierarchical, with economic and political power concentrated in the hands of a small number of people. Half of the cultivated farmland was worked by tenant farmers. Women did not have the right to vote. By MacArthur's standards, this social structure was unacceptable, and he took it as his mission to complete Perry's work. MacArthur intended to bring Japan further into accord with the ways of the Western world.

MacArthur believed the concentration of wealth and power in the hands of the Japanese aristocracy had led to the rise of militarism in Japan. He theorized that Japan's affluent classes had tolerated the expansionism that led to war because it was in their economic interest. MacArthur meant to topple these leaders from their positions of power, deprive them of their wealth, and restructure Japanese society. His ultimate objective was to remove what he saw as the conditions that had permitted the militarists to take power. Like Perry, MacArthur brought troops with him to enforce his will.

MacArthur began by dismantling the military leadership. Trials were held, and seven hundred military leaders were executed. He then turned his attention to the large trading companies that dominated the Japanese economy, the *zaibatsu*. MacArthur announced he would disassemble the largest ones. War reparations would be extracted from their holdings, and what remained was to be spread throughout the economy.

MacArthur turned first to Mitsui, the largest *zaibatsu* in Japan. The stocks of Mitsui-related companies comprised over 5 percent of the total securities of corporations in Japan. Most of these stocks were concentrated in the Mitsui holding company, and only Mitsui-affiliated companies owned securities in the holding company.

MacArthur decided he was going to eliminate the Mitsui holding company and released all of its securities on the Japanese stock market. He also planned to prohibit members of the Mitsui family from having any connection with their former businesses and to freeze their assets. The twenty-six major Mitsui affiliates would be divided into eighty-four smaller companies, and the former officers of these companies would be forbidden from engaging in any economic activity whatsoever.

These decisions held ominous overtones for Kiichiro Toyoda, because Mitsui-related companies held 14 percent of Toyota's stock. Kiichiro was notified by MacArthur's office in late 1945 that the company was being considered Mitsui-related by GHQ, and the GHQ staff was considering possible dissolution and seizure of assets of Toyota Motor Company.

When the proceedings were completed, the main holding company of Toyoda manufacturing operations was disbanded. The Toyota Motor Company stock held by the Toyoda family was released to the market, and Risaburo Toyoda was forced to resign from his position as chairman of the board. Nippondenso and Toyoda Spinning & Weaving were detached as independent companies, but Kiichiro Toyoda was permitted to retain his position, and no Toyoda assets were confiscated.

While reordering of the economy was underway, MacArthur's staff also moved forward with a second major aspect of their democratic reforms. MacArthur believed the working class in Japan was relatively powerless and that this was another relic of Japan's feudal past. The primary manifestation of the problem, MacArthur postulated, was the lack of Western-style labor unions in Japan. There were only four hundred thousand union members in Japan, and MacArthur pressured the government into enacting a law that authorized the formation of unions in companies all over the country.

While MacArthur and his staff believed that labor unions had been repressed in Japan, most Japanese people didn't understand why there was a need for unions. Japanese unions at the time included many communists—people who wanted to radically reform the structure of Japanese society. Most Japanese workers thought there was no distinction between communism and labor unions, and people who weren't sympathetic to communism didn't join them.

Conversely, American labor unions were based on the premise of class conflict within American society. It was presumed that company owners would operate only in their own interest and that workers had to protect themselves by banding together with other workers. American labor unions were formed according to job classification. Auto workers and electricians joined unions composed primarily of other workers who performed the same tasks. If workers' demands were not met, everyone in the same trade could withhold their services, having immense repercussions for their employers.

The American union model had never taken hold in Japan because Japanese workers didn't perceive class conflict within their society. Japanese culture was based upon mutual and interlocking social obligations among citizens. The reckless use of authority was held in check by the responsibilities of managers to their workers. Workers and owners did have different roles, but these differences were not seen as the basis for discord. Workers believed everyone in the company was working toward the joint goal of prosperity, and that if the owners achieved success with their enterprises they would reward their workers fairly.

The spirit of cooperation within companies was so complete that workers took their sense of personal identity from the companies they worked for rather than from the jobs they performed. An assembly worker at Toyota's Koromo plant thought he had much in common with other Toyota employees, but no connection at all with Nissan assembly workers.

Japanese business leaders had argued against the imposition of unions with GHQ, asserting they were inappropriate for the culture, and rife with communists as well. They insisted that fostering unions was encouraging communism, which was antithetical to enhancing democracy in the country. All of this was to no avail. MacArthur demanded that labor unions be allowed to organize, saying any dissension the communists might provoke would be an important exercise in the democratic process for the Japanese.

Kiichiro Toyoda received the news of the labor union regulations with a heavy heart. He had always identified closely with his workers, and now they would be pitted against him. He was a man who was far more comfortable getting his hands dirty on the shop floor than sitting in an office. In addition, Kiichiro was intensely interested in continuing his work of rationalizing the automobile production process. For that to happen, he knew the atmosphere within the factory was going to have to be one of mutual trust and cooperation. Without this milieu, the just-in-time production process would never be realized. Workers would see themselves as individuals who produced or assembled individual parts, rather than as team members who were dedicated to making cars.

Nonetheless, the new law had been passed, and with GHQ staff members were touring Japan with union organizers to enforce it, the point was no longer open to debate. As a courtesy, representatives of Toyota's work force visited Kiichiro and formally asked for his consent for them to organize, which he gave. The Toyota Motor Koromo Labor Union was established in early 1946, with the cooperation and participation of company management.

Given the harrowing economic conditions in Japan in early 1946, the first issue the union had to discuss was a monumental one. How was the Toyota Motor Company going to survive when the people of Japan could barely afford food, let alone motor vehicles?

While the officers of the GHQ were planning their sweeping reforms of Japanese society, American soldiers under their command were also having an effect on the Japanese population. The occupation army opened a department store in the Ginza section of Tokyo, and it contained all the advanced consumer products Americans were accustomed to. The store offered everything from electric razors and sophisticated radios to tailored clothing and sporting equipment. The U.S. dollar was the only currency accepted in the store, and it was off limits to Japanese, but Tokyo residents often stopped in front of the store's display windows. They were astounded by the opulent goods the store offered, and they could only wonder what the luxuriousness of American life must be like.

The Japanese got a second insight into American life when the comic strip *Blondie* was picked up by Japan's largest newspaper. Every day the strip exposed the Japanese to conveniences they had never seen before—clothes washers, electric vacuum cleaners, and lawn mowers. The Bumstead family had a large refrigerator, and, whenever he felt like it, Dagwood would pull armloads of food from it and construct huge sandwiches. Blondie went shopping frequently and always came home with so many packages she could barely carry them. The family went for pleasure rides in their car and took the dog along, and they were always going out for dinner. The Japanese, who had been forced to live Spartan lives for hundreds of years, were in awe of the abundance of American middle-class life.

Kiichiro Toyoda was confident the day would come when the average Japanese family would have this kind of lifestyle, and he was equally sure the automobile would play a key role in it. So he and his staff kept trying to get Toyota back into automobile production.

Shotaro Kamiya, who had left GM of Japan in 1935 to become Kiichiro's marketing director, was busy trying to re-create the Toyota dealership network. Kamiya had been drafted into the role of managing director of the centralized motor-vehicle distribution network established by the military during the war. The dealerships of individual manufacturers had been abolished and their personnel and facilities formed into a single, government-operated network.

After the war, Kamiya was selected as an auto-industry advisor to GHQ. In that position, he began lobbying GHQ officials to dismantle the centralized distribution network and return to the brand-specific outlet system. Kamiya thought they would be sympathetic to his appeal because they were Americans, and Americans understood the importance of automobiles. When it looked as if the Americans were about to approve the restructuring, Kamiya, having returned to his role of marketing director of Toyota, immediately began recruiting dealers for the company.

Kamiya knew all of the former Toyota dealers in the centralized network, but he had also gotten to know many Nissan dealers. Kamiya decided that once GHQ instituted the new system, it would be unethical for him to approach Nissan dealers about jumping ship. But if he were able to recruit dealers before the new system existed, then that was just good business.

Kamiya began making the rounds of dealerships, explaining Kiichiro's plan for returning to auto manufacturing and his dedication to constantly improving the quality of his products. Kamiya hinted GHQ might change the dealer system soon and invited the dealers to a meeting at Toyota's offices in the Koromo plant. Kamiya was a man of great persuasiveness, and many of the former Nissan dealers agreed to attend the session with their old rivals from the Toyota stores.

Kiichiro impressed everyone who came to the meeting with his sincerity and his firm belief in the future of the automobile business. He stressed how Toyota had worked closely with its dealers to resolve the problems with the first trucks. Toyota would always, Kiichiro promised, keep the needs of both its customers and its dealers in mind. More than anything, he said, Toyota would assist the dealers in ways Western manufacturers never had.

The dealers were impressed with Kiichiro's vision and promises of fair treatment that night, and many indicated their willingness to sign on when GHQ approved the restructuring. A month later GHQ gave its consent, and Kamiya scored a coup. The Toyota dealer network returned to life with a substantial increase in membership. Kamiya went out of his way to make former Nissan dealers feel like part of the family. It was good that he did, because dark days were ahead for the dealers.

Inflation was totally out of control in Japan in 1946. Consumer prices, which had tripled in the first six months after the war, began to climb even more rapidly. Almost five million Japanese soldiers had been released from the military, and there were no jobs available for them and little food. The government issued separation pay to them, but there was nothing to buy, so the money was worthless.

The government was forced to spend more than it took in to keep the country going, so it printed more money. Personal savings were rendered useless. A stretch of bad weather destroyed half of the annual rice harvest, and there was less than a week's supply of rice in the distribution system at one point. It was estimated that people were living on seven hundred calories a day. Everyone in Japan felt poor, hungry and, during the winter, cold.

For those who had jobs, wages were raised every month in an attempt to keep pay even with inflation, but there were no profits for companies to finance those raises. Almost every business was operating at a loss. The Reconstruction Finance Bank was established to keep companies afloat with loans, but that created heavy debts that drove businesses further into the hole. The Toyota Motor Company was no exception to these circumstances. The company managed to produce 5,800 trucks during 1946—as opposed to a peak of 16,200 a few years before—but Toyota was losing money.

With all of this seemingly endless social strife, Japanese workers began looking for someone who could give them answers—someone who could tell them tomorrow was going to be better. The newly sanctioned union leaders in Japan made just these promises. Their calls for worker solidarity and radical social reform began to sound far less fanatical than they had only a few months before. The 400,000 union members from the end of the war swelled to 2.7 million by May of 1946. By the following December they numbered 4.5 million.

Union leaders discovered that Japanese farmers, unhappy with the price the government was paying for their rice, had withheld portions of their harvest. Groups of workers shouting "Hand over the rice" began marching though the streets of Japan and rioting. Until the Japanese constitution was changed during the Occupation, Emperor Hirohito had been considered a god, and Japanese citizens bowed low before him. Now mobs of Japanese laborers stormed the grounds of the Imperial Palace chanting slogans of protest.

Japanese Premier Shigeru Yoshida was incensed with the havoc the GHQ-sponsored unions were bringing to his country, and he announced in 1947 that striking workers would not be paid. Union leaders responded by calling for a national strike on February 1, 1947. Estimates of the number of people who would join the strike ranged up to six million. At a time when the nation was barely functioning, the strike would be devastating to Japan.

Douglas MacArthur had watched the growth of the union movement, and the prominence of communists within it, with cool detachment. MacArthur was prepared to allow the Japanese to sort things out for themselves. But with chaos in the making, he reversed himself and threw his support behind Premier Yoshida. MacArthur prohibited the general strike, and when communists leaders in the large union of government workers kept pushing for it, he revoked their right to unionize.

The United States, shaken by the rapid development of the Cold

War and the increasing likelihood that communists were going to control China, decided that a sharp change of policy was required in Japan. Drastic reforms were to be halted, the purges of businessmen and the zaibatsu stopped, and programs were developed to address the deplorable social conditions in Japan. The country was to be fortified to make it a bastion of anticommunism in Asia.

One component of the modified economic-recovery plan provided for priority assistance to certain Japanese industries. The program directed funds and materials to the fields judged most vital to economic recovery: heavy industries like steel, railroads, and shipping. Limited truck production was permitted, but automobile production continued to be banned, as it had been since 1939.

Although GHQ made the final selection of industries to be given priority status, there was little support among Japanese leaders for reviving automobile manufacturing. Part of their opposition was based on immediate need. The Japanese population was struggling for survival, and automobiles clearly weren't vital items. But a factor far more onerous for Toyota Motor Company was also involved.

Harking back to the attitudes of the 1920s, Japanese business and government leaders were again insisting there was no future in the Japanese automobile business. American automobiles, the argument went, were simply too advanced for a Japanese company to compete with. That being the case, it made no sense to expend scarce resources on an industry ultimately doomed to failure.

Kiichiro Toyoda paid scant attention to the pessimism about Japanese automobiles. In January of 1947, he introduced to Toyota dealers a prototype of his first new car in eight years. The car was Kiichiro's radical new small car, called the model SA, and the dealers were clearly impressed. In a nation whose brief automotive history encompassed only sensible cars, the SA was a true novelty.

The aerodynamic body featured a sharply sloping hood with a split grille and prominent, rounded fenders. It was Toyota's first two-door car, having doors that opened from the front and a single windshield wiper that rotated from an attachment point on the roof. The engine was a small, 995-cc unit producing 27 horsepower, and the suspension was a four-wheel, fully independent design. It was a classy small car that looked like it would be fun to drive.

Although Kiichiro couldn't put the car into immediate production because of government restrictions, he was confident the ban on auto production would be lifted soon. Kiichiro asked his dealers to be patient, while also keeping his engineers busy with the preproduction work so the SA assembly line would be ready to roll when the embargo was lifted. In the meantime, Kiichiro kept the rest of his staff busy producing trucks.

Kiichiro put a new large truck called the BM into production in March, then introduced Toyota's first small truck, the model SB, in April. The SB truck had an external frame, unlike the unit-body SA, but the vehicles had the same engine. The SB truck was very well received and sold well, and Kiichiro was heartened.

Many of the people who ordered the SB said they intended to customize the small truck into a station wagon or four-door sedan, and Kiichiro took this to be evidence that the demand for automobiles was growing. But he also worried constantly about where he was going to get the money to finance the production of this new truck.

The staff of GHQ asked Toyota to produce fifty cars for them in June. The cars were for foreign trade delegations visiting Japan, and GHQ wanted full-sized vehicles for that purpose. Kiichiro was delighted to be producing cars again, even if he had to return to the old prewar model AC. The AC was of the size GHQ requested, and there were enough parts sitting around that Kiichiro didn't have to send his staff off on a mad chase for materials. Just to keep things interesting, Kiichiro added four model SAs to the production run.

When the fifty-four cars were completed, Kiichiro got the news he had been waiting to hear since 1939. Toyota had been granted permission to resume limited production of automobiles for the consumer market. Everyone at Toyota was ecstatic. After eight years in which events only seemed to get worse, here—finally—was some good news. Kiichiro's spirits soared, and once again it was like the old days. Kiichiro rolled up his sleeves and hurried around the shop, shaking hands and barking orders. Now there was real work to do again.

Shotaro Kamiya and his marketing staff told their dealers to start taking orders for the revolutionary new Toyota they had loved so much. The staff, remembering all of the publicity that had been generated with the logo-design contest in 1936, decided to stage another competition. This time the challenge was to create a nickname for the new car, and thousands of entries came pouring into Koromo.

Toyota Motor Company's headquarters was an exciting place again.

Even though he was now fifty-three and had a persistent case of high blood pressure, Kiichiro felt like a young man. He hadn't struggled all these years and poured his soul into the company to be a manufacturer of trucks. The creative possibilities of the automobile were far greater, and Kiichiro and his staff were thrilled that Japanese motorists would soon be able to drive their dynamic new car.

Perhaps it was naiveté or maybe it was just that people needed to feel elated after so many years of despair, but the fantasy the staff at Koromo spun—that everything was going to be different soon—lasted for two months. The economic realities of Japan, and the automotive industry in particular, were far too stark to disappear. Reality came to Koromo when, with the popular SB truck in great demand, Toyota couldn't get financing to put it into full production. Bank after bank turned aside Kiichiro's requests for funds until, in a most humbling moment, he was forced to go to his own dealers and customers asking for money.

Kiichiro had to demand a 50-percent deposit on the 200,000-yen selling price—when trucks had been selling for 3,000 yen ten years before—on every truck ordered. When that still wasn't enough, Kiichiro asked each of his forty-seven dealers to contribute 100,000 yen to keep the assembly line moving. Remarkably, all of the dealers complied.

With the SB truck in production, Kiichiro threw himself into getting the SA automobile ready to go. Kiichiro knew the SA would save the company, and he even liked the nickname that had been selected from the contest: the Toyopet. Kiichiro had complete confidence his vision of the new Japanese small car—a car that had been designed from scratch to be efficient and high-quality—would win the day.

Unfortunately, Kiichiro's belief was so unshakable he forgot about the dismal state of Japanese automotive technology. Rather than improving during the war, the technology had stood still or diminished, as manufacturers were constantly forced to improvise because of material shortages. There had been no time for research and development, and now there was no money to import Western technology. Overlooking these factors, Kiichiro's staff had designed their first unit-body car and their first fully independent suspension for an automobile.

The production of the SA went badly from the first. The body men, who hadn't produced anything but simple truck bodies for years, had tremendous difficulties with the unit-body construction. The independent suspension also posed problems. The production technology for making ball joints for the suspension was far too imprecise, and the engineers lacked experience in designing and manufacturing coil springs.

With his usual dogged determination, Kiichiro managed to get the cars off the line, and Kamiya and the marketing staff even made some exports to Egypt, but the SA wasn't the car that would save Toyota. Instead, as production costs soared, it became yet another drain on the company's practically nonexistent capital.

The Toyota Motor Company was in perilous financial condition at the end of 1948. The company had continued to borrow heavily to offset inflation, and by November of 1948 its debt stood at 782 million yen— eight times the company's capitalization. Truck sales had slowed, but Kiichiro continued production in the hope that the situation would improve. He couldn't just shut down the assembly line, for that would end the elaborate financial balancing act Toyota was performing to save itself from collapse.

Kiichiro was also strongly opposed to laying off workers. He had built the Koromo plant as a comprehensive company town in the countryside of Japan, and it represented the way he felt about his workers. He believed they were part of the Toyota family and they had supported the company through difficult times. Now, Kiichiro felt, the company was required to support them. It was his responsibility to keep his workers employed.

There were those in the company who thought Kiichiro was being financially innocent in his position towards the workers, but his stance became easier to defend as unions became more militant in Japan. The Toyota Koromo union had joined the Japanese Automobile Manufacturers Labor Union in March of 1948. The national auto workers' union was a powerful American-style trade group that prided itself on its combative strength. It was the most powerful union in Japan, and its leaders were the most radical. Kiichiro was certain that layoffs at Koromo would severely damage his relations with his workers and almost definitely lead to a strike. Despite the company's best efforts to maintain harmonious relations with its workers, economic conditions in Japan had driven a wedge between labor and management.

So the Koromo plant continued to produce trucks, which it sent to its dealers. Dealers were then forced to sell the trucks to people who couldn't afford them. To make the sales possible, the dealers had to offer extended credit terms. As these payments filtered back through the system, Toyota's cash flow became dependent upon the truck owners' making their monthly payments.

Many months the company couldn't make its payroll, and workers were told they would be paid as soon as possible. Sometimes paychecks were a month late. Toyota fell behind on its debt service and payment for materials as well. The economy was so fragile the company couldn't sell banks the promissory notes it held on purchased vehicles, even at a discounted rate. Then, just when Kiichiro thought things couldn't get any worse, they did. With the Japanese economy showing no signs of breaking the never-ending spiral of inflation, the U.S. government decided the time had come to enact harsh measures. Social conditions in Japan were so bad that anarchy was certain to occur in the near future if something wasn't done.

The man the U.S. government sent to correct the situation was Joseph Dodge, a Michigan banker with a reputation as a parsimonious ultraconservative. Dodge believed it was the job of banks to extend credit only to those who didn't need it, and he was sent to a country where the entire economy was being operated on credit and on freshly printed, but nearly worthless, money.

Douglas MacArthur had begun the Occupation by creating a program of social change that rivaled the New Deal in scope. That plan had been greatly curtailed in 1947 when conditions changed. Now, Joseph Dodge meant to terminate what little remained of the master plan. Dodge believed he who governed least governed best, and he was particularly opposed to government involvement in business—a hallmark of the Japanese economy. With most of the gross national product of Japan under some type of government control, Dodge didn't lack for government programs to discontinue.

Dodge stayed in Japan only three months, but in that time he put in motion a set of reforms that virtually halted inflation in Japan. Dodge's nonnegotiable instructions to Japanese officials were that the national budget was to be balanced at once, the exchange rate was to be fixed at 360 yen to the dollar, and all forms of government subsidies to industry were to be halted immediately. In addition, 250,000 government workers were fired, U.S. aid was cut, and wages and personal credit were frozen, while taxes were raised. In essence, Dodge took an economy habituated to subsidies and cut the allocations off cold.

The first outcome of what became known as the Dodge Line was the bankruptcy of tens of thousands of small and medium-sized companies. Heavily in debt, overstaffed, and underproductive, these companies disappeared the moment their credit lines were cut off. In a country where people traditionally spent their entire career with one company, hundreds of thousands of people were suddenly out of work. There were strikes all over the nation as the increasingly radical unions fought back. But since the Dodge Line had the support of the Occupation forces, social order was maintained.

The Dodge Line converted rampant inflation into recession overnight. Even people who hadn't lost their jobs were turned into paupers. The implications of the Dodge Line for Toyota were that truck buyers, whose monthly payments were keeping the company afloat, stopped sending their checks. In addition, the company was denied further credit under the Reconstruction Finance Act, and truck loans for potential buyers were halted.

The company needed to borrow forty million yen to meet its December 1949 obligations, and it anticipated the need for two hundred million yen the following month. Kiichiro and his financial people were out every day begging banks for money but, with Toyota's debt surpassing one billion yen, no one offered a single yen. Bankruptcy was days away.

Finally, Kiichiro found a financial savior in Takeo Takanashi, then head of the Bank of Japan's Nagoya district office. Takanashi knew that a great number of peripheral industries tied to Toyota—perhaps three hundred companies—would go under if Toyota folded. Takanashi stepped in and vowed to find a solution. Takanashi sought assistance from the president of the Bank of Japan, a man known as "the Pope" of the financial world because of his absolute authority.

The Bank of Japan had opposed the formation of the Japanese automotive industry from the beginning, insisting it was less expensive to import vehicles from the United States. When Takanashi visited the president of his company, the man challenged him to give even one reason why Toyota was worth saving. Takanashi explained the effect Toyota's bankruptcy would have on the subcontractors of Nagoya and then noted that the Bank of Japan's Nagoya branch had outstanding loans with many of these companies. The bank president grudgingly permitted Takanashi to arrange a loan through a consortium of banks.

While Toyota's financial people were negotiating with the banks,

Kiichiro was pursuing a different tack. Like his father, Kiichiro had little faith in banks or the large corporations that ran them. The Toyodas had built their companies on the labor of the simple country people of Nagoya, and Kiichiro went to these people to find redemption for the company. Kiichiro called his workers together, explained Toyota's dire straits, and then asked for their help. If the workers would agree to two 10-percent pay cuts, Kiichiro said, he would promise that no one would lose his job.

Kiichiro's heart was pure when he talked to his men. He was filled with the same determination that had enabled Sakichi Toyoda to take his *ie*, and his country, a step beyond the world they had known. Unfortunately, it was no longer the dawn of the Meiji restoration, and one man's tenacity was of far less consequence. Sakichi had been able to revive a project with a few thousand yen at the turn of the century. Now Kiichiro needed a billion, at a time when no one had even pocket change to spare.

Kiichiro and Risaburo Toyoda had fought bitterly at times, but Sakichi Toyoda had recognized their potential as a team. Kiichiro was bursting with ideas and spunk, while Risaburo possessed the wisdom to keep him on track. But Risaburo was gone from the company, and tragedy had claimed two men who had stepped into his shoes. The finance man who had taken over for Kiichiro during the war died while trying to put out a fire at a neighbor's house after an air raid. His replacement was claimed shortly thereafter in a truck accident. No one was left to keep Kiichiro on an even keel.

Kiichiro's workers accepted his plan. They would accede to pay cuts in return for guaranteed jobs. Everyone left the meeting filled with hope, but it was blind hope. Pay cuts were a drop in the bucket when Toyota needed oceans of relief. Even worse, with Nissan and other auto companies having laid off over 3,200 workers in the preceding months, the banking community took Kiichiro's plan to be further evidence of his financial irresponsibility.

While Kiichiro was signing his deal, the banks were working the numbers. They said Toyota's financial problems had come from overly optimistic production that created a large inventory of unsold vehicles. This attitude, the banks said, had to change. They agreed to provide financing, but it would be on their terms.

They calculated 850 vehicles a month as the maximum Toyota could afford to produce. With a plant production capacity of 1,400 vehicles a month, 1,600 workers would have to be dismissed. Toyota was to split into manufacturing and sales companies. The new sales company would order vehicles from the manufacturing company, which could produce only vehicles that were ordered. Ironically, the banks were ordering Toyota to institute a tenet of the just-in-time production system the company had designed more than a decade earlier. Vehicle production would be matched to demand. The final bank directive was that some members of management who had retired were to accept responsibility for the company's plight.

In March of 1950, the union learned unofficially of the bank's conditions, and they felt Kiichiro had betrayed them. Kiichiro had given the workers his word, and they had taken pay cuts. The union had been staging periodic work stoppages over the past year; now 94 percent of the workers voted to stage a full-scale strike if anyone lost his job.

On April 22, Kiichiro was filled with anguish. The time had come to tell his workers face-to-face that he had to break his promise. It was one of the most difficult things he ever had to do. He called the union leaders to his office and explained what had transpired. "This is very difficult for me to accept," he said, "but in order for the ship we call Toyota to avoid sinking, we have no recourse but to ask some people to leave. Until now, I have worked fervently on creating cars and was ignorant of how to manage the company. I take full responsibility for this."

Kiichiro told the men that two auxiliary facilities would be closed, 1,600 workers would have to leave the company, and those who remained would have to accept another 10-percent pay cut. He asked that 1,600 men resign voluntarily, but he was forced to admit he couldn't promise that those who left would receive their pensions.

The union workers stormed out of Kiichiro's office and carried out the preordained plan to strike. They rang sirens throughout the plant, and thousands of workers deserted their work stations. They surrounded the squat, wooden headquarters building of the plant, some of them climbing up onto the roof. The workers sang songs and shouted denunciations of the company, vowing never to accept the layoffs.

In the days that followed, production came to a near standstill. The company's already significant debts increased by a million yen a day. At every work site, every day, the union called out members of management and forced them to get up on stages and answer questions. Always, the union demanded the cuts be rescinded. The union even drafted a counterproposal under which production could be reduced without layoffs, but the matter was truly out of Toyota's hands.

As the strike entered its second month, the company sent letters to workers who weren't being laid off, asking them to please cooperate in the restructuring. The workers took the letters and burned them in a bonfire in front of the headquarters building, standing shoulder-to-shoulder and singing the "Internationale." The workers' anger was growing more intense every day.

Kiichiro was inconsolable. He couldn't stand to see the turmoil at the plant he had so meticulously designed, or to hear the taunts of the workers he had so carefully trained. Everything he had created was being destroyed. He stayed at home and shut himself off from the world. He tried not to ruminate, but he couldn't help it. His blood pressure soared to 180, and even the injections of medication he gave himself didn't bring it down.

In despair, Kiichiro sent a letter to the company's office at Koromo. "I'm thinking of quitting Toyota Motor Company," Kiichiro wrote. "It is the beloved child that I have raised, but it has already developed to the extent that it does not need me, its father. Now it has begun to act according to its own wishes. There are times when the best way is to do things all over again. Toyota Motor Company is at that stage. From the bottom of my heart, I want to disappear from the company."

On the fourth Sunday in May, an emergency meeting was held at Risaburo Toyoda's house in Nagoya. Risaburo was no longer officially connected to the company, but he was still *kacho* of the Toyoda *ie*. Kiichiro attended, along with his cousin Eiji; Tojiro Okamoto, the longtime family arbitrator between Risaburo and Kiichiro; and Taizo Ishida, the president of Toyoda Automatic Loom Works. It was a ghastly scene, as sad and silent as a funeral. Everyone knew something had to be done to break the company out of the deadlock, but no one wanted to be the first to speak.

Kiichiro finally spoke up. He had already decided the outcome in his mind, and he wanted to get this over with. Kiichiro said he was going to resign, and asked Taizo Ishida to take over for him. Ishida didn't have automobile experience, but Toyoda Automatic Loom Works was the most profitable company in the family group. Kiichiro believed that would make Ishida the most acceptable candidate to the banks, which now had so much control over the company.

Ishida was conflicted about agreeing to Kiichiro's request. Ishida had grown up in a world where Japan's hierarchial social structure was so unquestioned that he had an almost innate inclination to honor any appeal from the leader of his company—especially since the man was both Sakichi's son and the founder of the Toyota Motor Company. Conversely, it was precisely because of who Kiichiro was that Ishida hesitated.

Although Toyota was now a publicly held company in which the Toyoda family held only a minor financial share, the family was so respected in the environs of rural, traditional Nagoya that Toyota was still viewed as a family enterprise. Ishida feared that if he became the first outsider to head the company, he would find that his every decision would be second-guessed. Charges of "Kiichiro wouldn't have done it that way" rang in his ears.

Ishida told Kiichiro that he would be honored to lead the company until Kiichiro was able to return, but he asked Kiichiro to promise he would not allow others in the company to say things that were uncalled for. When Kiichiro nodded in understanding, Ishida said he would do his best for the company, and everyone left the somber room without additional discussion.

In early June, Kiichiro and Ishida went to the hall where the contract negotiations with the union were being held. Kiichiro had already started to separate himself from the company in his mind, but seeing all of the angry workers crowded into the room reminded him how sad it all was. Kiichiro was on the verge of tears, so he made his presentation brief. "I cannot remain in the company now that we are in this situation," he said. "But the company will collapse if we leave it as it is. Please cooperate and save the company." Kiichiro introduced Ishida as the new president, asked the workers to support him, and hurried from the grounds.

With Kiichiro's resignation, the workers finally came to accept how desperate the situation was. Toyota announced it would pay a pension to all those who agreed to retirement. The workers understood that no pensions would be paid, and everyone would be out of work if the company went under. Over two thousand men opted for retirement, surpassing the size of the needed work-force reduction.

Finally, on June 9, after negotiating around the clock for three days, the head of the union found a position that allowed the workers to save face. The union man said he would not accept the layoffs, which were in violation of the contract. But if the company denied admittance to the plant to men who had received dismissal notices, he would accept that.

Toyota Motor Company resumed production on June 10. The company had a new president, a watchdog from the banks overseeing its finances, an alienated work force, and crushing debt. The Japanese economy was still in shambles and materials were scarce. In the midst of this gloomy scenario, GHQ lifted all price and production controls on automobiles. The badly battered Toyota Motor Company was now free to face its competition in the marketplace.

8
TRANSITIONS

When Shotaro Kamiya was appointed president of the new, independent Toyota sales operation in April of 1950, he had a long and difficult road before him. Kamiya, as the former marketing director of Toyota Motor Company, was all too familiar with Toyota's financial plight. The banks' funding package would keep the manufacturing operation afloat for a while, but Kamiya's Toyota Motor Sales Company was on its own. GHQ's remaining anti-*zaibatsu* regulations prohibited Toyota Motor Company from investing in the corporation that would sell its cars. The only help the sales operation got was offices in the Nagoya, Tokyo, and Koromo; 353 employees drawn from Toyota's administrative department; and trademark rights for the company name.

Yet managing a new business with sparse resources was the least of Kamiya's problems. Much more pressing was the issue of when Toyota Motor Company would be able to supply the sales operation with a high-quality, reasonably priced passenger car. Kamiya had artfully wooed a large number of dealers into Toyota's network, and they were getting impatient. They wanted to know what was happening with the promised automobile production.

Kamiya recognized Toyota hadn't mastered the technology for auto production yet. But he couldn't tell his dealers that—particularly the ones who had jumped ship from Nissan, which was using licensed Western technology. So in the days after Kiichiro announced he was going to resign from the company, Kamiya went to him with a highly irregular suggestion. Kamiya told Kiichiro that while Toyota's trucks were winning a place in the market, he needed a car to sell. He then proposed that Toyota Motor Sales Company start selling Fords.

Kiichiro, saddened and angry about his impending departure from the company, told Kamiya the idea was worth investigating. Kiichiro had a fierce pride about wanting to enter the auto business without a foreign affiliation, but he had to admit that at the moment his dream seemed impossible.

Japan's progress in the automobile industry had come to a halt in the aftermath of the war, and Kiichiro imagined the Americans to be adding to their overwhelming advantage as each day passed. Perhaps, he thought, Japan really couldn't build cars without an infusion of foreign funds and technology.

Ford's assets in Japan had been frozen during the war, but they were released afterwards. The company held a clear title to the land it had purchased in Yokohama in 1935, and Kiichiro suggested Ford might be interested in building a joint-venture plant there. Since Ford was in the midst of constructing an assembly plant in England for a compact car called the Consul, Kiichiro suggested Toyota might be able to operate a Consul plant in Yokohama. The benefits for Toyota would be twofold: Kamiya's dealers would have a small car to sell, and Toyota would be exposed to the latest automobile technology.

Kamiya had contacts at Ford from the Ford-Toyota talks that had been halted by the war, and he approached these men again. The preliminary discussions were promising, as Ford recognized the latent potential of the Japanese market. Progress slowed, however, when Kamiya couldn't travel to the United States for further talks because of the strike at Toyota. When that was resolved, Kamiya made plans to go on June 23, 1950.

Kamiya was seen off at the airport by the recently retired Kiichiro and by Taizo Ishida, Kiichiro's successor as president of Toyota Motor Company. With all the turmoil of the recent months, the men could only hope Kamiya would return from Detroit with a partial solution to the company's problems.

Kamiya was at a hotel in Los Angeles, enroute to Detroit, when he heard an alarming bit of news on June 25. The army of North Korea had invaded South Korea, and the United States was going to war again as part of a United Nations force. None of the parties involved in the Ford-Toyota negotiations were certain whether this action would affect their plans, so Kamiya continued on to Detroit.

The negotiations went well at Ford, and the basics of a deal were agreed upon. Toyota would build Consuls in Japan, with Ford holding the majority ownership in the venture. In return, Toyota got export rights for the Far East after five years, with the company eventually acquiring world export rights.

Ford decided to dispatch four engineers to Japan to conduct a preliminary study. The engineers were selected, and Kamiya left, telling the men he looked forward to seeing them in his country. Before the engineers could pack their bags, however, the U.S. government issued a regulation prohibiting technical personnel in critical industries from leaving the country. Once again, a Toyota-Ford joint venture was halted by international conflict.

Everyone was hoping the war would be short, so Ford and Toyota continued their communications. Ford also agreed to uphold one component of the deal—accepting Toyota trainees at Ford's facilities in Detroit. Sakichi Toyoda had always instructed his men to study what the most advanced companies in a field were doing, and the people at Toyota were carrying on in his tradition.

The first man Toyota sent was Eiji Toyoda, Kiichiro's cousin. Eiji, who was now a thirty-seven-year-old managing director of Toyota, was proving to be as dedicated an engineer as Kiichiro, and he was highly respected in the company.

The purpose of Eiji's visit was to gauge the future prospects of the auto industry for Japan and to explore the possibility of Ford's supplying technical guidance to Toyota. Eiji felt as if he was coming to study at the right hand of the masters. Under the direction of Henry Ford, Ford Motor Company was ruled by engineers and manufacturing men. Toyota was run the same way, and Eiji felt as if he was making a pilgrimage.

Eiji had anticipated that the Fords, like the Toyoda family, would pass on their basic belief from one generation to the next. He expected to see Ford executives walking around the factories with their sleeves rolled up and their hands dirty, while the latest marvels of technology hummed away in the background. But Ford wasn't like that in 1950.

Henry Ford had turned eccentric and cantankerous in his last years, refusing to update his cars and allowing his factories to decay. Ford Motor Company was locked in a good-old-days mentality while the world passed it by. Henry Ford had nearly destroyed his company before family members forced him to retire. Now, Ford Motor Company was impoverished on a grand scale, and its physical plant was decrepit compared with those of other U.S. manufacturers.

Henry Ford's grandson, Henry Ford II, was in the process of rescuing the company at this time, but Ford's new leader wasn't a manufacturing man like his grandfather. Henry Ford II believed Ford Motor had to escape from the stranglehold of his late grandfather. The men Henry II enlisted in his cause weren't engineers; they were the new whiz kids of the postwar era—MBAs and professional managers. Henry II treated his factories with benign neglect and then told his managers to study their papers and find ways to cut costs.

When Eiji Toyoda arrived at the mecca of the automobile business, he was unaware of the changes taking place at Ford. Toyota had been promised their men would see the latest Ford had to offer. Eiji was eager to be dazzled by manufacturing virtuosity and couldn't wait to lose himself in the wonders of the River Rouge plant. This plant had been the most advanced and comprehensive manufacturing facility in the world when it was built in the 1920s, and Henry Ford had developed a forerunner of the just-in-time production system there.

On his first day at Ford, however, Eiji didn't see a single thing being built. Instead, he was sent to a classroom to listen to a lecture on budgetary management. Eiji hadn't traveled thousands of miles to hear this, so he feigned difficulty understanding the instructor's English and sneaked out. Then he asked his host if he could be sent to a factory instead.

Eiji felt right at home when he was dispatched to River Rouge, although the plant was of a scale quite unlike anything at Toyota. There were two assembly lines running, turning out a car every minute. But Eiji was startled to note that although the cars being produced had new body designs, the mechanics and running gear were the same as those that had been used before the war. He didn't understand how a company like Ford could be neglecting the engineering end of its business this way.

The plant was running at capacity because, with the huge demand for automobiles in the U.S. postwar economic boom, Ford was selling everything it could make. When this demand was combined with Henry Ford II's new management approach, Ford executives had decided that investments in engineering advances were superfluous. Minimizing such expenditures meant maximizing short-term returns.

Eiji spent most of his time at River Rouge wandering around, carefully observing what was going on and asking endless questions of the workers. They were always glad to explain what they knew to their inquisitive visitor, and Eiji took careful notes. He turned his visit into an engineer's grand tour. He inspected most of Ford's assembly plants in the region, then called on facilities that manufactured piston rings, carburetors, bearings, and valve lifters. He visited Chrysler and asked to see their car and truck plants. Eiji spent six weeks in Detroit, and then another six weeks inspecting machine-tool and parts plants throughout the Midwest and the Northeast, absorbing everything he saw.

Eiji felt like he was going to burst when he was replaced in the United States by another Toyota employee in October. As he prepared to make the long journey back to Japan, he looked over his notes and thought about the report he was going to make. He had indeed been awed by the scale of the operations in the United States. Ford was producing eight thousand cars a day at a time when Toyota, if it was lucky, got forty vehicles out the door. Yet the dated equipment in American auto plants startled him more than their scale.

Eiji could anticipate the first question his coworkers were going to ask when he got back to Koromo: How many years before we catch up with Ford? Eiji knew his answer had to be an uplifting one, because everyone at Toyota lived in constant fear that the U.S. manufacturers were going to return to the Japanese market and drive them out of business. He decided not to talk about the scale of operations in the States, but rather about the state of the manufacturing art he saw.

Ford, Eiji would tell his men, had made little technological progress in the last decade. In fact, he would even go out on a limb. He would say that Ford wasn't doing anything that Toyota didn't already understand. Competing with the West wouldn't be so difficult after all. Toyota only had to redouble its efforts to improve its products.

Eiji's trip had been an exhilarating one for him. Rather than being overwhelmed by the prowess of the second-largest automobile company in the world, he had been reassured. Toyota was on the right track. They still had a chance to catch up, especially since the company Eiji would be returning to would be nothing like the financial shipwreck he had left.

Even with its new loans, Toyota had been within spitting distance of bankruptcy when Eiji departed in July. Three months later, however, it was as if fate had once again smiled on the Land of the Gods. With the war in Korea raging fiercely, and with no end in sight, the U.S. military had enacted a policy that couldn't have been more fortuitous for Toyota. The military had decided that, rather than exporting trucks from the United States to Korea, it would be cheaper and faster to buy them in Japan.

Toyota, its parking lots awash with unsold trucks, had received orders for 3,329 vehicles within the course of a month. The Koromo factory was operating at full capacity. Men were working overtime! Financial projections indicated that the Toyota Motor Company would go from insolvency to solid profitability before the year was out.

Toyota Motor Company's unexpected prosperity was being overseen by its new president, Taizo Ishida, who was a distant relative of Risaburo Toyoda. Ishida had lived with Risaburo's family as a child, and the two men had come to share a common trait. They were both no-nonsense businessmen who knew how to run a company. Ishida had begun his career selling clothing in a textile store in Nagoya. When the operation went bankrupt, the owner was so despondent he committed suicide. That experience made Ishida a true realist whose life was ruled by numbers and calculations.

Ishida liked to say that his leaving Toyoda Automatic Loom Works, where he produced consistent profits, to become president of Toyota Motor Company was like going to see a fire, only to be handed the hose. Ishida's job was to extinguish the flames of inefficiency that were consuming Toyota, and he approached that responsibility just as Risaburo would have. He demanded strict financial accountability.

If the leaders of Toyota had learned anything during World War II, it was that having the military in charge of production was no way to run a manufacturing business. Toyota had survived that period, but now the U.S. military's procurements were posing a new, if indirect, form of control. Such a large portion of Toyota's output was going to Korea that a sudden end to the conflict would provoke severe repercussions. What would Toyota do, Ishida wondered, with all of the production capacity at the war's end?

Military production was as erratic as the weather, and consumer demand in Japan had been equally unpredictable because the economy kept ricocheting from inflation to recession. Kiichiro Toyota had responded to these changes by keeping factory production steady while simply stockpiling excess output until the market improved. The banks had made it abundantly clear to Ishida that this practice was forbidden. Now, production had to be adjusted continually to equal demand.

While the assembly line could be turned on and off as needed,

Toyota's work force couldn't be hired and fired as easily. The company had just been forced to lay off a third of its workers, and had suffered an extended and painful strike as a result. It was unthinkable in Japan, where career-long employment was the norm in large companies, to call these men back to meet increased demand, only to release them when the hostilities ceased in Korea or the economy went sour.

Ishida decided to institute a firm policy on handling Toyota's undulating production demand. Toyota could not afford to expand the permanent workforce—period. Increased demand would have to be met through overtime and the use of temporary workers and subcontractors. If peak output was to be achieved under these circumstances, Ishida knew that his production men, under the command of Eiji Toyoda, were going to have to improve production efficiency in every way possible.

If Taizo Ishida, with his rational business plans, was a latter-day Risaburo, then the man who would have to make his factory work with a restricted work force was his Kiichiro—Eiji Toyoda. Since his return from the United States, Eiji had been going around Koromo telling everyone who would listen that Japanese automobile companies could compete with those from the West. The workers who had stayed with Toyota through all of its hardships were never going to be satisfied with their current task of making trucks, so Eiji had a sympathetic audience.

When Eiji had been back at the factory for a few days, Ishida called him into the office for a talk. He said he was delighted that Eiji was so enthusiastic about getting a car into production, but he also reminded him of the financial realities of such a plan. There would be no additional permanent workers.

Eiji said he had already given this some thought. Manufacturing procedures would have to be systematized so every worker, whether permanent, temporary, or subcontractor, would produce craftsmanship of the same level. Automation would have to be employed wherever feasible. Although immediate circumstances were dictating these necessities, Eiji recognized they were actually another revival of Kiichiro's just-in-time production system.

Both men knew that Kiichiro Toyoda had been interested in rationalizing the production system for aesthetic reasons. He wanted his plant, and his cars, to have engineering elegance. Now, Eiji said, the production process would have to be far more than graceful. It would also have to be almost infinitely adjustable, enabling the company to meet fluctuating demand with a fixed number of workers. Eiji was certain it could be done.

Everyone in the automotive department was buoyed by Eiji's report on the state of the U.S. auto industry, and the ominous mood in the factory was starting to lift. The influx of business from the Korean War had bolstered the Japanese economy, stimulating motor vehicle demand. With good domestic sales supplementing U.S. Army procurements, Toyota was preparing to pay its first dividend since the war. Profits for the year were expected to exceed five hundred million yen. And there were rumors of new Japanese government support for auto manufacturers in the months ahead. Even the bankers agreed that the time had come for the company to expand. Toyota was going to take a decisive step towards initiating large-scale auto production.

In January of 1951, Eiji presented Ishida with a five-year modernization plan to double production capacity to three thousand vehicles a month. This was not simple bricks-and-mortar capacity building, however. The plan specified that production equipment would be updated while, simultaneously, the production process itself was rationalized. Ishida, who would not let a pencil be wasted, told Eiji he would obtain whatever money he needed for machinery to improve productivity.

Eiji planned to rework and update the standardized work charts that Kiichiro had created in the 1930s to ensure that each production worker knew how to carry out his assigned tasks precisely. The charts would specify the amount of time allowed to complete each task and the sequence in which work was to be performed. The charts were to be a starting point for streamlining each operation, with the expectation that workers would search continuously for ways to improve their performance.

The first stage of the program provided for the modernization of production equipment for trucks, which accounted for 94 percent of Toyota's sales, and all of its profits, in 1950. While new equipment was certainly needed, changes in equipment without corresponding experiments with production management would be futile. The Japanese motor-vehicle market was far smaller than that in the United States, and buying new American machines and mimicking American production methods wouldn't work.

The man Eiji Toyoda selected to implement the revolution in production methods was Taiichi Ohno, a section chief in the engine machine shop. Ohno had begun his career with the Toyoda family in 1933. Fresh out of Nagoya Higher Industrial School, Ohno went to work at Toyoda Spinning & Weaving in the town of Kariya, where his father was mayor. Ohno was a young man who didn't have an imposing presence, and his job was to supervise a large number of young women, so he had grown a prominent moustache to have a more authoritative air.

Ohno had arrived at the company when textile-machine technology was fairly advanced. All of the machines in the factory had automatic monitoring and shut-off devices, and Ohno spent his apprenticeship in a plant where each worker routinely oversaw the operation of multiple machines. Competition was so fierce in the textile business that every company in the industry was extremely efficient.

Ohno had moved to Toyota Motor Company in 1943, after Toyoda's textile and motor-vehicle companies were combined by the Japanese military. Automobile factories, Ohno had quickly learned, were very different places from textile mills. Production in textile mills was ordered and logical, and although the workers were not highly skilled, complications were few. A single yard of cloth produced little profit, so factories were geared to volume production. Everything about a textile mill was oriented towards speed, and there was no wasted motion.

Coming from such a background, Ohno couldn't have arrived at Toyota Motor Company at a worse time than 1943. Military oversight had completely disrupted the flow of materials, most of the employees were inexperienced people who had been conscripted, and the assembly process was being controlled by inertia rather than reason. Whereas U.S. auto plants were using twenty men on the engine cylinder-block line, Toyota was using a hundred.

Ohno couldn't stand the mess he found, and he had begun studying the production process to find ways to improve it. When Kiichiro Toyoda came to the plant in those days and saw Ohno doing his studies, he recognized an honored family tradition at work. The Japanese phrase was *genchi genbutsu shugi*, or learning through careful observation at the work site. It was the method Sakichi had started using when he decided to become an inventor, and it lived on in the company. Kiichiro would urge Ohno on, saying that Toyota only had a few more years to catch up with Ford or GM, or it would be too late.

Ohno had been told once that American workers, on average, were nine times as productive as their Japanese counterparts. Based on what he saw around him, Ohno guessed that U.S. auto workers had to be twenty times more productive. But he knew the U.S. advantage didn't hold in the textile business, where Japanese mills were among the most efficient. He concluded it wasn't a difference in people but a difference in methods, and the Japanese automobile industry had to learn how to work smarter.

Ohno taught workers to understand *kaizen,* or the striving for constant improvement, by first teaching them the observation technique of *genchi genbutsu shugi.* Ohno always carried a piece of chalk in his pocket when he made his rounds of the factory, and when he encountered a supervisor who couldn't figure out why a machine was working improperly, he would draw a circle on the floor. He would then tell the supervisor to stand inside the circle, quietly observing the machine until he understood the nature of the problem.

Although American auto factories were more efficient, Ohno wasn't tempted to adopt their methods, since he knew little about them. Instead, he began to adapt the practices and technology he was familiar with—the ones the Toyodas had helped pioneer in the textile world.

Workers at Toyota Spinning & Weaving were able to oversee the operation of up to ten machines at a time because the machines monitored themselves, shutting off when a problem developed. But in the machine shop at Toyota Motor Company, Ohno saw workers wasting time watching one machine do its work. Employees waited at the machines until an operation was completed, then carried the in-process component to the next machine, where another worker was waiting. The machines weren't automated in any way, and sometimes they weren't even synchronized to the flow of production.

The first step Ohno took was to reorganize the locations of machines in the engine shop, drawing on his textile-mill experience. First he put two identical machines into an L shape so that one worker could oversee two machines at once. When that worked, Ohno used a U shape so workers could watch three machines. Then he arranged the machines in squares, and the number increased to four. While these steps did make workers more productive, there was one fundamental flaw in the textile-mill model.

Textile machines produced finished goods, while automobile machines produced components that were then assembled to create finished products. Increasing the efficiency of individual machines only created stockpiles of in-process materials where there were bottlenecks in the production flow. Ohno came to see that the biggest shortcoming in the mass-production process was that components were being pushed into the flow of the assembly line by individual work stations that operated like independent entities.

A man casting transmission housings produced as many as he could, then sent them on to the next area without regard for the situation there. The man who machined the housings might have work backed up because one of his tools was broken or because the man at the station after him was having a problem installing the transmission gears. The workers saw themselves as individuals who made or installed a certain part, rather than as part of a team that shared the objective of constructing an automobile.

Ohno decided it would be far more efficient and economical for automobiles to pull component parts to them as they moved through the factory rather than for workers to push parts at the cars. That way, a part would be produced only when it was needed to complete the next step in the assembly process. Workers wouldn't make parts to create stockpiles. They would make them only when there was an immediate need for them.

Ohno saw this as the next step in Kiichiro Toyoda's just-in-time production, and he compared it to the system used in the supermarkets that were becoming popular in the West. In supermarkets, customers bought products only when they needed them, and grocers restocked their shelves only after customers had depleted them. The chain of supply was coordinated all the way back to the farmer, since foods were perishable. If the production and distribution system didn't operate on just-in-time principles, the food would spoil on the way from the field to the dinner table.

Ohno decided to approximate this process in the machine shop by having workers "order" the in-process components they needed from the previous work station. When the worker who was doing the final machining on a cylinder head needed more partially completed heads, he would take a *kanban* to the previous station. The *kanban*, which means "nameplate" in Japanese, was a slip of paper in a vinyl sleeve listing the type and quantity of parts the man was taking from the stock of the previous station. As *kanbans* were passed from station to station back through the production system, each worker began producing just as many components as were needed, just at the time they were needed.

As a next step, Ohno knew that he had to reduce the amount of time workers wasted waiting for machines to perform their functions. Simply having workers oversee multiple copies of identical machines, as was done in the textile business, would cause stock to build up at each work station. Instead, he decided to train the workers to operate a variety of machines so they could do additional processing on each component.

Ohno rearranged the machine shop so that, instead of having all of the lathes and all of the drill presses clumped together, the machines were positioned according to the flow of the work. A lathe was lined up next to a drill press, which was next to a boring machine, replicating each of the steps a cylinder head had to go through on its way to completion. Ohno then had each worker perform a sequence of operations on one cylinder head, using each of the machines, rather than one operation on numerous cylinder heads at one machine. When this multiple-process handling was combined with *kanban* controls, wasteful stockpiling plummeted.

Almost everyone at Toyota Motor Company was thrilled when Ohno's improvements reached this stage in the early 1950s, just as the company was realizing its salvation lay in efficiency. The most vocal exceptions were sounded by union leaders at the plant, many of whom were still in a combative mood after their recent strike. The union men interpreted Ohno's efficiency moves as attempts to increase the workload. Ohno tried to reason with them about the wastefulness of having men idly watching machines, but it was useless. The union lodged a formal protest with the company, but Eiji Toyoda and the others backed Ohno all the way. They knew this was imperative for the survival of the company.

The union leaders were joined in their protests by some senior workmen in the machine shop. These men had become highly skilled craftsmen on their individual machines, such as the lathes and the milling and boring machines. They took great pride in their abilities to produce high-quality components quickly and repeatedly. They resented having other men working their machines, and they rebelled against the idea of having to learn new skills to operate unfamiliar machines.

Ohno told the men that while he respected their skills, it was counterproductive for the company to have only a few highly specialized men working each type of machine. It was much more important for all of the employees to raise their skills to the same level. The company was like a multiple-oared boat, where if one oarsman pulled harder than the rest, the boat would never stay on course. Most importantly, Ohno said, there was no way for Toyota to catch up with the U.S. auto industry other than by increasing productivity while paring costs to the bone.

Toyota's improved efficiency was coming at a fortuitous time. The Japanese economy began expanding in 1951, and the government turned its attention to the automobile industry. The final draft of the peace treaty with the United States was nearing completion, giving added impetus to the government's plans. Automobile imports had been restricted by GHQ during the postwar reconstruction to control the flow of foreign currency out of Japan. When the treaty was signed and the occupation ended, those restrictions would expire.

Government ministries had played a strong role in the Japanese economy since the time of the Meiji Restoration, but with the purges of the *zaibatsu* they came to have particular prominence during the postwar reconstruction. The ministries, seeking to bring economic stability to Japan, first directed their attention to the steel and coal industries. When those more established industries were secure, support was offered to the automobile business again.

The Ministry of Commerce and Industry had developed a basic plan for the return of automobile production in 1948, but the Japanese economy wasn't strong enough for the ministry to move forward with it aggressively at that time. In 1949 the ministry changed its name to the Ministry of International Trade and Industry (MITI) and began looking at the Japanese economy in a more international context.

The Japanese government realized that with the country's lack of resources, the only way to bring real prosperity to the nation was to make it an exporting power. The only way to achieve that goal was to develop the industries that had the highest potential in the international market. At the midpoint of the twentieth century, MITI began to believe the automobile business had that kind of promise.

In March of 1951, MITI granted financial assistance to Toyota, Nissan, and Isuzu through the Japan Development Bank, and provided for tax exemptions on imported production machinery and business profits from foreign sales, as well as offering an accelerated depreciation schedule for new equipment. MITI's assistance was generous, but it brought a renewed outcry from those segments of Japanese society that had been opposed to a domestic auto industry from the start.

Only a few months earlier, the National Police Agency had decided to begin using patrol cars in its work, but the police didn't want to use Japanese automobiles. They said that in order to pursue suspects who attempted to escape from them in automobiles, police cars would have to have a top speed of sixty miles per hour. Since domestic cars couldn't attain that speed, the police requested permission to import American automobiles.

MITI rejected this request on the basis of restrictions on foreign currency leaving the country and asked domestic manufacturers to create higher-powered cars for the police. Toyota was the only company to accept the challenge. The Toyota test car attained the target speed, but its acceleration was poor and the police deemed it unacceptable. MITI was forced to allow the police to import cars, but it approved only half the number requested.

Pressure was also brought to bear on MITI by the taxi industry and corporations that used automobiles in their businesses. These groups were still dissatisfied with the size, performance, and durability of domestic cars, and they wanted the import restrictions lifted after the peace treaty was signed. Because of the objections being raised, MITI took no action on auto imports when the peace treaty was enacted in September of 1951, and 1,650 foreign cars flooded into Japan in the following months.

Eiji Toyoda had been watching these developments carefully. He knew Toyota had to get a passenger car on the market before it was overrun with foreign cars. Sixty percent of the passenger cars in Japan were used as taxis at the time, and that meant Toyota had to produce a suitable taxi quickly. The cars Toyota had developed in the late 1940s had proven too fragile for the rough treatment taxis got on Japan's poor roads. A new car would have to be developed almost overnight.

The plan Eiji created was to install a car body of new design on an existing truck chassis. It was the only scheme that could be accomplished quickly enough, and Eiji was certain the truck chassis would be rugged enough for taxis. Toyota still hadn't perfected the construction of dies for stamping presses, so the body work had to be farmed out to three different companies. Everything was very rushed.

The resulting car was called the model SF, and no one at Toyota was thrilled with it. It was a stopgap car, one designed to keep Toyota in the market until a new car could be designed from the ground up. Not surprisingly, public response to the car was cool. The SF was slow and sat high off the ground, and people said it looked like a baby carriage with an engine. The price was also far from competitive. The model SF sold for 1.2 million yen, whereas a much better Volkswagen— with a 40-percent import duty included—could be purchased for 740,000 yen.

Eiji Toyoda knew that the Toyota Motor Company had to get a new automobile into production if it was going to stake a claim in the automotive market. He consulted with others in the company and spent the New Year's holiday of 1952 mulling over the possibilities. Eiji believed Toyota was going to have to take radical steps if the company was going to break the pattern of jinxes that had plagued past models.

The company had committed itself to a five-year plan to reform production, and Eiji decided to extend that to the design and planning of the car as well. When he returned to the office on January 4, he called Kenya Nakamura into his office and gave the man a startling order. Nakamura, a manufacturing engineer, was to oversee the creation of a new passenger car for the company.

Manufacturing engineers, who worked in the factory, were thought to be of lower status than car designers, who worked in the engineering center. The designers kept their hands clean and did creative work, while manufacturing engineers got dirty as they put the designers' creations into production. Eiji Toyoda decided this was a misordering of priorities. The future of the company, he concluded, was staked upon how well it built cars, not how well it designed them. Therefore, it was time for the designers to start serving the needs of the production men.

Nakamura had been an enthusiastic supporter of auto production at the company, and Eiji liked that. But Nakamura's strongest qualification, as far as Eiji was concerned, was his extensive hands-on experience in the building cars. Eiji wanted a man who would know, before a car was designed, what was possible and what wasn't. The model SA with its monocoque body had been an expensive lesson for the company. After the SA was in preproduction, Toyota had learned it was a difficult car to build. With Japan's market now open to auto imports from the West, there was no time for such surprises.

Eiji also wanted an unlikely candidate for the assignment because the job itself was going to be unique. Nakamura would be the chief engineer of the new car, a position that hadn't existed before, and his post would be outside the normal chain of command at Toyota. He would have no permanent subordinates. Instead, after the basic car was defined, Nakamura would form a project team by selecting anyone he wanted within the engineering division. The team would be responsible for every aspect of the car from design through final production, and the members of the team would answer only to Nakamura in matters concerning the car. One of Kiichiro's trademarks at Toyota had been hiring good people and then giving them free reign. Eiji was continuing the tradition.

Eiji told Nakamura that the car should seat six people—a step larger than the model SF—and should be powered by a new 1500-cc engine, which was being developed separately. Most of all, Eiji said, the car should be competitive with the imported cars in the taxi and corporate-car markets—buyers who had said repeatedly they wanted nothing to do with Japanese cars.

Nakamura's first step, before talking to any engineers or technical people, was to call upon his customers. He took design sketches and photographs of existing cars and visited taxi companies and corporations. He showed the pictures to the taxi men and then asked what they liked and disliked about them and what features would encourage them to buy a car. He took ample notes and then returned to the factory to give the designers their instructions. Since imports might soon be flooding the country, Nakamura knew that if he didn't give the business market more than it wanted at less than it expected to pay, Toyota wouldn't have a chance.

Another person in Japan was also designing a new car at this time. He was Kiichiro Toyoda, whose life in the months since he had left Toyota could not be described as a retirement. Frustrated in his plans to produce a satisfactory car within the confines of a large company, Kiichiro decided—as his father had before him—that he would start his own small company. Kiichiro's plan was to create a car for export to Southeast Asia, one that would help bring the underdeveloped countries of that region into the automotive age.

Kiichiro set up shop in a remodeled warehouse in Tokyo. He managed to requisition one of Toyota's top designers, Shisaburo Kurata, to assist him. The men sat down and established the parameters for the automobile. It would have to be very inexpensive, and that meant it had to be small—but not too small, Kiichiro said. The backseat should hold three people. The styling should be modern, but not so modern as to make people question its reliability. Careful thought had to be given to eliminating potential shakes and rattles, and the engine should be virtually maintenance free. The car had to be simple to operate with a push-button automatic transmission so everyone, including women and young people, could learn to drive it with a minimum of time and expense.

Kurata listened to the long list of specifications and thought to himself that it would be impossible to build such a car, but he knew better than to say that to Kiichiro. Whenever he had told Kiichiro before that something was impossible, Kiichiro would get upset and answer, "Don't tell me that you can't do it."

Kiichiro left the designer to his work and then moved on to other projects. Kiichiro was raising a large number of quail at his home in Nagoya and selling their eggs on the wholesale market. He had other enterprises scattered from Tokyo to Nagoya, and every family member who wasn't working for Toyota Motor Company was in Kiichiro's employ. Kiichiro's oldest son, Shoichiro, had left the fish-sausage business in northern Japan and returned to graduate school. Now, as he was finishing his doctorate in engineering, Shoichiro found himself caught up in his father's new schemes.

Kiichiro had Shoichiro alternately helping with the plans to build a new car and working at Kiichiro's new modular-house company, Affluent Prestressed Concrete. Kiichiro had also asked his designer, Kurata, to teach Shoichiro about automobile design. So every time Shoichiro came to Tokyo, Kurata would give him a lesson. Shoichiro accompanied Kurata during prototype testing of the new car's engine.

Shoichiro also spent time at one of Toyota's parts suppliers in which the family had an interest, and Kiichiro decided Shoichiro should oversee the entry of that company into sewing machine manufacturing. To Kiichiro, who always did everything on a large scale, this frantic activity was all part of the young man's education.

While Kiichiro kept himself as busy as ever, he always returned to the automobile project. The irony of Toyota's miraculous economic recovery as a result of the truck orders for the Korean War, a month after Kiichiro resigned, were not lost on him. Kiichiro and Toyota had learned the ropes of the motor vehicle business with trucks, but Kiichiro didn't miss building them. They weren't enough of a challenge, and it was a point of honor for him to prove the Japanese could produce a

high-quality automobile that was also profitable. He was especially determined to prove that a Toyoda could do it.

Kiichiro kept up with what was going on at Toyota Motor Company, so he knew the company was making a good profit with its trucks.
Nonetheless, he was surprised when he received a visit from the assistant to Taizo Ishida, Toyota's president, one day in late 1951. The
assistant said he was there to deliver an important message from Ishida.
The communication was that, with Toyota Motor Company now on
sound financial footing, Ishida wanted Kiichiro to return to the company as president.

Kiichiro sat in silence, thinking about all he had been through with
Toyota and the banks and the government. Many of the memories were
unpleasant. But the prospects of getting a good Japanese car into production were infinitely greater with the resources of Toyota behind him.
Kiichiro went back and forth on the issues in his mind and then dismissed the messenger without a reply. There was no way he could
resolve this without a great deal of thought.

Taizo Ishida waited patiently for Kiichiro's reply. When it hadn't
arrived by February of 1952, Ishida went to visit Kiichiro. Ishida reviewed the current financial situation at Toyota and then repeated his
request for Kiichiro to return. Kiichiro answered quickly. He told Ishida
that he wouldn't return, because an automobile company that only made
trucks was no automobile company at all.

Ishida knew there was no point in arguing that the company was
poised to begin serious automobile production, for Kiichiro had seen
too many such plans evaporate in the past. Instead, Ishida appealed to
Kiichiro's sense of honor, reminding him of a promise he had made.

Ishida had strongly opposed Toyoda Automatic Loom Works' entry
into the automobile business in the 1930s, when he was a director there.
Kiichiro had stopped Ishida in the plant one day, telling him that Toyoda would produce fine cars soon and that Kiichiro would give him
one free when that day came. Ishida said that Kiichiro still owed him
that car and could provide it only by returning to the company.

Kiichiro may have simply needed some coaxing, but Ishida's appeal
worked. The men agreed Kiichiro would officially return as president
after the stockholders' meeting in July. Kiichiro immediately redirected
his energies to his return. He had meetings with all of the top people
who were working on the new car, he went around paying his respects
to various ministry officials, and he reviewed the plans for the produc-

tion modernization at the plant. Any bad feelings he had about returning to the confines of a large corporation seemed to fade away. As all of the parts for his return came together, Kiichiro turned to one piece of unfinished business that was still hanging on from the time of his resignation.

On March 17, Kiichiro invited the leaders of the Toyota Motor Koromo Labor Union to his home. He hoped time had healed the wounds between himself and the union leaders, but he wanted to make a personal appeal to them. Kiichiro felt the greatest challenge of his life was before him, and he wanted the workers to understand what an important part they would play in it. "We are returning to work on the automobile," Kiichiro said, "but we must move quickly or the Americans will come in all at once. We must ask the employees to do a rush job. I also ask for labor's cooperation." The workers pledged to do all they could.

Kiichiro knew that, this time, he really had a chance to make it work. The company was profitable, the workers had become more skilled, the machinery was being modernized, and the government was offering support. Then, just when he thought it had all come together, tragedy struck.

Kiichiro had been working on a memoir and biography of his father, and one cold day in March he announced to his designer, Kurata, that he was leaving the office for the day to do some writing. Kiichiro went to his writing retreat, a local inn where he rented a room. As he returned to his manuscript, Kiichiro—suddenly and without warning—was felled by a cerebral hemorrhage. He lapsed into a coma and died several days later on March 27 at the age of fifty-seven.

No one who knew Kiichiro had failed to be touched by his determination and his dedication. After large funeral services were held in Tokyo and Nagoya, everyone at Toyota Motor Company became more resolute about getting a new automobile into production. Eiji Toyoda went to visit Risaburo Toyoda to give him a report on Kiichiro's funeral. Risaburo was bedridden with tuberculosis and quite ill, and he was unable to attend the ceremony. Now even Risaburo was a believer in Kiichiro's cause. "Whatever you do," Risaburo told Eiji in a weak voice, "have Toyota make cars." Eiji swore to Risaburo that he would and left. Two months later, Risaburo passed away at the age of sixty-eight.

Kiichiro oldest son, Shoichiro, was preparing to leave for the United States at the time his father and uncle died. Shoichiro was carrying forward his father's plan to manufacture sewing machines. One of Toyota's parts suppliers was purchasing a die-casting machine for this purpose, and Kiichiro was going to spend six months at the Ohio factory learning to use it. Taizo Ishida told Shoichiro to cancel his plans. If Toyota Motor Company couldn't have Kiichiro, Ishida said, then it would have his son.

9
BEGINNING AGAIN

The Toyota Motor Sales Company was moving only two hundred model SF cars a month during the summer of 1952, and Shotaro Kamiya, its president, was getting worried. The manufacturing division of Toyota was diligently making improvements on the hastily prepared vehicle, but Kamiya didn't think his company could wait for that to produce results. Kamiya and his sales force needed something to happen now, so he went to see Taizo Ishida, his manufacturing counterpart.

Kamiya and Ishida did not have a cordial relationship, their differences being rooted in their vastly dissimilar personalities and obligation. Kamiya was an extroverted internationalist who had worked for Mitsui in London and for GM in Japan. He aggressively sought to build relationships with government officials and others in a position to help his company and was always pushing for Toyota to find ways to expand it sales.

Ishida, ten years Kamiya's senior, was a strong and reclusive nationalist. He hated socializing with his peers in the business and refused to hold positions in industry associations. He said the company's job was to remain solvent so it could pay its employees and its bills, and anything that didn't contribute directly to that was frivolousness, which was to be eliminated. The two men had criticized each other openly in public on occasion, so when they were forced to meet they talked only business.

Kamiya told Ishida that his sales were low because the Japanese taxi industry had a bias against domestic cars. They thought the vehicles were of lower quality and higher cost than Western vehicles. For proof, Kamiya cited projections that over ten thousand foreign cars would be imported into Japan during 1952, while less than five thousand domestic cars would be purchased. Imported cars were taking two-thirds of the

Japanese market, and Kamiya insisted Toyota make its cars more attractive by lowering the price of the model SF by 100,000 yen, to 1.1 million yen.

Ishida refused to lower prices. He had spent two years building solid profitability at the manufacturing company, and he didn't want to return to deficit pricing. Eiji Toyoda and Taiichi Ohno were working to lower costs by rationalizing production methods, and Ishida preferred to wait until results in the factory justified a price cut. Ishida told Kamiya that if he was unhappy with the price Toyota charged for its cars, Kamiya should buy his cars from another company—knowing full well that each man could do business only with the other.

Kamiya argued there wasn't time to wait for manufacturing technique to improve. Lower prices would increase sales and thus lower production costs through higher volume. Prices had to be set according to market conditions. Then it was Ishida's job to find ways to produce cars profitably for that price.

The men argued for a time, but, as always happened, Ishida yielded to Kamiya and agreed to the change. Although he would never admit it, many people thought Ishida, mindful of his lack of experience in the automotive business, allowed Kamiya to lead Toyota. Sales and manufacturing, by dictate of the banks, were separate entities, and Ishida's greater years required respect, but Ishida recognized Kamiya's talents, even if he didn't acknowledge them publicly.

The price cut did improve sales slightly, but they still weren't anywhere near the capacity for the SF at Koromo. Then the competitive situation in the Japanese taxi market changed. MITI had been encouraging Japanese manufacturers to establish cooperative ventures with foreign auto makers so they could acquire advanced technology. Since Eiji Toyoda had found deteriorating technology in the United States during his 1950 trip, Toyota was resisting this approach. But Nissan Motor Company announced in December of 1952 that it was signing a licensing agreement with the Austin Company of the United Kingdom. Toyota's biggest rival in the Japanese auto market was going to assemble British cars in Japan, and the first model would be on the market in five months.

This time Ishida was in complete agreement with Kamiya. The company had to cut prices again in an attempt to gain market share before the new car arrived. There were some people in Japan who wouldn't buy foreign cars because they wanted to support domestic companies, but those people wouldn't consider an Austin with Nissan nameplates to be a foreign car. Toyota cut the price of the model SF another 150,000 yen, to 950,000 yen, in January of 1953. The company probably wasn't going to make a profit at that price, but it was a gamble that had to be taken.

The taxi industry responded well to the unexpected second price cut, and sales of the SF improved considerably. Toyotas became even more popular when the new Nissan was introduced in May with a price 200,000 yen higher than Toyota's. Meanwhile, Toyota's engineers had been working to address complaints about the original SF's poor styling and performance. They developed a new 1,500-cc engine that doubled the power of the original 1,000 cc engine, and the body was made more attractive. The revamped car was introduced in September as the Toyopet Super. It was priced only 20,000 yen higher than the original SF, and it won more converts in the taxi market.

Toyota produced a record 3,572 cars during 1953, but it still had to rely on the sales of 12,422 trucks to make its profits. The quality and styling of the cars were improving, but costs were still too high. The lower prices of imported cars, which benefited from the savings of mass production, were putting a cap on domestic car sales. It was a vicious circle. Toyota's production runs were too low to bring down costs, and the selling price of cars was too high to increase demand. The only solution seemed to rest with Taiichi Ohno and his efforts to cut costs by streamlining the production process.

Truck production for the U.S. military, which had continued beyond the end of the Korean War, was aiding Ohno in his work. The U.S. military issued exhaustive specifications for the trucks they asked Japanese manufacturers to bid on, and the military refused to accept any finished vehicles that didn't conform. It wasn't a matter of how the trucks performed. If they didn't meet specifications, they were rejected. The exacting military inspections forced Toyota and its suppliers to improve their own inspection skills.

Ohno continued training his men to operate multiple machines simultaneously, but he was concerned they were still spending too much time watching the machines. He believed that machine work and human work should be distinctly different. Machines that had to be constantly monitored by humans were not adding full value to production. To achieve that goal, they should require human attention only when they were malfunctioning.

In addition, if workers stood by constantly helping machines do their work, the machines would never be perfected. Machine malfunctions would be considered routine, and no one would think to improve them. If workers had to stop doing something else to attend to a machine, however, attention would be focused on finding the root cause of the malfunction, and the machine would eventually be improved.

From his textile experience, Ohno was convinced there had to be a way for the machines to monitor themselves. Sakichi Toyoda had invented devices that automatically monitored the flow of yarn through a loom. In fact, these mechanisms had given Toyoda Automatic Loom Works its name. Ohno was confident he could make similar devices for automobile production machinery.

While Ohno was working to create an automatic monitoring device, one of Toyota's employees returned from a visit to Ford Motor Company. The man showed Ohno a mechanism, called a limiting switch, that Ford used to turn off machines after they had completed a set amount of work. Instantly Ohno recognized this type of switch could be adapted to monitor the operation of a machine as well as its output.

Ohno had his engineers create monitoring switches for the machines in the engine shop, and after some experimentation they worked well. There was no need for workers to watch machines equipped this way, since the machines stopped when trouble developed or when a process was completed. Ohno also added signal lights, or *pokayoke*, to the machines that would go on when they were malfunctioning. This visual control allowed repairmen to identify troublesome machines quickly.

The switches precipitated a large increase in productivity. Once a worker set a piece of work up on a machine, he could move on to another. If a machine stopped, it would be noticed immediately. Workers who had been able to handle only three or four machines before could now sometimes oversee ten to fifteen.

Having machines monitor themselves saved time, but it also caused in-process materials to back up behind malfunctioning machines that shut off—a result that was inimical to just-in-time production. Ohno recognized the only way to prevent the backing up was to stop the entire production flow when one machine went down. This wasn't a huge problem in the engine machine shop, but Ohno expected foremen in the assembly plant to object strenuously. Yet he knew the day would come when this procedure had to be part of the production process.

Ohno got the chance to expand his system from the engine shop to the assembly line when he was promoted to general manager of manufacturing in 1953. He went around the plant every day then, preaching there was no wastefulness so great as the wastefulness of overproduction. People smiled and agreed with Ohno, but not much changed.

Many workers thought Ohno was an eccentric. Military men had often worn mustaches during the war, but it was rare to see a Japanese man with one afterward. Ohno was the exception, and his facial hair became his nickname around Toyota: Mustache. "What's Mustache up to now?" was a common refrain at the plant as Ohno carried out his studies.

Ohno soon had his suspicions about the workers' objections to his plan confirmed. Radically transforming the vehicle assembly line was far more difficult than doing it in one machine shop. Engines and transmissions and other components poured into the assembly building from various locations, and orchestrating everything to arrive just in time was a monumental task.

Ohno realized that although all of the workers understood what he was trying to accomplish in principle, no one wanted to be the first to implement the system at his particular location. Stoppages occurred naturally at various points on the assembly line during the day, and the workers felt more secure having extra in-process stock available so they could continue their work. Ohno began combating this by making employees who produced excess stock take the unneeded material home with them. "Since the company does not need these things," he would tell the men as he filled their arms with parts at the end of the day, "you must take them home."

Ohno concluded he was going to have to force the system on everyone until they came to accept it. This was the only way the production system could be implemented, and without it, costs would never fall enough to make the company competitive. Eiji Toyoda, in particular, was supportive of Ohno's work, and within two years Eiji compelled a widely questioned principle on the operation of the factory. Whenever a problem developed in assembly, the entire production line was to be shut down until it was fixed.

As the work on production improvements continued, Kenya Nakamura's efforts as the chief engineer of the new medium-sized passenger car were going well. Nakamura knew the car would have to compete with foreign imports, so he gave it as many advanced features as possible. He specified an independent front suspension, rather than the solid-axle I-beam suspension that had originated on trucks. Many Japanese auto makers still used this system on their cars, despite its rough ride.

To distinguish the otherwise staid body design of the sedan, Nakamura added rear doors that opened from the center of the car toward the back rather than from the back toward the front. He thought this layout lent a certain elegance to the car. As the vehicle's chief engineer, it was Nakamura's prerogative to create this design. Nonetheless, both the front suspension and the doors made some managers in the company nervous.

The people from engineering and sales were afraid the all-important taxi market would not appreciate these features. Previous attempts to use independent front suspension had failed when it wasn't rugged enough for taxi use. Nakamura argued that the failures were because of production and materials problems, not because of inherent flaws in the design. Besides, he insisted, independent suspension gave a far more comfortable ride.

The people from the sales department said that, even if the new suspension was better, the problem was one of perception. Since the system had failed in the past, the taxi industry didn't trust it. In addition, the marketing men argued, rear doors that opened toward the back were inappropriate for a taxi. The drivers would have to get out of the front seat to close a rear door that was left open. With rear doors that opened toward the front, the driver could turn in his seat and pull the door closed.

Wishing to avoid an impasse on the issue, and not wanting to undercut their first chief engineer, Eiji and Shotaro Kamiya decided to put two new cars on the market simultaneously. Nakamura's car would have all the features he wanted, and it would be called the Crown. The sales department would get an update of the more conventional Toyopet Super, which had proven popularity in the taxi market, and it would be called the Master.

Another factor arguing for the compromise was time. The Koromo factory was in the middle of some important additions as the new models were nearing production. After years of having to farm out body work because of problems making dies for the stamping presses, Toyota was installing new die-making equipment. The Crown was to be the first Toyota automobile with a body made in-house. The equipment was part of the five-year plan for modernizing production, but it also represented an important barrier for the company to surmount. Everyone at Toyota was taking great pride in making a domestic car when other Japanese companies were using licensing agreements with foreign manufacturers. The more components manufactured in-house, the better it was for everyone's morale.

In addition to the die-making machines, body-stamping and spot-welding machines were added, as well as new conveyors for the paint and assembly lines. As the workers in the body department learned to set up and use their machines, Nakamura was constantly making special requests and ordering adjustments. More than forty experimental cars were produced, and then subjected to rigorous road testing. Whenever a flaw was detected, the design of the offending part was changed.

For all of the modern equipment being installed, some parts of the assembly still required hand craftsmanship. The body presses were not advanced enough to produce perfectly smooth panels, and imperfections had to be filled by hand. The workers made their own spatulas to apply the body putty, and they would gather in one place each morning to practice their technique until it was perfect. Since there were no automatic spraying machines for applying paint, paint was sprayed on manually, and the quality check for the finish coat was how well it reflected the stripes in the paint inspector's tie.

Finally, on New Year's Day of 1955, over two hundred company officials in morning coats attended the ceremony for the completion of the first Crown. Eiji Toyoda slid behind the wheel and drove the car off the assembly line. Everyone applauded and threw showers of confetti.

Two decades after Kiichiro had taken up the challenge, Toyota had completed a "real" passenger car under favorable conditions. The car had been built from scratch, with the time and money available to nurture it through the development stage. The assembly workers were experienced, and prototypes of the car were tested thoroughly. Now, the final test would come when hundreds of cars a month began flooding the marketplace.

Both the Crown and the Master went into full production later that month. As the sales department had predicted, the taxi industry cautiously bought the Master, with its proven I-beam suspension, despite the Crown's better looks and comfort. When Nissan introduced a new-model Austin that was smaller than the Crown and 150,000 yen more expensive, the Crown began to capture one part of the market. It became the car of choice for private companies and the few individuals who could afford automobiles.

The Crown quickly acquired a reputation as a comfortable and reliable car, and soon the taxi market began buying Crowns on a trial basis. After the Crown proved its durability to taxi owners, it became the standard medium-sized taxi almost overnight.

Shotaro Kamiya realized the Crown would lose its cachet as a high-class car when it flooded the taxi market, so the company swiftly planned an upgraded version, called the Crown Deluxe. The Deluxe featured more chrome, whitewall tires, a radio, a heater, an electric clock, tinted glass, and fog lights. By Japanese standards of the time, it was a luxury car directed at the private owner.

The private-owner market was small, but since the days of Kiichiro, Toyota had been planning for the day when it would undergo massive expansion. The marketing staff also knew the Crown Deluxe was important to the company's image, as Toyota was still making more trucks than cars.

With the Crowns doing well, Kamiya began intensifying Toyota Motor Sales' marketing program—especially that aimed at boosting private ownership of cars. He had created a special consumer-research department to conduct polls and forecast demand. These men worked closely with the product planning section of the manufacturing company to insure that future Toyotas would reflect known consumer preferences. But Kamiya was concerned the Toyota's dealer body, which primarily sold trucks to commercial customers, would have difficulty selling cars to first-time private owners.

Since its founding, Toyota's dealer body had been composed of one independent dealer in each of Japan's forty-seven prefectures. The dealers had more than one outlet in their territories, but each had exclusive rights to their region. Toyota owned none of the dealerships. In 1953, Kamiya decided to change that by opening a company store in Tokyo. The capital city accounted for 30 percent of the Japanese private-car market, so it was imperative that Toyota make a strong showing there. Kamiya overcame the strong objections of existing dealers by promising to use the outlet, called Tokyo Toyopet, as a laboratory for testing marketing techniques, which he would share with them.

Kamiya drastically altered the way automobiles were sold when he opened Tokyo Toyopet. He anticipated that first-time car buyers would be fearful of being taken if they had to haggle over selling price, so he instituted a fixed-price system. Salesmen were paid on salary rather than commission, and they had unique qualifications. Each was a college graduate who had joined Toyota Motor Sales as a regular corporate trainee. None of them had sales experience, but that was just what Kamiya wanted.

He wanted his men—the first college graduates to sell cars in Japan—to be refined, courteous, and reliable. He believed customers would buy cars from people they felt comfortable with and trusted. Kamiya also sent his salesmen out to sell automobiles door-to-door. The salesmen would call on every customer in their territory periodically, so that when someone was ready to buy a car, the Toyota salesman was a friend of the family.

Kamiya thought of the Tokyo Toyopet model when he was having trouble selling a new truck, the SKB, in 1955. This truck had been designed to compete with small, three-wheeled trucks, of which almost 100,000 were sold a year in Japan. Toyota's four-wheeled truck was approximately the same size as the three-wheelers, but of much better quality and utility. Yet Toyota hadn't been able to reduce production costs enough to make their truck prices competitive. The SKB was selling for 625,000 yen, while the three-wheelers were only 450,000 yen. Even though the Toyota was a better vehicle, people couldn't afford it.

Kamiya went to visit Taizo Ishida in late 1955 and offered him a deal. If Ishida would cut the price of the SKB by 12 percent, Kamiya said, he would create a new network of dealers to sell the SKB. Kamiya promised a marketing plan that would drive the three-wheeled trucks out of business, and thus increase Toyota's sales enough to make the truck profitable at the lower price. Ishida agreed, and Kamiya began signing up new dealers.

Kamiya staged another nickname contest for the SKB, this time bringing in two hundred thousand entries and tons of publicity. The winning name for the truck was Toyoace, and the dealers capitalized on the campaign with innovative marketing efforts of their own. They staged exhibits everywhere small-truck buyers would be—fish and vegetable markets, farming villages, and shopping districts. They formed Toyoace owners' clubs and handed out brochures in front of train stations. Soon, three-wheeled truck sales began to decline irrevocably.

While all of this was going on, Kamiya was always looking into the future. He was planning for that all-important day when the private-owner car market opened up. Kamiya laid the groundwork for selling Toyotas at department stores in Tokyo and Kyoto. Even if sales were small there, large numbers of people would be exposed to his cars. He thought of every inducement he could use to prepare the Japanese people for something that still seemed unimaginable to many of them in 1956—car ownership.

The largest driver-training school in Asia was located in Japan, and when Kamiya heard it was going bankrupt, he knew what he had to do. He called a board meeting and told his directors that Toyota's sales operation should buy the school. The school was on the block for four hundred thousand yen—an amount equal to 40 percent of Toyota Motor Sales' capitalization. The board told Kamiya they didn't know where they'd get that kind of money. Then Kamiya told them of his plan.

For a small fee, the school would offer unlimited lessons until a person earned his or her driver's license. The cars the students learned to drive with would be Toyotas, of course. Once they got their licenses, students would be offered special financing—with a low down payment—to buy a new car from a Toyota dealer. The board told Kamiya to go ahead, they'd find the money.

Even though the consumer auto market barely existed in Japan at the time, Kamiya was already looking beyond it. He knew the day would come when Japan would be saturated with cars. At that time, the company would have to export cars to grow. So he established an export department within Toyota Motor Sales. A man was dispatched to Brazil to study that market, with explorations of conditions in Africa and Southeast Asia planned. But Kamiya never forgot about the most important export market of all—the United States, the largest automobile market in the world. Kamiya, and everyone at Toyota, knew they would never be satisfied until they were able to compete with the Americans on their own soil.

Toyota was not the only Japanese automobile company developing new vehicles in the mid-1950s, and the industry was in considerable disarray as a result. Toyota had domestically produced cars on the market, Nissan and Isuzu and some smaller companies were assembling and selling knockdown foreign cars, and other concerns were importing assembled foreign cars. This jumble of products was matched by an equal number of opinions about what direction the government should encourage the industry to take. The halls of the Japanese Diet were rife with people arguing each point of view.

Some still insisted that government support for the domestic auto industry was a waste of resources, since American and European cars could never be equaled by a Japanese company. Others argued that a domestic industry could never survive unless foreign cars were banned entirely from the country. A third group thought that licensing agreements with foreign manufacturers were mandatory for Japanese companies to acquire the technology required to make world-class automobiles.

In May of 1955, MITI established what it saw as a compromise plan—banning the import of finished foreign cars, while allowing the assembly of foreign knockdown sets. MITI officials believed this plan provided the protection they thought the domestic industry needed, but still allowed for the acquisition of advanced technology.

MITI officials also thought, however, that too many domestic companies were entering the auto business. They feared proliferation would produce a rash of weak companies that would drive each other out of business. The ministry wanted to create a few strong companies—manufacturers that would develop a domestic market for automobiles and, more importantly, bring in foreign currency through exports.

At this time, there was a controversial proposal circulating through MITI. The plan suggested that true mass production could be fostered in Japan by developing a so-called people's car. The chief proponent of this plan was a man named Akira Kawahara, who had studied the European automotive industry. Kawahara discovered that the tremendous popularity of the Volkswagen had been instrumental in Germany's economic recovery after World War II. The Volkswagen, which literally meant "people's car," had been designed as a car for the masses by Ferdinand Porsche in the 1930s. Mass production of the car was part of Adolf Hitler's economic program, but that was scaled back with the beginning of the war.

The Volkswagen had become extremely popular in West Germany after the war, and by 1953 the company had built a plant in Canada and was exporting cars to the United States. Kawahara also discovered that the Fiat 500 and the Renault were playing similar roles in the economic recovery of Italy and France respectively. In each case, the small, austere cars were extremely inexpensive. Working people could afford them, and large-scale domestic sales supported the development of an automobile industry.

Kawahara calculated that when the cost of an automobile fell to 1.4 times the per-capita national income, the automobile market in a country mushroomed. At the time, the cost of a Volkswagen in West Germany was $892 and the per-capita income of the country was $600, a factor of 1.48. In contrast, the cost of a Toyota Crown was $2,639 and the per-capita income of Japan was $211, a factor of 12.5.

The gulf between Japan's income factor of 12.5 and the target factor of 1.4 was huge, but Kawahara kept juggling his figures. He hypothesized that per-capita income in Japan would rise to $500 in the near future. If the country could produce a car with a selling price of $700, or 250,000 yen, the magic barrier would be broken.

It wouldn't be a simple task reducing the cost of an automobile to 27 percent of the price of a Toyota Crown, but Kawahara pushed ahead with his plan nonetheless. Since the costs of materials and fuel were astronomical in Japan, he decided the car would have to be lightweight and fuel efficient. He specified a vehicle weight of 880 pounds, with an engine under 500 cc. The car should be able to attain a speed of sixty-two miles per hour, carry four passengers, get seventy miles per gallon, and travel 60,000 miles without major repairs. And the car should sell for 250,000 yen, based on production of 24,000 vehicles a year.

Kawahara recognized it would be impossible for a company to produce this car profitably—if it could be produced at all. To compensate, he wanted to hold a competition among Japanese auto makers. The company producing a car closest to his specifications would be given production subsidies. He assumed that subsidies would cease once production reached a certain level.

There was considerable resistance to Kawahara's plan within MITI, especially over awarding one segment of the market to a single manufacturer. As the debate continued unresolved, someone in the ministry leaked a copy of Kawahara's proposal to an influential newspaper. The paper was delighted to publish the exclusive story, and MITI got to gauge industry reaction indirectly.

The automobile industry went into an uproar when the story appeared. Experienced auto executives knew it was impossible to build a car that even remotely met the specifications Kawahara had selected—especially at the price he quoted. In addition, the proposal called for one company to produce twenty-four thousand cars annually, although all Japanese companies combined produced only twenty thousand cars in 1955. But what enraged the manufacturers most was the idea of MITI's providing special assistance to only one company while the rest were left to fend for themselves. The Japan Automobile Manufacturers Association objected vehemently, and MITI denied having had any intention of carrying the subsidy program forward.

Although the immediate furor over the proposal died down in a few months, the aftereffects lingered much longer. At a time when MITI wanted to prune the size of the auto industry, the controversy over the people's car actually caused it to expand. Recognizing the potential size of the market for the first time, and still hopeful that government support might be available later on, companies like Fuji Heavy Industries and some motorcycle manufacturers set up automotive departments.

As it happened, Eiji Toyoda had ordered his engineering staff to begin working on a prototype of something like a people's car in 1954. He wanted to create a front-wheel-drive minicar with an air-cooled, 500- to 600-cc, two-cylinder engine. He wanted to keep the weight under 1,300 pounds and the cost under 450,000 yen. With a year of experience on this type of car under his belt, Eiji knew better than the others how exacting it was to build a car with these specifications.

The weight of every component had to be minimized, and that required exotic materials and sophisticated techniques that taxed an inexperienced auto maker heavily. Little of Toyota's experience with other cars carried over to the experimental car, and progress was slow. Eiji was willing to be patient, but then the people's car story broke and manufacturers came rushing into the market. In an attempt to scare people off, Eiji bragged publicly that his minicar was almost ready, but it was all a bluff.

In actuality, Toyota Motor Company had a prototype of the minicar ready by the summer of 1956. The company wasn't certain when it would be ready for production, but Taizo Ishida, the president, estimated the car would have to sell for 450,000 yen—near the company's original projection. In the meantime, however, Shotaro Kamiya and his sales staff had conducted consumer surveys. The results indicated that if the price wasn't reduced to 360,000 yen, sales would never exceed 1,000 units a month. Ishida was dumbstruck. The company would lose a fortune if it sold the cars for 360,000 yen—or if it could only sell 1,000 a month at the higher price.

With no immediate solution at hand, Ishida reconsidered the company's position. The two cars Toyota had on the market, the Crown and Master, were both intermediate-sized. They were doing well in the mid-sized taxi market, but Nissan's Datsun 110 had the small-sized taxi market—where fares were lower—to itself. Proven demand for small taxis was increasing rapidly, while demand for the people's car was only theoretical. In addition, Shotaro Kamiya was screaming that if Toyota didn't enter the compact-car market immediately, Nissan would own it forever. Feeling like a man besieged from all sides, Ishida decided to face his most discernible enemy—Nissan—head on.

Ishida told Eiji Toyoda to drastically reduce work on the minicar, and to have his men create a new compact car posthaste. When Eiji asked how soon Ishida wanted it, Ishida said it had to be on the market in a year. And make sure you control costs, he added, because we will have to sell the car for 20 percent less than the Datsun 110.

Given the time and cost limitations, Eiji had no choice but to cannibalize existing models. The drive train would be picked up from the Crown, and the body design would be that of the Master, chopped off front, back, and sides to make it a compact. There was no way a compact could use an external frame as the Master did, though, and that meant another attempt to conquer unit-body construction, this time under a crushing deadline.

Controlling costs on the new car, called the Corona, was made easier by the new production equipment. Toyota Motor Company had obtained a loan of 846 million yen from the World Bank, which it had used to install additional automated equipment in machine processing and final assembly. Monthly production capacity had been boosted, and costs fell. Since 1951, the cost of casting had been reduced by 25 percent, stamping by 20 percent, and forging by 15 percent. Productivity had increased from two vehicles per employee to ten.

Toyota was also helped by advances made by its subcontractors and suppliers. In 1956 the Japanese government began providing 110 billion yen in long-term, low-interest loans to the auto-parts and machining industries. Production facilities were modernized, and the quality and reliability of auto parts increased rapidly. The funding the machine industry received meant Japanese auto makers could obtain production machinery locally, rather than having to import the machines from abroad and then modify them to Japan's smaller-scale production runs.

None of this, however, enabled Toyota to perform miracles, which is what creating a new car in a year would have been. Kiichiro Toyoda had managed feats like this with trucks in the 1930s, but the expectations of passenger-car buyers were far higher in the 1950s. The Corona was attractively priced at 620,000 yen when it hit the market in July of 1957. The car also received substantial marketing attention when it was distributed through the Toyopet dealer network that had been established for the SKB truck. Indeed, based on the excellent reputation Toyota had won with the Crown, the Corona grabbed 30 percent of the compact-car market in its first month.

But the Corona's impossibly short development time soon came to haunt Toyota. The car was overweight, underpowered and, with the new unit-body construction, insufficiently tested. People said goldfish could live in the car when it rained, and it broke down frequently. Worse still, in giving the car a 995-cc engine, the company had overlooked a Tokyo regulation limiting the engines in small-sized taxis to 910 cc. Then dealers put sleeves in the engine to lower the displacement, which only reduced power further. Taxi drivers, for whom the car was designed, were incensed.

Everyone at Toyota was heartbroken, and perhaps no one more so than the dealers, who were often undercapitalized and overextended. After the huge success of the Crown, the company's hard-won reputation was now being muddied. People were ashamed and embarrassed by what had happened, but they weren't pessimistic. The company had a tradition that went back two generations to Sakichi Toyoda. Immediate product improvement would have to be made to redeem Toyota's honor. Even as the first complaints were arriving, Eiji was assembling a crew to oversee the remake of the Corona. And if people doubted Eiji's determination, they only had to check with the Ministry of Finance.

In the midst of the storm over the Corona, Toyota had filed an application with the ministry to purchase a large plot of land owned by Tokai Aircraft Company in Koromo. Toyota wanted to use the land to build a massive new assembly plant. The plant would be designed with one specialization in mind—the large-scale production of automobiles.

As the Corona debacle broke in Japan, Shotaro Kamiya left the country on a business trip to come to the United States for Toyota Motor Sales. It was Kamiya's first visit to the States since 1950, and he immediately noticed a change that intrigued him. There were far more small cars on the road, all of them European imports. The United States was in the midst of the postwar boom, and the housing shortages created during World War II were being corrected through the construction of sprawling suburban communities. Suburban towns didn't have public transportation the way urban areas did, especially around Los Angeles, where Kamiya landed.

When families moved to the suburbs, the family car became transportation to work. That left the rest of the family stranded in a housing development, where stores and schools were likely to be located miles from the house. The only way a family in the suburbs could function was to buy a second car. But American cars were on their way to becoming too expensive for a family to own two of them. By the mid-1950s, the sales of compact European cars were doubling every year. The European cars had the market to themselves, as U.S. manufacturers didn't want to be bothered with these low-profit cars.

Shotaro Kamiya was running all of this through his mind as he traveled around the United States. He didn't have to do a lot of math to project that imported cars were soon going to capture 10 percent of the U.S. market. With eight million cars sold in the U.S. in 1955, a 10 percent cut of that was equal to ten years' production in Japan. Japan desperately needed foreign currency, and Toyota needed to increase its production to reduce unit costs. To the head of an automobile marketing company, it was an enticing opportunity.

But every time Kamiya thought seriously about exporting to the United States, he stopped himself. There was no way that a Toyota passenger car could compete in the American market. Yet the cars were getting better every year, and how would Toyota know if it didn't try? Then Kamiya looked at his figures again and became frightened. The U.S. Big Three had treated the small numbers of the compact-car market with disdain. But what was going to happen when—and his statistics showed clearly that it would—the imports captured 10 percent of the U.S. market? Surely the Big Three would finally balk and demand protectionist legislation. If the market was restricted before Toyota even got in the door, the company would lose its shot at the massive U.S. market forever. By the time his visit ended, Kamiya had decided that Toyota had to establish operations in the States as soon as possible.

Kamiya called a board meeting when he returned to Japan, saying that he wanted to begin exporting to the U.S. As he had anticipated, his idea was rejected out of hand. The gap between Japanese and American industrial, technological, and competitive capabilities, everyone insisted, was simply too cavernous. Everyone wanted to wait until Toyota became more competitive—probably five or six years down the line.

It wasn't for nothing that Kamiya was the president of a sales organization, and he carefully laid out his reasoning for them. He talked about the growth of the second-car market and his worries about restrictions on imported cars. Given that the United States was the home of the automotive industry, Kamiya said, such constraints seemed inevitable. Toyota couldn't be sure if its products were good enough, but once import restrictions were erected, any hope would vanish, regardless of how good the products became.

Eiji Toyoda spoke up and said he had great faith in the new Crown, and that he relished putting the car to the test. Then the manufacturing company's president, Taizo Ishida, spoke up with the winning endorsement. Ishida said he had been told by an American diplomat in Japan that the Crown looked like a great car, and he strongly recommended that Toyota try exporting it to the United States.

Two sample Toyota Crowns, one painted a dark color and the other light, were shipped to the United States from Yokohama harbor on August 25, 1957. Shotaro Kamiya and other Toyota officials in tuxedos, Miss Japan, and a flock of American reporters and photographers met the ship at the harbor in Los Angeles. It was a festive occasion: Toyota was in the United States only seven years after the company's near-bankruptcy.

Miss Japan placed bouquets of flowers on the cars after they were swung off the ship, as the photographers snapped their cameras. All the Americans crowded around the car and made complimentary remarks. They said that the fancy Crown Deluxe looked like a baby Cadillac and that they didn't know a Japanese company could make a great car like this.

Afterwards, the cars were taken to a service station in the Little Tokyo section of Los Angeles to prepare them for California registration. The first ominous sign was the long list of changes California officials demanded before they would issue license plates. The headlights, turn signals, taillight lenses, rearview mirrors and other safety-related parts had to be replaced to meet American standards. Certification, officials said, could take some months.

When the story about the arrival of the Toyotas hit the newspapers the next day, people immediately started calling and coming to the hotel where Toyota officials were staying. Everybody loved the car. They wanted to know how they could get a dealership—and how soon? The more enthusiastic callers were predicting they could sell four to five hundred cars a month, if only they could get a supply.

Kamiya was ecstatic. He sent a telegram to Koromo demanding production be increased to meet anticipated sales of one hundred thousand cars a year in the United States. Unfortunately, all of this transpired before anyone took the cars out for a test drive on an American freeway.

At the time, roads in Japan were paved—badly—in the major cities, but outlying roads weren't. Regardless of their surface material, all of the roads were narrow, winding and bumpy. There wasn't a single road in Japan where a car could travel fifty-five miles per hour. As Shotaro Kamiya and his staff soon learned, however, the United States was filled with such highways.

As soon as the Crowns got up to speed on a freeway, it became apparent the comparatively tiny 1500-cc engine was out of its league. American highways required an engine with endurance—like those huge American V-8s. Loud noises erupted from under the Crown's hood, power dropped sharply, and the engine began to overheat. Kamiya and his men pushed on with the cars, calling on prospective dealers along the way to San Francisco. But as the miles piled up, so did the Crown's oil and fuel consumption. For a car that was to be sold on its economy, the Crown wasn't proving to be economical at all.

Kamiya was terribly disappointed, and he sent word back to Japan to call off the whole thing. But Kamiya had done too good of a job convincing Toyota executives they needed to establish a beachhead in the United States. The company decided it couldn't pull back now. They had to open an American office before it was too late. Toyota was in the U.S. to stay.

Transforming a disaster into a success would become the responsibility of Eiji Toyoda and his engineering staff. The cars would have to be improved and remodeled and improved again until they were competitive in the market. It was as simple as that. In a vote of confidence and determination, Toyota Motor Sales, U.S.A., was founded on October 31, 1957. Capitalization was one million dollars, and Shotaro Kamiya, the wonder-worker of the sales division, was awarded the daunting job of president.

10
THE THIRD
GENERATION

Kiichiro Toyoda's oldest son, Shoichiro, was a thirty-three-year-old director of Toyota Motor Company when plans for the company's new assembly plant were coming together in 1958. Taizo Ishida, the company's president, decided it was only fitting that Shoichiro be put in charge of construction. This was, after all, Toyota's first plant to be designed primarily for automobile production. Ishida dispatched Shoichiro to Europe to study automobile factories there in preparation for the job. When he returned, Shoichiro conferred with other engineers, men who had visited U.S. assembly plants recently. There had been a boom in U.S. plant construction, and these men had an excellent overview of the latest production technology.

When Shoichiro was well versed in equipment and layouts, he went to Ishida to ask what specifications the company wanted for the new plant. Ishida gave Shoichiro only the briefest instructions. He told him where he thought the most fortuitous location for the main entrance would be. He said not to locate the cafeteria north of the smokestack because of prevailing northerly winds. And he said to make absolutely sure that, ten years in the future, the plant would still be one of the world's best.

Toyota was in an intense struggle to establish itself in the fiercely competitive Japanese automobile market, where everyone was looking for anything that would give them an advantage. Time was of the essence. Toyota was taking yet another gamble building the plant, particularly after the problems with its latest car. But there was only one way to do things in such an atmosphere, and that was to do them all the way. The timetable would be as outrageous as it had been for all projects in recent years. The plant was to be built, equipped, and running in less than a year.

The question of production capacity at the plant, called Motoma-chi, was still being debated as the construction equipment moved into position. Toyota was only selling two thousand cars a month in 1958, but Eiji Toyoda was pushing for an unthinkable monthly capacity of ten thousand at the new plant. His argument was that auto sales had tripled in three years, so it was not unreasonable to expect them to increase fivefold in another five years.

Everyone at Toyota was caught up in the spirit of their adventure, and people around the plant were quick to agree with Eiji's assessment. Outside the factory, however, there was much disagreement. Dealers, envisioning thousands of cars being pushed off on them, urged the company to reconsider. President Ishida ultimately intervened with a compromise. Build the plant for five thousand units, he said optimisti-cally, but include expansion room for another five thousand.

Construction was carried on at a frantic pace, and Shoichiro came to resemble Kiichiro when he was building the first company plant at Koromo—tracking through the mud and learning where every pillar went. But Kiichiro had started the company, and Shoichiro was aware that he was a young man walking into a thriving concern. He had much to learn, so he wasn't one to bark orders. Instead, he became a careful listener who would hear both sides and suggest the best alternative. Shoichiro was a quiet man, but he had a warmth the employees appreciated.

Planning was rushed at Motomachi, yet the company still managed to introduce a number of production innovations. The conveyor line was designed so a car could be pulled off if defects were discovered. The car would be repaired and then put back on the line without in-terrupting production. Pits were dug under the line at stations where workers had to install parts underneath the cars. Always, new equipment was installed whenever possible—including television cameras to aid in production-line control.

Painting operations continued to present problems because of the hot, humid summer weather in the Nagoya area. Shoichiro took this on as one of his projects. He persuaded the company to install air-conditioning—which was rare in Japan at the time—in the paint booths, and he studied various conveyor-line speeds. When none proved universally appropriate for the changing seasons, he designed a variable-speed-control switch for the line in that area.

As an outgrowth of the mutual-assistance association Toyota's suppliers had formed during the war, the company continued to have close relationships with them. Taiichi Ohno knew the suppliers were going to play a big role in perfecting the just-in-time production system, and it occurred to him that building Motomachi presented an important opportunity. With Toyota undertaking a major expansion, the suppliers were also going to have to enlarge.

Taizo Ishida urged the company's suppliers to build close to Motomachi, so the flow of parts to the plant could be controlled more easily. The idea was widely accepted, and the area around the new plant began to resemble an automobile city, with virtually every major Toyota supplier located within a short distance of the company's plants. Since its inception, Toyota had been a company with a distinct regional character, which now was reflected in the prominent physical presence of the company and its suppliers in the region. In recognition of that, the local government renamed the locale Toyoda City, later changing the name to Toyota City.

Motomachi was put into operation on August 8, 1959—eleven months after construction had begun and just into the second half of a year of remarkable economic prosperity for Japan. Despite a recession in 1957, the Japanese economy had been expanding at an average of over 9 percent a year since 1955. For 1959, it looked like it was going to be 14 percent. Annual sales of Japanese trucks had risen to 224,000, as merchants and shop owners switched from three-wheeled vehicles to small trucks. Annual car sales were up to 165,000.

The latest economic expansion came to prove Eiji Toyoda partially right in his production projections. Motomachi was operating at its 5,000-vehicle capacity two months after it opened. Annual combined truck and car production passed 100,000 vehicles for the first time in 1959. But it wasn't 5,000 cars pouring out of Motomachi each month. Trucks continued to be 70 percent of Toyota's production, but no one was conceding defeat.

There was a revision of the Corona in development, and Eiji Toyoda still had men working on Toyota's version of the people's car. Yet there wasn't a second to lose, for there were foreboding developments in the domestic auto market. Nissan had introduced a revised Datsun, called the Bluebird, to compete with the Corona. The Bluebird was a smashing success; as a result, Nissan passed Toyota to become the largest auto producer in Japan for the first time since 1956.

*   *   *

Nissan was also outselling Toyota in the United States, but the numbers involved were minuscule. Toyota Motor Sales had shipped nearly two thousand Crowns to the United States after its offices opened, but most of them were gathering dust on dealers' lots in 1959. The company had taken steps to improve the Crown's performance, but that hadn't improved sales. While the Crown Deluxe was indeed luxurious by Japanese auto standards of the time, it was stark and underpowered compared with other cars in the U.S. market—particularly those in the Crown's price bracket of $2,300.

Toyota Motor Sales had located its offices in a defunct auto dealership in the Hollywood section of Los Angeles. There were about thirty employees, as well as a small staff at the company's parts warehouse in Long Beach. The stock of the warehouse was meager, but that wasn't a real concern since only 288 cars had been sold. The warehouse manager often took parts orders himself and then delivered the parts or dropped them off at the bus depot for transport.

The company opened a few field offices in people's homes around the country and handled dealer inquiries through them. After the initial flurry of interest in selling Toyotas, inquiries dropped off precipitously. Some Big Three dealers added Crowns to their stock, but there were also a number of used car lots with a Crown or two on the front line.

Toyota sent over a revision of the Corona called the Tiara; it didn't sell, nor did a pickup truck. The only vehicle that produced any income was the Land Cruiser, a rugged four-wheel-drive jeep Toyota had developed for the military during the Korean War. The Land Cruiser had a huge engine by Japanese standards—3,878-cc and 95 horsepower—and it was an extremely heavy-duty vehicle. Toyota had been exporting the Land Cruiser to South America and Asia, and the vehicle sold modestly well in the United States. But not nearly enough units were moving to offset the massive losses the company was piling up in the States.

By then, just as Kamiya had predicted, European compact cars had claimed almost 10 percent of the U.S. market, and the Big Three decided enough was enough. Ford, Chrysler, and General Motors all introduced compact cars in 1960. Import sales were cut in half. Only Volkswagen, which had carefully developed a strong dealer body throughout the country, and whose car was distinctly different from the rest, managed to escape devastation.

The Japanese truck market was keeping Toyota profitable, with the

Sakichi (sa-kee-chee) Toyoda.

The first Toyoda loom, patented in 1890.

Kiichiro (kee-ee-chee-ro) Toyoda,
Sakichi's son.

Risaburo (ree-sa-boo-ro) Toyoda, Sakichi's
adopted son.

The first Toyoda vehicle, the GI truck.

Dealer candidates attending a demonstration of the model AA car in 1936.

Auto production was begun, then halted, at the Koromo plant in 1938.

When banks ordered Toyota to layoff 1,600 wokers in 1950, the workers called a strike.

The 1953 Model SF was intended to fight off a feared invasion of imported cars in Japan.

The 1955 Crown was considered Toyota's first "real" car.

Taiichi Ohno perfected the just-in-time production system.

Toyota established its first U.S. office in 1957.

With the encouragement of the U.S. ambassador to Japan, Toyota began exporting to the States in 1958.

The first Corona suffered from its hasty development.

The 1960 Corona was a radical design departure.

Toyota's "people's car" was behind the market when it was introduced.

The 1964 Corona was Toyota's first international car.

The 1966 Corolla broke open the consumer market in Japan.

Kanban cards are displayed on cars during assembly.

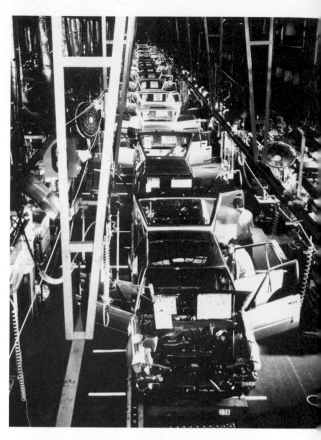

Cousins Eiji (ay-gee) Toyoda (*left*) and Kiichiro (kee-ee-chee-ro) Toyoda with a Model AA and a Lexus LS400.

manufacturing and sales companies earning over six million yen in profits between them. But it still hadn't cracked the car market in the United States, and some people were beginning to have serious doubts it ever would. Toyota sold only 316 cars in the United States in 1960. It only made matters worse that Nissan sold 1,640.

Shotaro Kamiya decided to approach Ford Motor Company about reopening joint-venture talks, this time about a car to be sold in the United States. He renewed his old contacts with Ford, and discussions started. The deal Toyota proposed was for joint production of their much-delayed people's car. Toyota would produce and sell the car in Japan with Ford's technical oversight, and Ford would market the car in the United States through its dealers. Toyota would bring Ford into the Japanese market, and vice versa. Toyota would own 60 percent of the company; Ford would have 40 percent. In what would become the sticking point of the negotiations, however, Taizo Ishida insisted on an option to buy out Ford's share of the deal in five years.

Ford's engineers visited Japan this time, and they were clearly impressed by what they saw at the new Motomachi plant. After decades of not being taken seriously, Japan now had an automobile plant with enough technology to equal a factory in the States. But Ford and the other U.S. car makers had just dealt a heavy blow to foreign cars in their home market, and Ford had a strong small-car operation in Great Britain. Ford wasn't in any hurry to complete a deal with Toyota, regardless of how good its factory was, and the company considered the proposal for over a year before Ford's board vetoed it.

While Ford was thinking the proposal over, Toyota had to stem its losses in the United States. Shipment of passenger cars was halted, and Eiji Toyoda came to Los Angeles personally to handle the layoff of half the work force. Toyota would maintain its U.S. beachhead through Land Cruiser sales, but it resolved not to put another car on sale in the U.S. until it had a product that met international standards. The company expected that to take five years.

While Toyota was attempting to get its operation in the United States off the ground in 1960, the company was also battling to regain its spot as the top auto maker in Japan. The mid-sized Crown continued to sell well, but the company needed to get its revised Corona into the compact-car market, which the Nissan Bluebird was dominating. The new Corona was to be a total remake. Kenya Nakamura, the chief engineer on the Crown project, oversaw the new Corona, assisted by a young designer who had just returned from studying in Italy.

Nakamura had successfully argued for a new front suspension on the Crown, and he went further for the revised Corona. Both the front and rear suspensions were radical departures, ones designed to give the car an extremely smooth ride. The body design, too, was revolutionary. Unlike past Toyotas, which always had a look of solidity to them, the new Corona was light and airy. Gone were the dome-like roof and thick pillars between the windows, replaced by large expanses of glass topped by a roof that was more like a wafer. The car looked elegant, nimble, and taut.

The sales people hated the new model as soon as they saw it. They thought the car looked far too delicate for the rugged tastes of taxi owners. Nakamura became incensed about this objection. He tried to explain that the automobile world was changing in Japan, and that the company would never get anywhere if all of its products were designed primarily for the taxi market. The sales people dismissed Nakamura with a shake of their heads.

Nonetheless, the new Corona went on the market in April of 1960, and it was immediately popular with private owners. As the Bluebird and Corona battled for buyers, the mass media dubbed it the "BC Wars" and began reporting sales figures as though they were scores in a championship sports match. The free publicity could have been a godsend for Toyota, but it turned into a noose when the Corona proved to be another defect-riddled car.

An alignment problem in a body-welding jig used to manufacture the Corona was locking tension into the body when the car was assembled, and windshields began shattering while people were driving the cars. The new suspension, which had been tested in the United States to insure a good ride on smooth American highways, turned out to be all wrong for Japan. The springs were too soft for rutted Japanese roads, causing people to hit their heads on the roof when the car went over a dip. Furthermore, just as the sales department had argued, the body was too delicate for the taxi market.

Corona sales stopped dead, and Bluebird dealers did everything they could to foster that. The dealers took Coronas as trade-ins and then used them for advertising purposes. They put lines of Coronas in the front of their lots, posting large signs on the windshields describing the defects that had prompted the owners to dispose of the cars. All of this only fueled the growing conventional wisdom in Japan that said: Nissan for passenger cars, Toyota for trucks.

Shotaro Kamiya asked the manufacturing company to began planning a new Corona immediately. A new engine was selected, the suspension was altered, and the body welding was corrected. But Toyota's image had been badly tarnished. The next Corona model to hit the streets would be improved in numerous ways, but executives at Toyota Motor Sales Company knew it was going to be a tremendous challenge to get people back into the car.

Seisi Kato, who had been lured away from GM of Japan by Shotaro Kamiya in 1935 to join the fledgling automotive department of Toyoda Automatic Loom Works, was given the assignment of creating a marketing campaign for the revamped car. Kato brainstormed with his colleagues at Toyota Motor Sales and conducted consumer research. The feedback he got was unanimous—everyone thought the Corona was a fragile and unreliable car.

Kato decided the only way he could change the popular perception of the Corona was to attack its negative image head-on. He would create a massive TV advertising campaign in which Coronas would be tortured beyond belief, only to keep on running. The first ad in the series called for a Corona to be driven up a ramp and launched into the air.

On the day of the filming, the stunt driver failed to appear, and no professional replacement could be found. Anxious to get on with it, a loyal advertising department employee volunteered to drive the car. Japanese cars weren't equipped with seat belts in those days, so the man was lashed into the driver's seat with strips of torn cloth. As a safety measure, he brought along a pair of scissors to cut himself free if the car crashed and caught fire.

When the cameras were ready, the driver hurtled up the six-foot height of the ramp at top speed, propelled the car into the air and braced himself for his return to earth. The car bounced repeatedly on landing, but it remained upright and was able to be driven off as though it had just come from the showroom floor. It was dramatic stuff.

A later commercial showed a Corona being pushed forward off a cliff. The car performed three somersaults on its way down the hill, shattering its glass as the roof and part of the hood caved in, before it came to rest, right side up, on a collection of oil drums that had been placed at the bottom. The car had been unoccupied, but a driver crawled into it and drove the mangled car away. Corona sales improved tremendously, but this model would never catch the Bluebird.

Toyota Motor Sales Company had turned to television commercials to redress the reputation of the Corona because it realized what a powerful force the medium had become in the country. Japan had undergone massive changes since the end of the war, and they extended far beyond the introduction of TV. Traditional farming villages were disappearing in Japan, and people were migrating to where the jobs were— in the newly industrialized cities. Only 28 percent of Japan's population lived in cities at the end of the war; by the 1960s the number surpassed 60 percent.

Life had often been bleak for people in the cities in the years after the war. Tokyo had been devastated, and Japan as a whole was in a state of deprivation. When life for the average Japanese citizen improved, it was only slightly. The Japanese government's first priority had been reconstructing its industrial base. Wages were kept low, and consumer prices and taxes high, as the country funneled all available capital into acquiring new plants and machinery. Pension plans were meager, so people were forced to save for their retirement, which increased the amount of low-cost capital available to industry. This approach continued throughout the 1950s, as the industrial infrastructure was improved at the cost of people's lifestyles. It worked so well that Japan became the largest producer of steel in the world in 1957.

The Japanese people tolerated this approach until the late 1950s, when latent discontent was inflamed by the signing of a revision of the U.S.–Japan Security Treaty. Early drafts of the treaty allowed the U.S. military, after consultation with the Japanese government, to take military action to halt internal unrest within Japan. Although this and other objectionable provisions were deleted, the treaty still permitted the United States to house nuclear weapons at its bases in Japan. Many Japanese felt the treaty had been signed without sufficient public debate. The political left in Japan, which had been dormant since the Korean War, came back to life. Soon the most massive protests in Japanese history were occurring regularly.

Almost every day during May and June of 1960, hundreds of thousands of union members, students, white collar workers, intellectuals, and housewives protested at government buildings. President Eisenhower was forced to cancel a planned visit to Japan because of security concerns, and shortly afterwards 300,000 demonstrators surrounded the Diet building. Under Japan's parliamentary government rules, Prime Minister Kishi was forced to resign to halt the unrest. He was replaced by Prime Minister Ikeda, who quickly began searching for a way to restore order to the country.

A number of European governments had been restricting imports from Japan at the time, saying the country's low wages caused Japanese goods to be priced artificially low. Prime Minister Ikeda reasoned that increasing wages would serve two purposes: it would diminish social unrest at home and reduce export restrictions in Europe. If the increased exports resulted in lower production costs at home because of higher volume, the real cost of the wage hikes would be minimized.

In December of 1960, the government announced a sweeping plan to double the wages of salaried Japanese workers over the next ten years. The program, part of a larger strategy to liberalize trade and expand the Japanese economy, was predicated on annual economic growth of 7.3 percent over the coming decade. Both the wage and economic-growth targets were met, and the first large-scale middle class in Japanese history was created. And in becoming middle-class, the Japanese people quickly acquired a taste for many of the conveniences of Western life, which they had been deprived of for years.

People built new homes of concrete and steel, rather than of wood, paper, and bamboo. Gas, electricity, and kerosene replaced firewood and charcoal as the sources of energy and heat in most homes. Low tables and *tatami* mats for sitting on the floor were displaced or supplemented by tables and chairs. Even fashions changed as the Japanese began wearing Western-style clothing, with its ease of movement. Synthetic fabrics and advances in dyeing led to more colorful and inexpensive ready-to-wear clothing that consumers took to readily.

New packaging and processing techniques made a wide variety of foods available regardless of the season. Prepared foods also became available and, combined with a reduction in working hours, created the concept of leisure time, which had been unknown in Japan. This induced consumer demand even further. There was a tremendous boom in electric appliances as people bought TVs, washing machines, and stereos. By 1961, the percentage of the average household budget devoted to discretionary spending in Japan reached 22 percent, higher than West Germany.

Each of these changes happened gradually, and to different degrees in various parts of the country. Because change was piecemeal, and sometimes unhurried, it was often difficult to gauge the extent to which people's tastes had changed—especially in regard to one of Japan's most modern products, the automobile.

The Japanese government had first put forward the idea of a people's car in 1955. This utilitarian vehicle was intended then to develop one segment of the economy—the auto industry—while also raising the lifestyle of the average family by supplying it with personal transportation. The concept had been proven in several European countries, and the notion still seemed valid to Toyota in the early 1960s. The company had invested six years of difficult development work in a people's car and couldn't just walk away from it.

When it became obvious Ford was not going to consummate a joint-production venture with Toyota on a people's car, Toyota decided to move ahead forcefully on its own. Progress had been made on the vehicle, and it was another way to gain precious market share. A number of preproduction changes had been introduced into the design of the car over the years—front-wheel drive had been abandoned in favor of rear-wheel drive—but the basic concept remained the same. The people's car was to be the most basic and stripped-down car that it was possible to produce and still call it an automobile. The tiny engine required that weight be kept to a minimum, so the car had to be unadorned.

In preparation for putting the car into production in 1961, Toyota held its traditional nickname contest. This time over a million entries were received, and the winner was Publica, a Japanese contraction of the English words "public car." A new assembly line was built adjacent to the main factory at Motomachi, and a new machine-tool shop was added. The Publica was priced at 389,000 yen, based on sales of 3,000 cars a month. The company anticipated, however, that sales would rise to 10,000 cars a month in short order.

The Publica was everything it was designed to be when it made its debut in June of 1961: small, efficient, and plain. It was a reliable car, and it was cheap. But the public response was indifferent. It seemed that during the car's long development time, many potential buyers had managed to advance into the middle class without the aid of a people's car. Now that they had improved their lifestyles, they wanted a car that was middle-class like them. They wanted a car with charm and personality, one that represented where they hoped to go in life rather than where they had been.

Toyota had another redesign job on its hands. The private-owner market had spoken, and Toyota would be quick to respond. The Publica would be transformed into the Publica Deluxe. Chrome trim and accessories would be added, and even a convertible would be appended to the line. Rather than producing another Volkswagen, Toyota would revise the Publica into something unique. It would be a small, extremely efficient car that also had class. It was an intriguing idea—a logical extension of what Kiichiro Toyoda had imagined back in the late 1940s, when he had his staff design the ill-fated model SA. The Publica Deluxe would be a small car that was very good at being small. The idea had promise. Meanwhile, though, Nissan was becoming the Godzilla of the domestic auto market.

Toyota's annual truck production passed the two hundred thousand mark in 1961, and Taiichi Ohno and the rest of the production staff were making real progress in their rationalization efforts. The just-in-time production system had been instituted throughout the company, and Toyota began asking its suppliers to adopt the system as well.

After decades of struggling to make dies and die molds for body production, the company had achieved a remarkable breakthrough. The stamping of body panels, like fenders, on massive presses was a process the Americans had perfected. But the American method was designed for a market where eight million cars were sold annually in the early 1960s. American stamping presses were intended to operate the way all U.S. mass production machinery worked. They produced an endless stream of identical parts in fits of near-perpetual motion.

It took two to three hours to change a die on an American stamping press, but the time wasn't a problem because dies were seldom changed. Entire plants were devoted to a single automobile model, so their stamping presses produced a single line of body parts for a year. Toyota, however, didn't have that luxury. They weren't selling enough individual models of their three car lines—the Crown, the Corona, and the Publica—to have dedicated equipment, and the dies on their machines had to be changed frequently. For Toyota, a stamping press with a die that took three hours to change was virtually a single-purpose machine, and they had been outlawed at the company since the time of Kiichiro Toyoda.

The Toyota engineering staff resolved this dilemma by creating dies that fit into the presses in the same manner that a cassette goes into a tape recorder—the whole unit popped in and out. When this method was perfected in the early 1960s, Toyota workers could change a die in fifteen minutes. Now, multiple car lines could be produced on the same stamping and assembly lines with only minor adjustments.

The need for constant facilities expansion was reduced, and the production process became easily adaptable. When cars were built for the U.S. or other markets where the steering wheel was on the left side of the car, the alterations from the Japanese right-side standard was accomplished within the normal flow of production. Toyota had developed the ability to "mass-produce" cars by making numerous small lots of different models.

These kinds of advances, combined with continuing efforts to perfect the just-in-time production method, made Toyota's plants highly efficient. Toyota was producing close to twenty vehicles per employee in the early 1960s, versus two per employee in 1950. At times of peak demand, plants were routinely operating at more than 115 percent of capacity—not factoring in overtime—over extended periods. Adding to the efficiency was the fact that, after sporadic labor problems during the 1950s, labor-management relations were now harmonious.

The national auto-workers union had gone bankrupt in 1954, after an extended strike against Nissan. Afterwards, the Toyota Motor Workers' Union became a company union once again. Mistrust lingered on the part of workers until a sequence of events swept it away.

As 1960 approached, the United States was pressuring Japan to open its market to the import of assembled cars, which had been banned since 1955. Japanese auto workers, who had just been promised a doubling of their wages over the next ten years, lived in constant fear that American automobile imports would obliterate Japan's auto industry. In addition, Toyota was locked in a tremendous battle with Nissan for market share. Since both management and labor were concerned about staying in business, the two parties began holding discussions about how they could work more cooperatively.

Representatives of Toyota's union and labor-relations office decided to travel to the United States to study how the UAW worked with the Big Three. The two sides shared room and meals during their trip, something that would have been unthinkable ten years earlier. As the men got to know each other, the beginnings of friendship developed. Yet the most significant agent of change was what Japanese workers learned about American unions.

Since the Japanese labor movement of the 1940s was largely led by communists, Japanese workers believed unions were essentially political in nature. Strikes were intended, they thought, not so much to force the company to improve working conditions or wages as to foment revolt. When they talked to UAW members, the Japanese workers were shocked to learn the Americans were interested solely in improving their own lives, not in bringing down the social structure.

The Toyota workers recognized this was an important lesson to relay to their coworkers at home: the union should negotiate concerns rather than issuing ultimatums. The Japanese workers also concluded they could be even more successful with this technique than the Americans were, because they enjoyed a unique advantage that was absent in the American factories.

Ever since Eiji Toyoda had first thought to appoint a manufacturing man as the chief engineer of each new car project, the status of assembly-line workers at Toyota had been elevated tremendously. Chief engineers, designers, and planners became frequent visitors to the assembly line, where they eagerly questioned the workers and took extensive notes. Eiji had proclaimed that production was the most important thing that happened at Toyota. By extension, that meant the mission of the designers and engineers was to enable the production staff to do the best job possible. The Toyota delegation that visited the United States noted this attitude was distinctly absent at American plants, where the workers were treated as the least important employees.

In the aftermath of their U.S. visit, Toyota's management and workers were successful in finding joint solutions to their problems and this relationship was formalized in 1962. The company and the union signed a labor-management declaration, pledging to work for mutual prosperity and for the resolution of problems based on mutual trust.

When all of these positive developments were combined with the solid profitability of the manufacturing and sales companies, outsiders judged Toyota to be an admirable enterprise. Yet just as Sakichi Toyoda had never been able to sit back and relish the fruits of his latest success, the people at Toyota were far from content. Every time a Toyota man heard someone say, "Nissan for passenger cars, Toyota for trucks," he was filled with rage. Reflecting on the catastrophe in the United States only made it worse.

*   *   *

Shoichiro Toyoda was made managing director of the corporate planning office after Motomachi was built, and he knew it was going to fall
to his end of the business to cure what was ailing Toyota's cars. The
company was putting cars on the market at competitive prices, but the
quality wasn't there on introduction day. Cars were being developed
too quickly and under too much pressure, as everyone in the company
felt the hot breath of the competition on their necks. The result was
defective cars. Toyota had always sprung into action, repairing defects
and continually improving products whenever flaws surfaced, but that
wasn't enough anymore.

Shoichiro came to realize that the company was practicing *kaizen*
too late in the game. Repairing cars after they were on the market
demonstrated Toyota's loyalty to its customers, but it was destroying
its public image. When people made an expensive purchase like an
automobile, and especially when it was the first automobile they ever
owned, they expected the car to be perfect. Toyota now had to constantly improve the *process* of making its cars. Problems had to be identified and eliminated during planning, production, and testing. If such
a program was carried out assiduously enough, Toyotas would hit the
streets defect free.

It would have been impossible for Toyota to consider such a program only a few years earlier. Since Toyota had never executed a joint-
production deal with a Western manufacturer, the workers had to learn
about automobile production as they were making cars. Mistakes were
numerous and costly using this approach, but everyone was learning
enormous amounts. Each time the bugs were worked out of a new
model, the learning curve took a dramatic sweep upwards. Now Toyota
had learned enough to graduate to the next level.

When Shoichiro Toyoda set out to discover how quality controls
could be applied directly to the production process, the first name he
encountered was W. Edwards Deming. Deming was a scientist who had
worked at a U.S. War Department think tank at Stanford University in
the 1940s. Deming's task there was to propagate the work of Walter
Shewhart, a physicist who had done pioneering work in statistical methods of quality control at Bell Laboratories in the 1920s.

Statistical quality controls replaced individual inspection of each
finished product coming off an assembly line with random-sampling
inspection. Shewhart developed a chart that specified when product
variations in inspected pieces were normal, and when they indicated

defective manufacturing. When randomly selected products from a lot fell within normal variations, the entire lot was approved. If they exceeded normal variations, the entire lot was inspected. Production managers also used these readings to make alterations in production machinery.

The War Department had so much confidence in Shewhart's work that it created the Stanford program to conduct mandatory training in his system for defense contractors. Deming expanded on Shewhart's work during this time, as he came to believe quality inspections should not be conducted at the end of the production line. Deming thought quality should be checked and controlled by each worker on the factory floor during the manufacturing process. He also believed quality control programs had to involve all departments in a company, not just manufacturing. Deming called this system "total quality control."

Deming saw a marketing department exercising quality control by conducting consumer surveys to insure the company didn't produce products for which there was no demand. Production-planning departments practiced quality control by creating schedules and production methods that anticipated and avoided error-causing production snags.

Deming wanted to continue teaching this system to U.S. companies after the war, but few were interested. Corporations were selling everything they could produce in the overheated economy, and the new clan of MBAs who were running American industry were interested only in how they could speed up production. Deming finally gave up, taking a job with the U.S. Bureau of the Census.

In that position, Deming was sent to Japan several times to assist the Japanese government in census taking. Deming's heart wasn't in the work, but he managed to connect with a number of Japanese engineers who were very interested in quality control. The reputation of Japanese goods as being inferior was universal at that time, and Japanese industrialists were ravenous for information about improving their products. Lacking natural resources, Japan couldn't exist without exporting. Therefore, it was imperative that Japanese goods gain worldwide acceptance.

Deming gave some lectures, which prompted companies to try his approach. Quality improved instantly and dramatically in these companies. Soon Deming was publishing books on quality control in Japan, which became bestsellers. After being ignored in the United States, Deming became a god in Japan, with companies flocking to learn about and implement his methods. Deming was so pleased with all of this that he donated the royalties from his books to create the Deming Prize, an annual award given to the Japanese company that instituted the most effective programs in quality control.

Toyota had instituted some aspects of Deming's approach to quality control on their own in the early 1950s. Japanese technology and materials were so rudimentary at the time that defective final products were commonplace. Toyota had to integrate informal quality inspections into each step of production, or vast numbers of cars would need to be repaired at the end of the assembly lines. The company simply couldn't afford to do anything else. If the root causes of defects weren't identified during production, the number of acceptable finished vehicles would slow to a trickle.

As Shoichiro Toyoda reflected on this situation, he recognized two elements were needed to convert Toyota's haphazard quality program into total quality control. It had to become more systematic, and it had to be extended to every department. Deming emphasized that true quality production began with solid support from the top management of the company. If it existed there, Deming believed, it would filter down. As Kiichiro Toyoda's oldest son, Shoichiro recognized it would carry enormous weight within the company if he committed to a total-quality-control program.

With Shoichiro's encouragement, Toyota adopted a three-stage plan to have a total-quality-control program fully operational by 1964. To give added emphasis to the program, Shoichiro also made a personal commitment to having the company win a Deming Prize shortly thereafter. Toyota hired a number of quality-control experts and academic consultants and then began a long effort to teach the program to all of its employees.

Since the more theoretical aspects of total quality control were highly statistical, they required an enormous amount of complicated— and sometimes obscure—record keeping and calculations. As the months wore on and the novelty began to disappear, some people at Toyota began to resent this enormous intrusion into their already overloaded schedules. There were regular accountability meetings at which department heads had to give presentations. Often they were severely criticized by the quality-control experts. Then the engineers would rise up in revolt, saying that the plan was recreation for the scholars, who were being paid far too much as it was.

Nonetheless, Shoichiro remained firm in his support, which became more justified as improvements occurred. During the first year, in-process defects in the plants were reduced by 50 percent. Although Taiichi Ohno, the just-in-time production expert, had initially been opposed to the program, he became a convert. Ohno recognized that just-in-time production was fully compatible with total quality control.

Total quality control called for eliminating defects at the source. Just-in-time production called for eliminating component-part overproduction at its source. In both cases, the source was an individual work station in the production process. Therefore, when the two systems were combined, the entire production process would be halted whenever there was any kind of problem at a work station. That way, everything produced met two criteria: it was needed to complete a car, and it was defect-free.

As the quality-control system spread throughout the assembly plants, Shoichiro conspicuously avoided the men who were deeply involved in creating the latest model of the Corona. The chief engineer on the project was a man named Atsushi Tajima, a former aircraft designer who was one of the first army engineers Kiichiro hired right after the war. Tajima let Kiichiro know he was far too busy to get involved.

As part of their redesign work, Tajima's men had resurrected an approach that Kiichiro Toyoda had used after the G1 truck was introduced in 1935. When the G1 trucks broke down continually, Kiichiro and his men spent months out in the field. They interviewed dealers about customer complaints and had them keep strict repair records. Often factory mechanics performed the repairs themselves. This way, Kiichiro learned exactly which components needed to be improved on the trucks.

Now the men on the Corona team were following the same procedure, but for a different reason. They wanted to learn what people didn't like about the old Corona so they could design a car consumers would like. The new Corona was being built from the ground up, and after three disappointing models everyone was anxious to make this one right.

The team conducted interviews and surveys, produced prototypes, and performed road tests. All of this wasn't just to please buyers in Japan. Toyota was now an exporting company, and the new Corona was to be the company's first car designed for the international market.

This would be the car, everyone hoped, that regained Toyota's honor in the United States.

The request Corona researchers heard most frequently during their surveys was that even if a car was compact sized, people wanted it to feel safe and sturdy. The Corona engineers decided the easiest way to impart this feeling to their new model was to make it wider. They planned to increase the width from sixty to sixty-two inches, but they encountered immediate objections. The sales people argued that such a car would be classified as an intermediate-sized taxi, rather than a compact, and would require higher fares.

Toyota Motor Company was at a turning point. The Japanese taxi market had been buying the bulk of its automobiles since the 1950s. This market, in fact, had made auto production possible in Japan, and companies that ignored its requirements did so at their peril. Nonetheless, Shotaro Kamiya knew Toyota couldn't develop the private-owner market in Japan, or in the international market, if they continued to allow their designs to be dictated by such constricted requirements. The new Corona would be wider, and the guaranteed sales in the taxi market would be written off.

The Corona designers felt like a yoke had been lifted from their necks. At last they were free to create a compact that was truly aimed at the consumer. The final car, it was decided, would have a modern, international design. The car would be the first Toyota to have four headlights flanking a square grille, and large, tricolor taillight lenses with separate segments for the brake, turn-signal, and backup lights. Horsepower would be increased to seventy and top speed to eighty-seven miles per hour.

Durability and performance were emphasized in every aspect of the vehicle's design and this was reinforced by rigid quality inspections during production. As the car neared its introduction in September, the manufacturing company was certain it had produced a world-class car. The sales company, however, was still concerned about public perceptions of the Corona line. To conclusively dispel any lingering doubts, the sales people planned another one of their special campaigns for the car.

The first expressway in the Nagoya area had just opened, and Toyota Motor Sales Company staged a highly publicized endurance run on it to introduce the car. Over the course of fifty-eight days, three Coronas traveled sixty-two thousand miles on the expressway. The cars were run around the clock, using forty-five drivers. As the news media dutifully reported, not one of the cars broke down.

The new Corona was a big success and immediately began stealing sales from the Bluebird. With several updated Crowns on the market—including one with a V-8 engine—as well as the Publica Deluxe, Toyota sold over two hundred thousand cars in 1965. Toyota was once again the largest auto maker in Japan, and the Corona displaced the Bluebird to become the best-selling car.

With the Corona on the market successfully, Shoichiro Toyoda was overseeing the implementation of the final stages of the company's total-quality-control program. The plan was working so well that Shoichiro decided to submit an application for the Deming Prize. The application process was lengthy and complex, and it had to be based on the improvements that had been obtained in a specific product or function of the company.

The Corona was the finest example of improved quality Toyota had, but Shoichiro's staff hadn't worked with that project team because they had been so busy. Nonetheless, Shoichiro had his men look into the Corona project, and they came back with a surprising report. Kiichiro Toyoda's old method of working closely with dealers and customers to improve products could be seen as a model of total quality control. When this approach was combined with other improvements within the company—and particularly those on the assembly line—the Corona made a strong case.

Toyota Motor Company submitted an application for the Deming Prize, based partially on the Corona, in May of 1965. Auditors and inspectors from the Union of Japanese Scientists and Engineers, which administered the award, came to the company and conducted a detailed review of Toyota's program. The inspection went on for weeks, and no one was sure what the outcome would be. Unlike Nissan, which was headquartered in Tokyo, Toyota was still regarded as a provincial company from the hinterlands of Japan. Sometimes Toyota's workers thought that too, and now they weren't certain that their company was advanced enough to win the prestigious Deming Prize.

Everyone was hoping they would win, if only for Shoichiro Toyoda's sake. Shoichiro had overcome a lot of resistance to put the total-quality-control program into effect, and it would look bad for him if the company's application was rejected. As the tension mounted, a group of nervous quality-control managers surrounded Shoichiro one day and asked if they would be fired if the company lost. "If that happens," Shoichiro told them, "then I will ask to be fired too." No one lost his job in the end. Toyota and the Corona won the Deming Prize in November of 1965.

11
RETURNING
TO AMERICA

The Big Three had claimed half of the American compact-car market the moment they introduced their first small cars in 1960. Ford alone sold over 417,000 Falcons that year. The American people had been buying automobiles from Ford, General Motors, and Chrysler for generations, and there was no question in their minds who made the best cars in the world. The first automobile may have been made in Europe, but it was the Americans who created the automobile industry. Americans had bought imports when they needed a second car and nothing else was available, but when the Big Three began producing compacts, American motorists purchased them by reflex.

The conventional wisdom was that the U.S. small-car market was now closed to imports. Volkswagen might manage to hang on for a few years because the Beetle—at times, the largest-selling car model in the world—was so original. But all the other foreign cars were expected to disappear as the American companies exerted their historic dominance. Rather than continuing to gain market share, however, the Big Three began losing it almost as soon as it reached the 50-percent mark. Sales slowed and then fell as motorists became disenchanted with the American compacts very quickly.

The problem was that the Big Three weren't very interested in making small cars. They were massive companies with colossal fixed overheads. Their work forces were brimming with senior employees earning high union wages, with hundreds of thousands more collecting pensions and medical benefits. Their plants were aging and their production methods were rife with inefficiencies. American manufacturers simply couldn't afford to build small cars, because small cars meant small profits—and sometimes even a loss on every car sold.

American compact cars of the 1960s were Detroit's efforts to drive the foreign competition out of the country. The Big Three only wanted to neutralize their competition, make some meager profits or lose as little as possible, and get back to their real business—making large and highly profitable cars. Accordingly, the original design work for the cars was minimal. Production costs were trimmed wherever possible. The companies essentially created new small bodies and crammed as many existing components into them as they could—as Toyota Motor Company had been forced to do when it entered the automobile business.

Unlike Toyota, however, the American manufacturers never tried to make their small cars profitable by improving production efficiency. Instead, the Big Three reduced costs incrementally by cutting corners on the cars themselves. Less expensive materials were used whenever possible, even if that meant a saving of only pennies a car. The resulting cars were neither well designed nor well executed, and it didn't take owners long to figure that out.

No one was more acutely aware of these deficiencies than the American management of Toyota Motor Sales. Many members of the staff had left jobs with the Big Three to come to Toyota—almost always against the advice of friends and former coworkers. Toyota had promised these people the company would be returning to the American market with a car that met the highest standards. Now the staff was traveling to Japan to preview the new Corona and to judge whether the company had lived up to its word.

Advance word from Japan on the Corona had been quite good, and everyone was pleased with the car when they saw it. It was a solid and attractive, and it drove well, but the people from the Los Angeles office wanted some changes before the model was brought to the United States. They wanted carpeting for the interior, rather than the more practical rubber mats, and additional interior trim—things to dress the car up.

Simplicity is highly valued in Japan, and Toyota's designers had a difficult time understanding the American concept of creature comforts. Nonetheless, the U.S. staff won some concessions on the interiors. But getting the new engine they wanted was far more difficult. The Japanese engineers had labored to create a balanced car; now the American staff wanted them to pull out the specially designed 1,500-cc engine and replace it with a 1,900-cc motor that Toyota used in Japanese trucks.

The 1,500-cc engine was a "horsepower" engine, one that put out most of its power at high engine speeds. Its initial acceleration was sluggish, but its acceleration at passing speeds was much faster. Conversely, the 1,900-cc engine was a "torque" engine, one that put out most of its power at lower engine speeds. This engine had a high rate of initial acceleration, which dropped off at passing speeds. The 1,500-cc engine would get better gas mileage, but the 1,900-cc would get people away from a traffic light faster.

The U.S. staff argued that American roads and drivers required the power of the 1,900-cc engine, and that fuel mileage was of secondary concern. Since Japanese gasoline prices were six times those in the United States, and Japanese cars were taxed by engine size, Toyota's engineers found this difficult to accept. More important, the changes would be costly—at a time when the company couldn't reasonably expect initial U.S. sales to exceed thirty thousand cars a year.

Shotaro Kamiya of Toyota Motor Sales intervened on behalf of his American staff. Kamiya recognized how important it was to make a strong showing during Toyota's return to the States. As always, it was better to spend the extra money now in order to recover the profits later. The new engine was approved, along with the interior changes that included repositioning the arm rests and giving the seats more travel to accommodate larger American physiques.

The new Corona arrived in the United States in April of 1965, four years after Toyota had pulled out of the market and a year short of the anticipated five year absence. The car was roomier and more powerful than its competition, and it was one of the few imports to offer an automatic transmission. as an option. The car was priced at $1,860, compared with $1,600 for a Volkswagen with half the power and far less comfort. Everyone in the company was sure they had a winner.

In many ways, the U.S. office was working from the ground up when it took the Corona to the market. With only the Land Cruiser to offer, the U.S. operation had been more a novelty in the market than anything. Now Toyota had to become a serious player. The plan was to make a convincing showing in a few local markets before expanding nationally. This strategy would give the staff the chance to gain experience, while also allowing the company to develop inventory.

Sales efforts were concentrated in Los Angeles, San Francisco, Portland, and Seattle. The West Coast had proven more accepting of imported cars, and it had the shortest transportation routes from Japan. The company wanted to create the image of being a substantial manufacturer to people in these markets, who were unfamiliar with its cars, yet advertising funds were limited.

A perfect solution arose when major national magazines, such as *Time, Newsweek,* and *Life,* began publishing zoned, or regional, editions. Toyota could get the credibility of advertising in respected publications, at rates it could afford, and the ads would be restricted to areas where the Corona was available.

The quality and price-competitiveness of the Corona made it easier for Toyota to add dealers, and the company started a cooperative advertising fund to expand its budget. Scraping together five thousand dollars in production money, the company filmed one sixty-second commercial and then cut it to ten- and thirty-second versions. Each version was aired repeatedly in the four key markets in an attempt to build name recognition.

Then a man who had bought three Toyotas filmed an unsolicited testimonial and sent it in. He said he liked his Toyota so much that "once you get your hands on one, you never want to let it go." The company's ad agency edited this line down to "Get your hands on a Toyota and you'll never let go." This would become a Toyota advertising slogan for the next six years.

With so much effort having been put into preventing defects during the manufacturing of the Corona in Japan, the American staff became dismayed when cars kept coming off the transport ships in Los Angeles with body damage. Hiroshi Imai, who had just returned to the U.S. office as import manager after spending two years in Japan, set out to investigate. He discovered that damages averaging eighteen dollars a vehicle were being caused by carelessness as the cars were lifted off the boats on slings. Imai was well versed in the principles of total quality control, so he knew the solution was to eliminate the damage at the source.

Imai went to the shipping company's office and tried to explain Toyota's philosophy. Imai said he wanted to work with the company to improve their handling practices so the damage would be eliminated. Toyota was only a minor customer of the shipping line at the time, and the company wasn't very interested in Imai's offer. The head of the shipping company said he knew more about shipping than Toyota did, and if Toyota didn't like it they could take their business elsewhere. Imai did that, contracting with a shipping firm in Japan. But he also concluded there was only one true solution to the problem, so he made preparations for Toyota to enter the shipping business.

Imai knew that for total quality control to be used in transportation, special ships would have to be built. The ships would allow cars to be driven onto them, rather than lifted on in slings. Then he devised an unloading plan. The cars would be unloaded on each level of the ship in a counterclockwise direction. That way, the driver's door wouldn't strike anything as the car was removed from the ship. Later, these ships and a stevedore education program would cut Toyota's vehicle damage rate to the lowest in the industry—under three dollars a vehicle.

As the Corona was being introduced in the United States in 1965, the Japanese economy was booming beyond anyone's wildest dreams. Wage increases in the country had averaged 10.3 percent a year since 1960, and the traditional bonuses given to workers each year had increased from two to three months' wages. There was also full employment of the population for the first time in Japanese history. The birth rate had remained low, and many families were sending their children to college for the first time, delaying the entry of young people into the labor market and creating labor shortages in parts of the country.

The Olympics had been held in Tokyo in 1964, giving the nation both a psychological and economic boost. The Japanese people were proud their country had been awarded this prestigious event, signaling a full return of Japan into the international community of nations. The country had spent a staggering 1.01 trillion yen preparing for the games. Sports facilities, luxury hotels, and Japan's first skyscraper were built in Tokyo. Transportation was improved through extensions of the subways and construction of a new system of freeways. Even after the games were over and the tens of thousands of foreign visitors were gone, Japan seemed to be a more urbane place.

The Japanese automobile industry had grown along with the economy, but it still hadn't broken through into the true mass-production volume that would be expected in an industrialized nation of almost one hundred million people. Workers' wages were rising, and car prices were falling as a result of increased volume and improved technology, but a Ministry of International Trade and Industry prediction was proving false. MITI had theorized that once car prices fell to a factor of 1.4 times per-capita income, auto sales would skyrocket. The Publica, however, was selling for a factor of 1.17 times per-capita income in 1965, and even the Publica Deluxe was selling for a factor of 1.29, but sales remained modest.

Events in the auto industry were contradicting the price-triggering phenomena that had occurred in consumer electronics during the late 1950s. When the price of major appliances and televisions fell below 50,000 yen during that era, sales increased exponentially. Television sets sold for 150,000 yen in 1957, and only 7.8 percent of all Japanese homes had one. But in 1965, with TVs selling for under 50,000 yen, sets were present in 90 percent of Japanese homes.

Even with a number of affordable minicars on the Japanese market, private ownership of automobiles rose from only 2.8 percent of the population in 1961 to 9.2 percent in 1965. There was still plenty of potential market demand to be satisfied, and the number of suburban communities in Japan was growing. With people relocating to escape rising urban real-estate prices, automobiles were becoming more of a necessity than a luxury. Yet no one had come up with the automobile that opened the floodgate on consumer demand.

Toyota Motor Company was on its way to selling 236,151 cars in 1965. This was a propitious number, for it put Toyota on the cusp of the position it had struggled for. Automobile production in 1965 would comprise 49 percent of the company's total output. Toyota was close to being an automobile manufacturer that also made trucks. Shotaro Kamiya knew normal sales growth would edge the company past 50 percent soon, but he also wanted to be in position with the right car when consumer demand took off.

The new Corona was selling well, and it completely restored the company's reputation as a maker of high-quality products, but at 1.74 times per-capita income, it was still too expensive a car to have mass appeal. Conversely, the Publica had a low price, but even the Publica Deluxe wasn't dragging people into the car market for the first time. If people really wanted or needed a car, but didn't have a lot of money, they would buy a Publica or a Deluxe. But there was a much larger pool of people in Japan at this time who were just thinking about buying a car.

These buyers had no compelling need for an automobile, but they would have liked one. Yet, they couldn't afford a nice car like a Corona, and the Publica didn't excite them enough to motivate them to buy. Purchasing a car was going to be a stretch for them economically, and to take this step they were going to have to be seduced. When a car showed up that was irresistible, these people would rush to the showrooms.

A careful observer of this phenomenon was an engineer at Toyota named Tatsuo Hasegawa, who had been to the United States and witnessed the automobile culture there. He was keeping up on all the new models Western companies were producing, and he was particularly impressed by a new car that Opel had produced in West Germany called the Kadett. The Kadett was the antithesis of the VW Beetle, which it was designed to compete with.

The basic design of the Volkswagen was almost thirty years old now. The company updated the car each year, but it never attempted to alter its legacy as a utilitarian machine. The air-cooled engine was noisy and anemic, and the body was intentionally homely to symbolize the car's sensible intentions. The Kadett was a modern version of the VW. It had a strong water-cooled engine, good performance, and a pleasing look, but it was still inexpensive. More than anything, the Kadett had lots of zip and was fun to drive.

The Kadett was on the forefront of a new generation of carefully engineered small cars that were coming out of Europe, and it inspired Hasegawa to start thinking about a new model for Toyota. He wanted to build a car that fit in between the mini Publica, with its 700-cc engine, and the Corona, which was large for a Japanese compact and had a 1,500-cc engine. Hasegawa wanted to make a car with a 1,000 cc engine that was youthful and classy and fun. It would be affordable, but it would never seem to be cheap.

What Hasegawa wanted to create was a 1960s white-collar version of the people's car. Kiichiro Toyoda had tried to make a good small car with mass appeal with the Model SA in the late 1940s. He had been ahead of the company's production capabilities at the time, and the car was never made successfully. Hasegawa had tried the same thing with the Publica, when he was that car's chief engineer, but he had been behind the market in creating a down-scale car. Hasegawa thought he had his design and market senses coordinated this time, and he began lobbying for the project.

It was not easy for a chief engineer to win approval for the production of a new car, with the billions of yen in development and plant costs involved. But Hasegawa knew what the procedure was. Decisions in Japan were arrived at by consensus, so he started working to achieve that. Hasegawa talked to the head of the technology division, who couldn't see a market for the car. Using that cue, he went to see Shotaro Kamiya at the sales company. Kamiya thought the car had modest possibilities and said he would support the idea.

Hasegawa thought he was in the clear then and went to see Fukio Nakagawa, who had replaced Taizo Ishida as president of Toyota Motor Company. Nakagawa had come to Toyota from Mitsui Bank, so he was mindful of the company's finances. He said he would support the car, but it would have to use the existing 1,000-cc engine that had been used in the second generation of the Corona.

Hasegawa was greatly distressed by this restriction. His whole concept of the car revolved around a new, lightweight, high-performance engine that would be the car's heart and soul. Hasegawa was a persistent man who didn't accept defeat easily, so he paid a call on Eiji Toyoda, who was now the vice president of the company.

Many people had expected that Eiji, who was highly respected, would succeed Taizo Ishida as president of Toyota. But Ishida had decided that, at fifty-three, Eiji was still too young for the job. Nonetheless, because of both his accomplishments and his birthright, Eiji had tremendous influence when it came to the engineering and production of automobiles. He was still an engineer at heart, despite his high rank, and he understood Hasegawa's concern. If Hasegawa would find a truck model the old engine could be used in, Eiji said, he would win Nakagawa's approval for the new engine.

In addition to making the car attractive, Hasegawa wanted to load it with advanced engineering features. The car would have twin carburetors, disc brakes for the front wheels, and a four-speed transmission with a floor-mounted shifter. Three-speed transmissions with gear-shift levers mounted on the steering column were the rage in Japan. The change from a floor-shift, which had originated on trucks, to a column-shift had been seen as an advance in the 1950s. But Hasegawa successfully argued that the trend was being reversed in Western countries, and Japan should take the same step. A four-speed transmission required more shifting, but it greatly improved the acceleration of cars with small engines.

The car was also to be the first Toyota with MacPherson-Strut front suspension. This design, which combined a coil spring and a shock absorber into one unit, was extremely compact and made room for other engineering changes under the hood. Hasegawa's men had a difficult time mastering the design and production of these units, and he asked Eiji if they couldn't be purchased outside instead. Eiji refused, restating a basic company philosophy: the production of all basic technology had to be mastered in-house. It took over a year of experimentation before Hasegawa's men perfected the system.

Toyota Motor Sales Company realized there was a growing demand for compact-sized automobiles with greater luxury and comfort, so Kamiya urged Hasegawa to include such features. Kamiya asked him to make a car that people would be proud to own. Hasegawa decided to make an automatic transmission optional and made provisions for air conditioning to be fitted to the car as an accessory. Then he added a lot of little touches like two-speed windshield wipers and backup lights, as well as a flow-through ventilation system that would keep the air fresh inside the car.

While all of these features were being added to the car, Toyota was acutely aware that people still had to be able to afford it, so value engineering was to be stressed at all stages of production. Every facet of the company was enlisted in this drive, including outside parts suppliers. Production costs had to be minimized so the new car, to be called the Corolla, would be price-competitive with the less adorned minicars.

The company constructed a new plant for the car, with modern equipment including automatic welding and painting lines. One of the most important pieces of equipment would be a new computerized control system that would manage all of the manufacturing processes at the plant. The computer would be used to schedule production and to monitor cars as they were being built. Most important, the system would also be connected to the engine plant and to the plants of vendors who supplied seats and wheels.

This computerization was an important advance in just-in-time production. Suppliers would be notified hourly of the quantity of parts to be delivered at a specified time. They would also be informed of the sequence to be used in loading parts on their delivery vehicles, enabling Toyota to unload the parts and move them to the assembly line in an order that corresponded with the requirements of each car as it came by on the line.

As the Corolla was in the advanced stages of its preproduction design work in early 1966, Shotaro Kamiya of Toyota Motor Sales received an unexpected bit of news. Nissan Motor Company was about to introduce a new model, called the Sunny, which would be in direct competition with the Corolla. Toyota had known that Nissan had a new car in the works but had made some incorrect assumptions about what kind of car it would be.

Nissan had never produced a minicar to rival the Publica, and Toyota had speculated that the new Nissan would be of this class. Now, however, Kamiya learned the Sunny was going to be slightly larger than the Publica and, like the Corolla, would have a larger 1,000-cc engine. Toyota had wanted to make a grand debut with the Corolla, but now the Sunny, which would be on the market months before the Corolla, would make Toyota's car seem like an afterthought. Kamiya summoned Eiji Toyoda to his office for an important strategy session.

In past head-on model competitions with Nissan, Toyota had always tried to compete on price. Whatever price Nissan sold for, Toyota would be slightly less. As Kamiya and Eiji talked, however, they realized that every indicator in the domestic auto market showed it going upscale. The Publica didn't sell well, but the Publica Deluxe sold better. Neither car, however, had enthralled the public. But a Toyo Kogyo subcompact, called the Mazda Familia, which was better equipped and more expensive than the Publica Deluxe, was doing well in the market. Given these developments, Kamiya and Eiji decided to make an abrupt departure from past marketing practices. This time, they would go upmarket on Nissan rather than underpricing.

Kamiya knew the Corolla would have far more features than the Sunny and that it would be slightly larger and heavier. He thought these differences would make the Corolla feel more luxurious. But he also knew the company couldn't trust its marketing campaign—or its future—to such subtle and subjective differences. Kamiya needed a symbol that would represent the Corolla's distinct advantages in a succinct fashion, so he asked Eiji if Toyota could make the Corolla's engine 100-cc larger than the Sunny's 1,000-cc.

Eiji said it would be difficult, but not impossible, to make the change this late in the planning process. But he had another, more pressing concern. Did Kamiya understand that cars with engines over 1,000 cc were taxed at a higher rate in Japan? Kamiya said that, of course, he was aware of it, but he didn't see it as a problem. If the whole idea was to take the Corolla upmarket on the Sunny, the higher tax would be just another status symbol for the car. Corolla owners were so discerning in their tastes that they didn't mind paying higher taxes to own a superior product!

Chief engineer Hasegawa was dumbfounded when Eiji told him in March that the engine had to be enlarged by 100 cc. The 1,000-cc engine was in its final stages of testing, and production was scheduled to begin in six months. The change would mean a major redesign of the engine, since the cylinders would have to be bored out and all of the pistons, connecting rods, and affiliated parts would have to be redesigned and retested. It was a preposterous idea. Eiji told Hasegawa to stop complaining and get to work.

The Corolla was introduced in November of 1966, six months after the Sunny had gone on sale. Toyota Motor Sales launched the car with the largest advertising campaign in the history of Japan. Television was used extensively, and each ad employed the Corolla's slogan, "The extra 100 cc gives extra comfort."

The standard Corolla was priced at 432,000 yen, and the Deluxe at 495,000 yen, figures 5 percent and 7 percent higher than the competing Sunny models. With its extensive list of features that were lacking on the Sunny—disc brakes, four-speed transmission, strut suspension—the Corolla outsold the Sunny by margins of up to 35 percent from the day it was introduced. Toyota had successfully gone upmarket on Nissan.

More important than beating Nissan, though, was what the Corolla did for Toyota's overall sales. The Corolla and Corolla Deluxe—priced at 1966 per capita income factors of 1.16 and 1.33 respectively—finally brought consumers into the private-owner market in droves. The Japanese had proven to be crafty consumers. Even though they could afford the Publica, they hadn't bought it because it wasn't the product they wanted. In 1967, the first full year the Corolla and other cars in its class were on the market, passenger car sales in Japan increased by 33 percent, to 1,129,131.

The new Corolla, with all of its features and a price under $1,800, arrived in the United States in 1968. Toyota's U.S. sales more than doubled that year, to 71,463, and the number of dealers increased to 699. In 1969, when Toyota had an $18.5 million dollar ad budget in the U.S. and a growing reputation for building economical, high-quality cars, sales reached 130,000.

Toyota's sales represented only one-tenth of 1 percent of the U.S.

market, so nobody saw the company as a threat to General Motors. But suddenly the idea of competing with Volkswagen, the undisputed leader of the import market since the 1950s, wasn't so intimidating. The design of the Volkswagen was becoming dated, and Toyota's cars offered many features the Beetle lacked.

Toyota's sales efforts were aided by the birth of the consumer movement in the States and the tons of bad publicity it generated about American cars. Ralph Nader had given the movement high visibility when he published his book *Unsafe at Any Speed* in 1965. Nader charged that Chevrolet's entry in the compact field, the Corvair, was so poorly designed it was dangerous. The book attracted a lot of headlines when it was published, and then again when GM was forced to admit it once employed a law firm that hired a private investigator to look into Nader's personal life.

The book seemed to unleash a barrage of pent-up consumer dissatisfaction with American cars. The Senate Judiciary Committee undertook an investigation into automobile insurance in 1967, but so much testimony was presented about automobile problems in general that the hearings took on a broader focus. Over the course of three years, the committee investigated all aspects of the automobile business. Hundreds of witnesses gave damning testimony, all of which was widely reported. One of the most sensational disclosures was General Motor's revelation that it had received over 410,314 letters of complaint about its cars between 1967 and 1969.

The sale of imported cars blossomed in the wake of this kind of publicity, and exiles from the Big Three continued to pour into Toyota's Los Angeles office as the staff expanded. Former coworkers still told these people they might as well be joining the French Foreign Legion and still asked if they realized they were committing career suicide, but many of the Americans liked the vastly different milieu they found at Toyota.

Norman Lean left a job in the service division of Ford to come to Toyota in 1969. The forty-two-year-old Lean became Toyota's service manager because he thought the company had promise. He was shocked by an unexpected benefit of his new job. Lean discovered that dealing with customer-service problems could be an enjoyable experience. It had never been that way at Ford.

Ford Motor Company, with its huge output and mass-production methods, saw its dealers' new-car-prep mechanics as the factory's final inspection station. Ford turned out the cars, shipped them to their dealers, and told them to fix any defects they found before they delivered the cars. Owning a Ford dealership in those days was a guarantee of instant wealth, so no one ever objected. The dealers simply hired mechanics to spend hours going over brand-new cars, fixing all the things the factory had missed. What the new-car-prep mechanic didn't catch would be fixed later under warranty.

For American manufacturers in general, warranty claims were much like accident claims to an insurance company. They were a necessary expense in the course of conducting a larger business. Auto manufacturers made their money building cars; insurance companies profited from their investments. Insurance companies didn't get involved in training people who had accidents to become better drivers, and auto manufacturers didn't pay much attention to warranty claims as data for identifying design flaws and product weaknesses.

With Ford paying so little attention to identifying the root cause of problems, the new-car owners Norman Lean dealt with as a Ford customer-service representative were always angry. They had just spent thousands of dollars for a new car, and they always had a two- or three-page list of defects they were ready to confront Lean with. Lean's orders were to find out what it was going to take to make the customer happy. His job was to be a pacifier, not a quality-control inspector.

When Lean started dealing with Toyota customers, he was amazed to discover that they were angry far less frequently. Certainly, there were problems with the cars, like brake and cold-start problems. But they were specific mechanical problems, not laundry lists of trim falling off and control cables that weren't connected. These "fit-and-finish" complaints were the kind that caused people to believe their cars weren't well made. They were also the kinds of problems that were greatly reduced on the assembly line by a total-quality-control program.

Lean's first order of business at Toyota was to make sure the customers got their cars fixed. But an equally important task was to discover why the problem had occurred in the first place. Toyota engineers in Japan were eager to know what went wrong with their cars so they could eliminate these flaws from future models. This not only reduced production and warranty costs, but it also kept customers happy. Suddenly, Lean discovered the "war" was gone from warranty dealings with customers.

Toyota Motor Sales, U.S.A., stepped-up its national expansion at this time. The company had decided to establish a network of independent distributors around the country. Local wholesalers, who were familiar with their territories, would recruit their own dealers, encouraging faster growth and better market penetration.

One of the first people Toyota approached was James Moran, who had been the largest Ford dealer in the U.S. before he stepped away from day-to-day responsibility for his operations. Moran had started out in Chicago in the service station business, before becoming progressively more successful with Hudson, American Motors, and Ford dealerships, along with Renault, Triumph, and Jaguar distributorships. Moran was about to go into semiretirement with a Pontiac dealership in Miami when Toyota approached him about becoming their southeastern U.S. distributor.

Toyota had approached Moran a few years earlier, but he had politely declined. He was making a good living, and he wasn't even sure what a Toyota was. Now Toyota asked Moran if he wouldn't at least take a drive in one of their cars, and he agreed. There was only one Toyota dealer in Miami, and Moran drove over and asked if he could test-drive a car.

Moran took the car out on the interstate, and he was amazed by its balance and tightness. Durability, however, was a different matter, so Moran decided to give the car the ultimate test. While driving at fifty-five miles per hour, he threw the car into reverse. To Moran's amazement, nothing broke. Moran took the car back to the dealer and told him how impressed he was. The dealer said the only trouble was getting people to drive the car—that once they drove it they almost always bought it.

Moran was intrigued by now. He showed Toyota officials from Japan around his Pontiac dealership, then met with them at the DuPont Plaza hotel in Miami. Moran knew Toyota had a good car, but he was concerned about his ability to recruit dealers. Selling Japanese cars in the Southeast in the late 1960s wouldn't be an easy task, and Moran wanted to know what the company was going to do to help him.

The Toyota officials told Moran about their total-quality-control program, and how defects were eliminated from cars right on the assembly line. Moran said that was quite different from the Ford and General Motors plants he had been to, where there were always lots full of new cars waiting to be repaired before they could be shipped. Then the Toyota people told Moran something that really shocked him.

They said Toyota considered its dealers to be its most important customers, and that if he was unhappy about anything, he would be welcome to discuss it personally with the company's top management in
Japan.

Moran's Ford dealership had sold 52 percent of the cars sold in
Chicago—more than the combined sales of forty-two other dealers in
the area—and he hadn't once sat down with a top officer of Ford. Ford
executives were like gods to their dealers, and gods never solicited opinions from their minions. Ford's position was that you were just a dealer,
and you should be grateful for that. Although dealers had daily contact
with Ford's customers, Ford never solicited the dealers' advice about its
products.

Finally, the men from Toyota asked Moran what he would do if
they shipped him ten thousand cars. Moran said he'd find a way to sell
them, and the deal was concluded. Moran called all of the dealers he
knew, telling them to stop by and see him when they were in Florida
during the winter. The dealers would come and hear Moran's pitch: He
had a car they might not have heard of, but they should take a look at
it. He could set them up in business for only twenty-five thousand
dollars. They had to buy only about fifteen hundred dollars' worth of
parts and keep only three or four cars in stock.

The dealers said they couldn't make any money on three or four
cars and asked how many they would be able to get. Moran said he
could give them only fifteen or twenty a month at first. The dealers
would head for the door then, saying that they were used to making
forty to sixty thousand dollars a month and that Moran's offer wouldn't
be worth their time.

So Moran went on the road, making cold calls on any outlet that
looked promising. He took on a couple of gas stations and even a
bicycle shop, but he kept going to the smaller, but established, dealerships as well. His pitch about how well Toyota was going to treat its
dealers was well received. At that time—before federal laws protecting
dealers were passed—most Big Three dealers lived in constant fear of
being terminated and often didn't know whether they would be around
the next year.

The clincher, though, was when Moran would look the dealers in
the eye and deliver his closing line. He'd say that Toyota was so tuned
in to the developing small-car market in the United States that he could
promise the dealers they would be multimillionaires in five years.

As dealers signed on, Moran found some inexpensive production facilities and began turning out a barrage of Toyota TV commercials. He had been the first person in the United States to sell automobiles personally on television in 1948, and he knew the power of the medium well. He bought ninety films in Hollywood for a hundred thousand dollars and began showing them on TV along with his commercials. Everyone said Moran was crazy, but the movies sold a lot of cars. (Two years later he resold the films for five times what he had paid for them.)

All of Moran's programs were working well, until he went up to Jacksonville, Florida, to inspect a boat-load of cars that had been unloaded. The windows of many of the cars had been left open, and the interiors were soaking wet. Discarded lunch bags and soda bottles were scattered about, and the cars were covered with rust chips from the inside of the ship. They looked as if they were ten years old. All of the cars were the same model, a two-door hardtop, and all had either a black or black-and-red interior. Moran began to wonder if he hadn't made a serious mistake.

Moran got the cars cleaned up and then worked with Hiroshi Imai, Toyota's import manager, to plan a new dock facility where the cars would be handled more carefully. He also planned to talk to Toyota about jazzing up the interiors and the product mix. But in the meantime, he got to work selling cars. With Moran's contribution, Toyota sold 208,000 cars in the United States in 1970. In five years, Toyota had gone from twenty-first place in the U.S. import market to second, trailing only Volkswagen.

12
SMOG WARS

By 1971, the Toyota Motor Company had dozens of models on the international market and, led by Corona and Corolla sales, was achieving remarkable prosperity. The company had further expanded its product line and production facilities by establishing ties with Hino Motors, a maker of large trucks and buses, and Daihatsu Kogyo, a maker of small vehicles.

MITI had encouraged a consolidation of the burgeoning Japanese motor vehicle industry to strengthen it in anticipation of a liberalization of foreign investment laws. The ministry wanted to restrict each manufacturer to a single size of car, but the industry rejected this. Instead, the auto makers formed alliances among themselves, resulting in a smaller number of more diversified manufacturers.

The company Kiichiro Toyoda had struggled to establish against formidable odds, and against all naysayers, was now a major multinational corporation. Even more astonishingly, Toyota had become the third-largest manufacturer of motor vehicles in the world. Having surpassed Volkswagen and Chrysler, Toyota's production now trailed only General Motors and Ford.

During 1971, sales were just short of two million vehicles. Sixty percent of those vehicles were sold in Japan, with the remainder exported to virtually every corner of the free world. Toyota's success, twenty-one years after near-bankruptcy, was representative of the larger success Japanese companies had achieved in the world market. Japan's reputation as a maker of inferior goods was long dead, and the products of Japanese companies now set the standards of quality in a variety of fields.

Japan's flourishing export business, however, created imbalances in

its foreign trade, especially when the domestic market constricted during periods of recession, causing imports to drop and exports to expand.
Japanese financial institutions began accumulating large amounts of foreign currency, which totaled $5.5 billion in 1971. Japan's trading part-
ners objected and began exerting pressure to raise the value of the yen
relative to other currencies. The exchange rate, they argued, had remained unchanged since the end of the war at 360 yen to the dollar,
and it was time to revise it.

The foreign trade situation in Japan became more urgent when the
United States, Japan's largest trading partner, entered its fifth year of
inflation and growing trade deficits. Gold reserves in the United States
had fallen below the amount of the country's external dollar liabilities,
and confidence in the dollar was falling around the world. The dollar
was the only benchmark currency in the international monetary system,
and the global economic balance was at risk.

With the American economy showing no signs of improving, President Richard Nixon decided to take drastic steps to strengthen the
U.S. economy in August of 1971. Nixon temporarily suspended all con-
versions of the dollar into gold or other currencies, imposed a 10-per-
cent surcharge on imports, and enacted a ninety-day freeze on domestic
wages and prices. This announcement caused Japan's stock market to
plunge to a record low and set off massive buying and selling of dollars.
The economic backlash in Japan was so severe it became known there
as the "Nixon Shock."

The panic in Japan over the 10-percent surcharge was exacerbated
by the realization that the yen would inevitably have to be revalued. Japanese exports, which had driven much of the country's economic expansion, would become more expensive. The low prices of Japanese products
had been their selling point on the world market, and whether the country was prepared for it or not, that was going to have to change. The
Japanese government entered into economic-policy negotiations with
nine other major nations concerning the revaluation of the yen, but as
the talks dragged on, Japan's economy remained in chaos.

Toyota officials were powerless as they observed these machina-
tions. They didn't know how to price their exports from day to day,
and they couldn't plan their export volume effectively. Then the International Longshoremen's Warehouse Union went on strike in the
United States during the summer of 1971, closing all the country's
ports.

Hiroshi Imai, Toyota's U.S. import manager, had anticipated the possibility of the strike. There hadn't been a longshoremen's strike in the United States in some time, so strike rumors had been rampant. One of the major issues in the dispute was the handling of cargo shipped in containers, a point on which labor and management were sharply divided. Imai knew the closing of the ports during a strike would strangle Toyota's U.S. operations, potentially bankrupting some of the company's dealers.

Many of Toyota's dealers had only been in business for a few years and had meager financial reserves. Their buildings and inventories were heavily mortgaged. The process of finding dealers who would stake their livelihoods on selling an unknown Japanese car had been long and difficult. After all of this, Imai knew the company couldn't leave its dealers stranded without cars.

Imai had traveled to San Francisco in the spring of 1971 to visit Harry Bridges, the legendary head of the International Longshoremen's Warehouse Union on the West Coast. Bridges had enormous power within his union, and Imai decided to go right to the source. He asked Bridges directly if there was going to be a strike. Bridges responded ambiguously, but he advised Imai to "get prepared."

Imai immediately began searching for alternate ports, traveling to Mexico City to meet with officials of that country's port authority. The Mexican officials said they would be happy to have Toyota's business, and would offer every assistance they could. Imai then contacted Harry Bridges of the longshoremen's union, asking what accommodations Toyota could make to achieve the union's cooperation with their plan. The unions said they would agree if Toyota used American drivers to transport the cars up from Mexico. Toyota acceded and then got the approval of the U.S. government.

Imai made other arrangements to bring cars into eastern and western Canadian ports, although his negotiations with East Coast unions about transporting cars into the United States were not as successful. During the strike Toyota had to stockpile cars in northeastern Canada, praying it would end before thousands of cars were snowed in for the winter. Using these alternate plans, Toyota managed to prevent its U.S. dealers from completely running out of stock. When the strike ended in October, cars poured back into the country, and the International Longshoremen's Warehouse Union made Imai an honorary member because of his cooperation.

More cars were available, but the 10-percent surcharge on imports remained in effect until December. Japan agreed to revise the exchange rate to 308 yen to the dollar then, a 15-percent increase in value. So when the surcharge was lifted, Toyota's U.S. prices did not fall; instead, they were increased by another 5 percent. Thus the Corolla, which had been sold on its low price and high value, was no longer price-competitive, and it was this model that was flooding into the country as the backlog from the strike broke loose.

Everyone at Toyota Motor Sales, U.S.A., began working overtime, trying to brainstorm a solution to their high prices and large inventory. The focus of their U.S. marketing efforts to date—price—was no longer applicable. The company finally resolved to institute a crash advertising campaign, one directed away from the price of the cars. After some intense lobbying from the U.S. office, they had a sporty new model called the Celica to sell, and there was a new pickup truck as well. Toyota had deliberately kept the number of its U.S. dealers low to help insure their profitability, and now it introduced new incentives for them.

When all of these measures were enacted, the company managed to increase its sales by 49 percent over 1970, to 309,363. Nonetheless, production had been planned around continued growth, which had disappeared. Cars were piling up in inventory, and dealers were refusing to accept any more shipments. There was no other choice; production had to be cut in Japan.

Just when the company began to give up hopes of catching Volkswagen in the United States, the situation changed. An income-tax reduction that was part of the president's economic reform package kicked in, and the economy picked up. But the biggest boost Toyota received came from its U.S. rivals. The American auto makers all hiked their prices, canceling out the advantage they had gained with the rise in the yen. Thanks to the Big Three, Toyota was price-competitive in the United States again.

Toyota officials in Japan were thankful to have the revaluation of the yen resolved, and sales in the U.S. stabilized, so they could return their attention to the business of making cars. That was not to be, however, as a new controversy had developed in Japan—one that would eventually take many years and half of the company's engineering staff to resolve.

An inevitable side effect of Japan's rapid industrialization was an increased concern among citizens and government leaders about environmental pollution. These concerns had first surfaced in the 1950s as a result of several highly publicized incidents. In 1953, a number of residents of Minamata were stricken by mercury poisoning as the result of discharges from a fertilizer plant. A few years later, cadmium was found in another waterway near a mining company. As these incidents became known, citizens began protesting at other industrial sites—for example, fisherman staged a demonstration at a wood pulp factory thought to be polluting the Edo River in 1958.

The government responded to these incidents by promulgating the Pollution Countermeasures Basic Law in 1967. This measure set standards for the control of air, water, and noise pollution, with the proviso that any countermeasures had to be in harmony with the healthy growth of the economy. Although the law intended to avoid inflicting undue financial hardships on industry, it was also a reflection of the rudimentary state of scientific information on the causes and control of emissions at the time.

Pollution attracted less attention in the late 1960s, as industries began to investigate and correct sources of pollution without government oversight. In 1970, however, two highly publicized incidents brought environmental pollution back onto the front pages of newspapers and into the halls of government.

Because Japan's land mass is small and its population is homogeneous, there are a handful of widely read national newspapers that have tremendous influence. When these newspapers took up the cause of industrial pollution, it became a highly politicized issue. After having worked so hard to make Japan's phenomenal economic success possible, some segments of Japanese society began to rebel against it.

The first incident occurred when the National Medical Students Union studied the levels of lead in the blood of people who lived near a busy intersection in Tokyo. The results showed a number of the test subjects had toxic levels of lead, and auto emissions were presumed to be the source.

The National Police Agency responded by conspicuously directing traffic away from the intersection, and MITI announced plans to encourage auto makers to manufacture cars that would run on unleaded gasoline. The cabinet also established the Central Pollution Control

Countermeasures Headquarters in July of 1970, just as another incident took place.

One hot and humid morning in a Tokyo suburb, forty girls from a middle-school sports team were holding a practice session. The girls were running around vigorously in the summer heat when a number of them began to complain that their eyes and throats were burning. Others concurred and said they were having trouble breathing as well. Suddenly, ten of the girls fainted and had to be rushed to the hospital. The girls recovered quickly, and medical officials were hard-pressed to explain these spells. Since the school was located near a busy highway, the fainting was ultimately attributed to air pollution from automobiles.

The incident provoked sensational headlines the next day, with stories quoting experts as saying Japan had developed the same photochemical smog that plagued Los Angeles. There are few geographic or weather similarities between Tokyo and Los Angeles, and Los Angeles smog exceeded .35 parts per million one day out of three at that time. Such a level had never been reached in Tokyo. Nonetheless, the word *smog* entered the language and consciousness of the Japanese.

Newspapers and television news programs began announcing smog alerts on a regular basis, and episodes of students fainting on school playgrounds multiplied. Physicians who examined these children frequently attributed the attacks to air pollution, although attending circumstances suggested mass hysteria might also be at work. Ninety percent of those afflicted were schoolchildren, and although it was recognized that photochemical smog peaked around noon, their attacks always took place early in the morning. In addition, children never suffered from these spells on school holidays.

A public outcry arose over environmental pollution, and it became the main topic of debate at that summer's session of the Diet. Hearings were held and expert testimony presented as the news media and the public demanded a rapid solution to the problem.

There was some question whether mobile sources, such as automobiles, or stationary sources, such as factories and power plants, produced more emissions. Ultimately, automobiles, the quintessential symbol of Japan's industrial success, were assigned most of the blame. One of the first steps the government took was to remove the clause "in harmony with the healthy growth of the economy" from Japan's antipollution law.

The United States had been investigating air pollution for years at this time, having enacted its first automobile-emissions-control law in 1961. Since those standards were relatively mild, they were easy for U.S. auto makers to meet by adding a few pieces of hardware to their engines. But the standards became much tougher in 1970, with the passage of the Clean Air Act. Also called the Muskie Bill after its sponsor, Senator Edmund Muskie, this law required U.S. auto makers to reduce two of the three emissions from automobiles to one-tenth their current level by 1975 and the third to that level by 1976. With the emissions debate in Japan beginning just as the Muskie Bill took effect, it was a foregone conclusion among Japanese auto manufacturers that they would be held to the same standards.

As engineers at Toyota began studying ways to reduce car emissions, they were entering an area with which they had little familiarity. Their greatest previous challenge in working with engines had been extracting sufficient power from them without diminishing fuel economy. Gasoline was taxed heavily in Japan because almost every drop of oil in the country was imported, and the government wanted to control the flow of yen from the country. On the other hand, there were many uses of oil the Japanese government actually encouraged. After a series of strikes and other problems in the domestic coal industry, Japan had switched from coal to oil to power its postwar industrialization. Oil was cheap and readily transported on massive new oil tankers. Oil ran the machines that had brought prosperity to Japan, and all of them would come to a halt without it.

While the pollution scare was reaching its apex, the oil actually did stop flowing into Japan when the Arab oil producers cut production in the fall of 1973. It was as if Japan had run out of air to breathe. The country had only a fifty-day supply of oil when the Middle East oil embargo began, and no one knew when more oil would be available or how much it would cost. The price of oil hadn't increased appreciably in decades, so everyone had known a price hike was inevitable some day. But no one had guessed the oil producers would use an embargo to precipitate price hikes.

What made the embargo especially threatening to Japan was its political overtones. The Arab-Israeli conflict was influencing what was going to happen with oil, and the outcome of that controversy was anyone's guess. It would be one thing for Japan to pay more for oil. It would be an entirely different matter if Japan couldn't get oil at all.

The first response to the anticipated oil shortage in Japan was anxiety and remembrances of wartime hardships. This was upgraded to horror when a Japanese official mistakenly said the country only had a few weeks' oil on hand, and a stampede of consumer panic buying ensued. Over two hundred housewives lined up outside an Osaka supermarket one morning, awaiting its ten o'clock opening. Within fifteen minutes after the doors were unlocked, the store's supply of toilet paper was exhausted. Patrons who were unable to buy toilet paper rushed to the next closest store, where they found another mob of shoppers. Soon the phenomenon spread from store to store, and from town to town.

There was no reason to expect the supply of toilet paper was endangered, but news of its disappearance spread. Toilet paper hoarding was followed by runs on detergent, soap, soy sauce, and kerosene. Speculative reports of suppliers and distributors stockpiling consumer goods in anticipation of price increases began filling newspapers. The prices of everything, already elevated by chronic inflation, became exorbitant.

Gasoline prices were the most unstable, and this caused automobile sales to almost halt. Dealer lots began overflowing with cars for which purchases had been canceled. But even if demand for cars had continued, car companies could not have kept up full production. Automobile-industry suppliers soon lacked fuel to operate their plants and petrochemical materials to manufacture plastic and rubber products. There were shortages of paint pigments for cars. No one could even get enough steel.

Production schedules were abandoned as procedures that had prevailed during the war reappeared. The availability of materials began to dictate production. There were times when otherwise finished cars couldn't be driven off the assembly line because manufacturers had no tires for them. Sometimes new cars had to be sold without spare tires.

These shortages were accompanied by massive cost increases for manufacturers, as petrochemical and aluminum product costs rose by up to 50 percent. Workers' paychecks had to be increased by 30 percent to keep them even with inflation. Car makers were forced to raise their selling prices in response, and Toyota increased prices 7 percent in November of 1973 and an additional 10 percent in January of 1974. Car sales dropped 25 percent in December compared with the previous year. Then, in an attempt to control inflation by lowering consumer spending, the Japanese government increased motor vehicle taxes twice in the first half of 1974, and auto sales dropped 36 percent from the preceding year. Toyota's lots brimmed with unsold inventory.

Toyota checked with its U.S. office on the situation there, and no one was certain what to say. Reports in the mass media speculated that the world might run out of oil by the end of the century. Anyone who found the slightest bit of credence in these stories had to conclude that the internal combustion engine was about to become extinct. Even though Toyota's U.S. sales had shown strong increases each year, the staff at the U.S. office never forgot they were playing catch-up ball on the home field of Ford and General Motors. They were trying to sell economy cars, but their selling prices increased monthly. Everyone in the U.S. office gulped and told Japan to cut production more.

Toyota Motor Company had been in business for thirty-seven years, but it was as if the company were emerging from the financial collapse of 1950 again. Eiji Toyoda and other officials felt the company might face extinction, and they fell back on the same strategy that had salvaged them before: costs had to be slashed. There had never been any indulgence in the company's use of materials, and work-force reductions of permanent employees were not acceptable. That meant savings could only be produced through improved production efficiency. Toyota's lean, just-in-time production system would have to become leaner still.

The company immediately undertook a massive cost-reduction and production-adaptation program. The first thing to go was plants devoted exclusively to the production of a single car model. The company had developed the ability to mix products on the assembly line early on, but this practice was unnecessary when some Toyota models were selling in huge volumes. Now, since no one knew what direction consumer demand was going, or how widely orders were going to fluctuate from month to month, every plant had to become highly flexible, prepared to produce what was needed, when it was needed.

Energy-conservation teams combed every facility in search of ways to lower utility costs. Line employees expanded their total-quality-control focus to include resource conservation at each step of manufacturing. The production department discovered that scrap from rolls of sheet metal could be used to make smaller parts, saving two and a half tons of steel a month. Before the color of paint going through the hoses on automatic painting machines could be changed, the hoses had to be purged, so whatever paint was left in the hoses at that time was wasted.

The hoses were shortened to reduce that loss. Many parts from suppliers came with rubber dust covers to protect them in transit. Those covers were now recycled rather than discarded when the part was installed on a car. Cheaper paper was used for company documents, and both sides of the paper were printed on.

The only thing certain in the automobile market was that as gasoline prices went up—and with gasoline sometimes not even available—cars were going to have to become more fuel efficient. Engineers were assigned to study every aspect of reducing the weight of automobiles. They found ways to remove a pound or two everywhere—transmissions, seats, batteries, exhaust pipes. Other teams studied the combustion efficiency and design of engines.

The bright spot Toyota Motor Sales Company found in this situation was the wild expansion of one car market. The dollars that were flowing out of oil-consuming countries after the price hikes were funneling into oil-producing countries. Toyota had been exporting only thirty thousand vehicles a year to the Middle East when the embargo started, but the company expanded its operation there immediately.

Demand for consumer and industrial goods exploded in the Middle East as petrodollars piled up. Producers from around the world rushed into the market, and traffic jams developed in Middle Eastern harbors. Ships couldn't be unloaded quickly enough, and sometimes they had to sit at anchor for two to three months before they could get a berth. Seeking to avoid becoming entangled in these harbors, Toyota began shipping vehicles to the east coast of Africa on large transport ships. There the vehicles would be transferred to smaller ships that could be unloaded more readily in Saudi Arabia and the other Gulf states. Sometimes ships would no sooner dock than customers would rush on board to buy automobiles for cash. When the vehicles were unloaded, they disappeared into the desert.

Eiji Toyoda, who had been named president of Toyota Motor Company after Fukio Nakagawa died suddenly in 1967, always insisted the company maintain a long-term perspective. He never saw this as a one-time effort to dispose of excess production. The price of oil wasn't going to fall, and that meant the Middle East would remain an important market.

Eiji ordered service facilities expanded in the area, and he chartered forty cargo planes to send parts in by air freight to avoid the congestion at the docks. Staff members were dispatched from Japan to study the

Middle Eastern markets, trying to discern how the company's vehicles had to be modified to satisfy local requirements better. Cars and trucks were subjected to endurance runs through the desert and modified accordingly. Steering wheels and dashboards were made more resistant to the heat of the desert sun, and engine-temperature gauges were modified so they wouldn't give false readings because of the high ambient temperatures.

After Toyota took these steps and expanded its local dealer organization, its Middle East sales began doubling every year. When the situation stabilized, what had once been a minor Toyota market came to account for 16 percent of Toyota's total exports. In a few years, the Middle East became the company's second-largest foreign market after North America.

The fuel crisis had profound implications for the automobile emissions research that was underway in Japan and the United States. Engineers were trying to reduce three different pollutants: carbon monoxide, hydrocarbons, and nitrogen oxides. Yet steps they took to reduce one substance often served to raise one of the others—particularly nitrogen oxides, the pollutant they had been given an extra year to control. The most obvious solution was to take a number of steps to control each of the three substances, but that was a disaster. Every change engineers made to reduce emissions decreased fuel economy.

Emission-control devices installed to meet the mild standards of the early 1970s hindered performance so greatly that manufacturers were forced to put cutoff devices on them. Government emission tests were conducted under specific ambient-temperature and vehicle-speed conditions. To avoid the power and economy losses of the devices as much as possible, manufacturers constructed their devices so they operated only under the temperature and speed conditions employed in certification tests.

Everyone in the industry knew this was a poor solution to the problem, but it was the best they could do at the time. Meanwhile, U.S. manufacturers kept appealing to the Environmental Protection Agency to extend its deadlines. Each time, the EPA turned them down. The oil crisis of 1973 changed that. The immediate need to decrease fuel consumption began to be considered in tandem with the need to reduce emissions. The U.S. Court of Appeals, in response to a suit filed by the manufacturers, ordered the EPA to reconsider. The EPA relented and extended both the 1975 and 1976 standards by one year.

When the United States delayed their standards, the Japanese Auto Manufacturers Association began pressing the Japanese government for a similar postponement. Eiji Toyoda was the president of the association at the time, and he told a seemingly endless series of investigative panels that the manufacturers simply needed more time.

The most severe complication Toyota was facing was the company's proliferation of models and engines. The company had become so successful, and its product lines so diverse, that it was now suffering as a result. Engine emissions varied considerably with each engine and each car it was installed in, and Toyota had fifteen engine types with ninety-five variations. The same engine installed in two different cars produced different levels of pollutants and required different corrections. This made it difficult to decide whether to reduce emissions by altering the combustion process within the engine, or to clean up dirty emissions from the engine in the exhaust system with a catalytic converter.

Toyota tried several converters produced by independent manufacturers, but with only limited success. Converters that worked well with the smooth-running V-8 engines used in American cars failed in Toyotas. The more intense vibrations produced by smaller Japanese engines tended to shake the converters into self-destruction.

Toyota was also prohibited by one converter manufacturer from disassembling any converters to do composition analyses. Thus individual converters had to be shipped back to the States constantly so the manufacturer could inform Toyota how the materials in the converter were responding to various engine modifications. Finally, Eiji Toyoda reverted to a long-standing company principle. Toyota would develop its own converter technology in-house.

Toyota had retained a few emission-control experts from academia in the early days of its research, but they had since left the project. Emission technology was in its infancy in Japan, and the academic consultants were familiar only with stationary-source emissions, such as those from power plants. Toyota assembled a massive team of researchers and engineers to learn about converters as they were developing them. Eiji's charge to the men was harsh. He told then not to take a piecemeal approach to the problem. From the start, they were to take the long-term view. Their job was to meet the most stringent requirements of the regulations as soon as possible.

Those from the engine division were in charge of monitoring the emissions the engines produced. This group would later be joined by engineers from Nippondenso, a former Toyota subsidiary, who would create new engine-control devices. Other Toyota employees worked on the external design of the converter package, while Toyota Central Research Laboratory handled the composition of the catalytic elements within the converter.

The coordination required among the researchers and engineers was staggering. The engine people had to ensure that engine emissions were stable enough to avoid contaminating the catalytic elements in the converter. The body-design people had to create a layout that would keep the converter, which reached temperatures up to one thousand degrees centigrade, from setting the car on fire, while also isolating it from roadway damage. Market researchers had to insure that the final packages would be cars people would buy, while the manufacturing people worried about how the systems would be produced.

Eiji Toyoda kept trying to explain these complexities to the investigating panels, but without much success. The public and media pressure on auto makers was enormous, and Eiji was in a personally precarious position. On loan from Toyota to head the Japanese Auto Manufacturers Association, he had to speak as the emissary for all of its members. He felt that he couldn't promise anything more than the least advanced manufacturer could accomplish, yet this position was interpreted as Toyota's being obstinate about meeting the requirements of the law. To make matters worse, other members of the manufacturers association began to break rank.

Toyota and Nissan, after living in fear of the giant American manufacturers for years, were now the General Motors and Ford of Japan. They were massive, diverse companies with tremendous economic strength. The Japanese auto market was still as fiercely competitive as ever, however, and the small manufacturers were always looking for an opportunity to gain an advantage on Japan's Big Two. When Toyota, the largest of all, said it needed additional time to get its numerous models to pass emissions certification, several smaller auto makers seized on this position as an advantage they could exploit.

Honda Motor Company had always been an outsider in the Japanese auto industry. Beginning life as a motorcycle manufacturer, the company achieved sensational results in the world of motorcycle racing, deriving tremendous power from its small engines. The company advanced to auto production in the early 1960s, despite strong opposition by MITI. The ministry was trying to consolidate the auto industry, and it didn't want anyone else joining the fray. Honda ignored MITI and proceeded anyway.

Honda followed the traditional niche-market route in entering the business. Drawing on its racing background, it constructed minicars with tiny 531-cc engines that produced a robust forty-four horsepower. With a power-to-weight ratio resembling that of a race car, Honda's two-seat sports cars caused a sensation when they appeared. Having achieved that success, Honda began adding models.

When the U.S. and Japanese governments established emission-control regulations, Honda had only a few models in production and a tremendous amount of experience in fine-tuning engines. Soichiro Honda, the company's president, recognized this as a tremendous opportunity for his company. If Honda could get its very limited number of engines and models to pass the emission standards before the large Japanese manufacturers, it would be a public relations bonanza.

Honda gambled on taking a different approach to emission controls than the others. The company decided to draw on its background in maximizing engine power in an effort to decrease emissions during the combustion process. The most direct way to lower emissions was to decrease the amount of fuel an engine used. But if the air-fuel ratio became too low, the gasoline in the engine wouldn't burn. Honda resolved this by creating the Compound Vortex-Controlled Combustion (CVCC) engine. The CVCC burned a rich fuel mixture in chambers adjacent to the main combustion chambers, which would then ignite a very lean mixture in the main chamber.

The CVCC design worked so well in Honda's test cars that Honda officials made a surprise announcement at an Environment Agency hearing in Japan in June of 1973. Just after Eiji Toyoda completed his testimony that the industry needed additional time, Honda declared it didn't understand the problems the other manufacturers were having. Honda's CVCC was so effective, they said, it could already meet the 1975 standards—two years ahead of the deadline!

Honda's announcement brought sensational headlines in Japan, as it did in the United States shortly afterwards. While American manufacturers were demanding the U.S. standards be delayed, Honda repeated its bold declaration to a Congressional committee. In the commotion that followed, no one listened when other manufacturers said that although the CVCC might meet the 1975 standards, it didn't meet the far more difficult 1976 nitrogen-oxides standards.

Matters only got worse when another one of the smaller Japanese manufacturers, Toyo Kogyo, said their Mazda cars would also meet the 1975 standards with a revolutionary rotary engine. This engine, which used far fewer moving parts than a traditional reciprocating engine, had become the darling of the automotive business several years before. The Mazda engine was an update of an old German design that had never been put into mass production.

Like the CVCC, the Mazda engine wouldn't meet the 1976 standards either, but the mass media neglected this aspect of the story. Nor could it be known at the time that the engine would soon fall from favor when it was discovered to have poor gas mileage. All that mattered at the moment was that these engines could be offered as proof of heel-dragging among the largest auto companies in the world.

Toyota took tremendous abuse from the Japanese mass media in the months that followed. Not only was the company the largest, and thus the most visible, in Japan, but it had become a favorite target of the press. When a number of Toyota models were recalled in 1969 as a result of a problem with brake-line corrosion, the company, along with other auto makers in Japan, had been blasted as a maker of unsafe products. Now the outcry against Toyota was resurrected.

President Richard Nixon announced in June of 1974 that, because of economic and fuel-conservation concerns, the U.S. would delay the enforcement of the Muskie Act an additional two years, until 1978. Honda and Mazda were minor players in the U.S. market, and their testimony about their engines had not carried much political weight. That was not the case in Japan. Given the outcry in the press and among government officials, the Japan government decreed that its 1975 standards for carbon-monoxide and hydrocarbon emissions would remain in effect.

13
TURBULENT
DAYS

The automobile business was wildly unpredictable internationally in 1974. There would be surges of car buying alternating with periods of flat sales. The United States slipped into a recession after the oil crisis, and dealers were overstocked in most of the country but sold out in pockets where the local economy had remained strong. Intermittent materials shortages continued in Japan, and Toyota cut its allocations to the United States, while also raising prices twice.

In the face of this uncertainty, the automobile market was undergoing a distinct change. The Toyota Corolla became the best-selling car in the world in 1974, selling 677,455 units—35 percent more than Nissan's Sunny, which was in second place. The full-size Chevrolet was in third, followed by the Volkswagen Beetle. Three of the four top-selling cars in the world were compacts. In the United States, the stronghold of the large car, 50 percent of all cars sold in 1974 were compacts.

Americans were shifting to more fuel-efficient cars, but after having been raised on spacious and comfortable American automobiles, it wasn't stripped-down econoboxes they wanted to buy. They wanted smaller versions of large American cars: vehicles with comfortable interiors, good stereos, peppy acceleration, and an attractive exterior. And trucks weren't just for business use anymore. Americans—and particularly young ones—wanted pickup trucks with bucket seats, alloy wheels, ornate paint jobs, and extended truck beds to hold campers or off-road motorcycles.

The spartan VW Beetle was still in fourth place on the international sales chart, but it had owned first place for many years. Volkswagen was planning to export its new Rabbit to the United States to replace the Beetle in 1975, but it would be too late then. Toyota would ac-

complish what had seemed impossible five years before. The Corolla
would displace the Beetle as the best-selling import in the States.

The Corolla was doing well in 1974, but Toyota's American office
needed new models badly. Competition in the U.S. small-car segment
was starting to resemble the fierce market battles that were the norm
in Japan. Chevrolet introduced its new Chevette, Ford and Chrysler
expanded their compact offerings, and Datsun and Honda added spe-
cialty cars. The Japanese manufacturers, particularly, were creating special high-fuel-mileage models. The U.S. government had begun
publishing fuel-economy ratings, and a spot near the top of the list was
a tremendous boost to sales.

With this kind of competition, Toyota was managing to increase
its U.S. sales each year, but only by modest amounts. Nonetheless, even
with sales flat or falling in Japan, Toyota was the only auto manufacturer
that was consistently showing a profit. Thanks to its lean, just-in-time
production and to its manufacturing flexibility, the company had become both extremely efficient and highly adaptable. Competing manufacturers, who had previously paid scant attention to Toyota's
manufacturing methods, began making visits to Toyota City. How, they
wanted to know, was Toyota profitable in a bad market, when they
were all losing money?

The man all the visitors wanted to meet was Taiichi Ohno, whose
production system was now fully implemented—although, under the
principles of *kaizen*, it was also always being improved. Ohno was not
surprised by the timing of this outside interest. Automobile manufacturing had been a growth business for decades, and it had been comparatively easy for an established and competent company with good
products to be profitable. It was during a severe downturn that inefficiency, which had been masked by high volume, drove companies into
the red.

Manufacturers always thought production efficiency was synony-
mous with production volume—that if they produced enough of something its price would end up being competitive. Some years before,
Ohno had visited a Toyota supplier from whom the company was
buying seventy thousand parts a month. The plant manager bragged to
Ohno, "We have enough manpower and capacity to cope with your
orders even if you need a hundred thousand parts."

"Then," Ohno asked, "do you currently close your operation ten
days a month, since we are only buying seventy thousand parts?"

"We wouldn't do anything that silly," the man answered. "We are building a warehouse for the excess production."

Ohno explained to the manager that if he built the warehouse he would probably lose his contract with Toyota, since the additional overhead would make his parts too expensive. The idea, Ohno said, was to have only the equipment and workers needed to produce what was actually sold. Future production increases should then be obtained by improving the efficiency of the workers already on hand, rather than by adding additional men or equipment. That way, when sales declined, the company could remain profitable, since its overhead hadn't been increased to meet peak demand.

These were the kinds of stories Toyota visitors heard in 1974, as the Toyota staff tried to explain succinctly a production method that had been conceived four decades before, and fleshed out over the past two decades. In fact, until other people started calling it the Toyota Production System, it didn't even have a name. People at Toyota thought of it as improving efficiency, and when they wanted to refer to it, they called it, in deference to Ohno's nickname, The Mustache's Methods.

Although these visitors came to learn how Toyota had remained profitable in lean times, the truth was that Toyota had lived with small profits for years, while continuing to perfect its production system and its cars. But now the stage was set for the company to reap the benefits. If it could get additional models on the market, Toyota would be able to score tremendous gains in market share. Unfortunately, the new models were slow in coming. Half of Toyota's engineers in Japan were occupied with the emission-control project.

It took Toyota's emission-control team until November of 1975, the latest date allowed under the law, to introduce its first models to meet Japan's 1975 emission standards for hydrocarbons and carbon monoxide. Honda and Mazda had been selling cars that met these standards for a year, and they flaunted their accomplishments mercilessly in their advertising. The Japanese mass media and government also were unstinting in their charges of heel-dragging against Toyota. Even Toyota's dealers began to turn against the company when the bad publicity was exacerbated by the reduced performance and fuel economy of the company's emission-compliant vehicles.

Eiji Toyoda was embarrassed about putting these disappointing cars on the road, but he had no choice. The 1975 emission laws were in place, and if Toyota wanted to remain in business, it had to meet them. The company could expend only so much effort improving the performance of the 1975 cars, since there was a new emission standard for nitrogen oxides taking effect in 1976.

Japanese scientists had presented studies at emission-control hearings in 1974 saying that nitrogen oxides from automobiles were combining with pollutants from stationary sources to create a unique pollution problem in Japan. They said the Japanese people were suffering from an unusually high rate of chronic bronchitis as a result, and they urged that nitrogen-oxides standards be made tougher than those in the U.S.

Auto makers countered that the scientists' data was flawed and that nitrogen oxides were the most difficult emission to control. But the scientists' testimony was accepted, and the strict ambient nitrogen-oxide levels became the standard. It was predicted that the amount of ambient nitrogen oxides would be reduced to a level far below that deemed acceptable in the United States. To achieve these ambient levels, tailpipe measurements of nitrogen oxides were required to be the lowest in the world.

Scientists outside Japan later confirmed that the findings presented at the hearings were incorrect. Although there was a high rate of chronic bronchitis among Japanese, it was not caused by nitrogen oxides. The Japanese government refused to alter the regulations, however, even though realistically the hoped-for ambient readings were impossible to achieve. It is a characteristic of Japanese bureaucrats to save face by not admitting to mistakes. They preferred to force Japanese auto makers to meet the stringent tailpipe standards—even if they wouldn't produce the envisioned ambient readings or reduce chronic bronchitis. With the mass media and public opinion behind them, they had plenty of support in this position.

After these hearings, Honda and Mazda again stepped forward and said, although they couldn't meet the proposed tailpipe standards in 1976, they could come close. Eiji Toyoda protested that these companies had only limited model offerings, but his pleas fell on deaf ears.

Toyota swallowed its pride and bought a license to use the Honda CVCC engine in its cars. The engine proved to be a waste of money, however, when it couldn't pass emission standards in Toyota's body configurations. Honda, not surprisingly, was not interested in sharing much information with Toyota about the engine beyond the basic documents provided for in the license. Nonetheless, Toyota's efforts, along with those of other manufacturers, were taken by a few government officials—if not the public and the press—as a sign of good faith. The extremely tough 1976 standards were delayed until 1978, but interim standards were put in place for 1976.

Any sense of comfort Toyota's engineers felt about having to meet only interim standards in 1976 was short-lived. Eiji Toyoda took the additional research time away from them as soon as it was granted by the government. Eiji was incensed that Toyota continued to be criticized for stalling on emissions compliance, and he was determined to redeem the company's honor. The company, he ordered his engineers, would not only meet the interim standards in 1976. They would also meet the 1978 standards by 1977, making Toyota the first manufacturer to be in compliance with the law.

The responsibility for meeting Eiji's directive fell on the shoulders of Kiyoshi Matsumoto, a young engineer and engine specialist. Matsumoto had traveled to the United States as a part of an emissions study team in 1966, but he thought emissions were an American problem then. When Eiji told Matsumoto in 1971 that Toyota was to develop its own catalytic converter, he had protested that he wasn't a chemist. "There are no chemists at Toyota," Eiji had said, "so you must learn."

There were 2,240 Toyota engineers on the emissions project at that time, and those working on catalysts had tested 10,000 different catalytic materials for possible use in their converter. By 1975 they had narrowed their choices, but a tremendous amount of work remained. There were decisions to be made about a new fuel-injection system to replace the outmoded carburetor, as well as a new lean-burn combustion system Toyota engineers had created. Always, every selection was complicated by the necessity of earning certification for each of the 125 car-and-engine combinations that were then in production.

With Eiji's new 1977 deadline in place, Matsumoto knew he had to find a way to eliminate trial-and-error testing on all the potential combinations. That work was extremely tedious, and there simply wasn't time for it. He found a potential solution in a computer program the U.S. National Aeronautics and Space Administration had developed for the design of space craft. Called the Failure Mode Effective Analysis (FMEA) program, this software enabled engineers to identify design problems by running tests on a computer that simulated the actual operation of a system.

The FMEA program had never been used before in the automobile industry, but Matsumoto saw it as the only chance he had to meet Eiji's deadline. All of the performance and design specifications for emission-related components from a few cars were fed into the program. The program was run, yielding predictions of specific component failures. The engineers tested the same systems on actual cars, and they were amazed by the results.

The program worked perfectly, accurately predicting the performance of each component. The emissions team quickly assembled workers to feed all of the pertinent specifications from every car into the computer. They would be able to do their testing in weeks now rather than months. The chances of meeting Eiji's deadline increased dramatically. The beleaguered Kiyoshi Matsumoto could hardly believe it. There hadn't been a day when he hadn't thought about quitting his job and leaving the company. His wife had urged him on, saying, "Even if the progress seems slow, the gods know of your efforts." Now Matsumoto thought she may have been right.

The engineering team continued to have the most difficulty with mid-sized and larger cars, which produced more emissions. By concentrating most of their efforts on these cars, Matsumoto hoped to reach a breakthrough that would speed their work on the smaller cars. That point occurred when the team made an important discovery about the effect of an engine's air-fuel ratio on emissions.

Technicians at Toyota Central Research Laboratory noticed that, regardless of the catalytic material they used, catalysts were most effective when the air-fuel ratio in the engine was carefully controlled. The magic spot, called the theoretical air-fuel ratio, was fourteen and a half parts of air to every part of gasoline. If they could maintain this precise ratio, they could control all three pollutants with a single, multiple-element catalytic converter. In essence, the three pollutants, processed through the catalytic elements, canceled each other out. Matsumoto was delighted by the discovery, which he called the three-way catalyst.

A combination of platinum and rhodium proved to be the most effective catalytic elements for the converter. A problem remained, however, with controlling the air-fuel ratio. The effectiveness of the converter dropped dramatically when the ratio strayed from the theoretical level, so a highly precise electronic fuel-injection system had to be created.

Nippondenso had developed a fuel-injection system, and the company agreed to create an effective oxygen sensor for the exhaust system, which was needed to ensure the accuracy of the fuel injection. There were already oxygen sensors on the market, but questions remained about whether these sensors could withstand the one-thousand-degree-centigrade heat generated by an exhaust system with a catalyst. Eiji Toyoda, as always, insisted the company develop its own critical products in-house.

By early 1977, Nippondenso had perfected the oxygen sensor that was the last link in the long chain of emission-control devices Toyota needed. By using various combinations of fuel injection, lean-burn engines, oxidizing converters, and three-way converters, every model in the Toyota lineup was able to meet the severe 1978 standards. Eiji Toyoda was ecstatic when the first of these cars went on sale in June of 1977, six months ahead of the government deadline.

The emissions battle had been a long and expensive, but even though the government regulations had been met, it wasn't over yet for Toyota. The three-way catalyst significantly reduced the performance and fuel economy of the cars it was used on, and the noble metals in the catalyst increased production costs. This was inefficient and wasteful, and therefore unacceptable to Eiji. He ordered a core of engineers to remain on the project.

Eiji's hand had been forced by the regulations and public opinion, making him engineer cars to suit the government. Now he would do it Toyota's way. He told his men to use the advanced knowledge of engine and combustion technology that had been gained to find a way to eliminate the use of the three-way catalyst whenever possible. Eiji didn't want these inefficient devices on his cars if he could help it.

In the coming years, Toyota would use its new technology to reduce emissions in the engine enough to equip many cars with less restrictive single-element converters, increasing performance and economy. In the Japanese market, where high-technology components are a strong selling point, Toyota would use its knowledge to introduce two high-performance engines that would give it the lead in engine technology over Nissan. This would lead to Toyota's introducing multiple-valve engines in the United States long before any of the Big Three.

Those developments were in the future, however, and at the moment Toyota Motor Sales Company could only rejoice that thousands of engineers and technicians had been released to resume work on new-model development. Toyota had dug itself into a hole with all of the emissions research. Competitors had released dozens of new models, and Toyota was going to have to hurry to catch up.

The American automobile market had remained depressed while Toyota's emissions work was underway in Japan. Motor-vehicle sales in the United States had reached almost 14 million during 1973; by 1975 they had fallen to 10.5 million. Toyota Motor Sales, U.S.A., managed to record modest sales increases in this environment, as the market stayed soft through 1976. People who could afford to buy cars were purchasing small, fuel-efficient ones, but many more people simply weren't buying. Even though they may have wanted to save money on gasoline, the savings would never equal the price of a new car.

Through all of this gloom, one factor continued to work in the favor of auto manufacturers. Sooner or later, people had to replace their deteriorating cars. This was especially true since two-income families had become a necessity in the United States. The number of women in the workforce had doubled since 1955, and, lacking public transportation, most families needed two automobiles.

The pent-up demand in the U.S. auto market finally exploded in 1977. Toyota sold 568,000 vehicles, a 45 percent increase over the previous year. The emissions battle having been won, the company had thirty models on the market. Many of them offered five-speed transmissions and other advanced features. Prices had increased only 2.8 percent, and thanks to the knowledge gained during the emissions research, those vehicles offered an average 12 percent increase in fuel economy.

Toyota sold a lot of economical Corollas in 1977, but it also sold a lot of its upmarket cars. The more embellished pickups had arrived, and the sporty Celica was a huge hit. The Celica had won the Import Car of the Year Award from *Motor Trend* magazine in 1976, and it was adding tremendously to the company's profitability. The Celica liftback, priced in the five-to-six-thousand-dollar range, was one of the biggest sellers. With a new Celica due in 1978—the first created in the company's American design studio—everyone was expecting another big increase in sales.

Toyota's period of tremendous growth in the United States began to look like a one-year aberration when 1978 came. The United States was suffering from another bout of inflation and unfavorable trade balances. Meanwhile, the Japanese economy was slowing down at the same time that its exports were becoming stronger than ever in the international market. This caused a 78 percent increase in Japan's trade surpluses, with the country accumulating $30 billion in foreign currencies during the first eleven months of 1978.

The increasing trade imbalance caused the value of the yen to appreciate at an unprecedented rate. The yen was trading at 263 to the dollar in October of 1977. By November of 1978, it had been revalued to 176 yen to the dollar, a 37-percent increase in the yen's value. Japanese products, on which Americans were spending $18.6 billion a year, became more expensive with every passing day.

Toyota had to increase its prices four times between September of 1977 and April of 1978 alone. By the end of the 1978 model year, the average price increase for all Toyota models was $1,011. Only one car in its 1979 lineup would be selling for under $4,000. Sales dropped 7 percent during 1978, and members of the American staff began to worry.

It wasn't just the increase in the value of the yen that had people alarmed. While Toyota's sales had fallen in 1978, those of the Big Three were still riding the buying wave that had formed in 1977. Americans had forgotten all about the gasoline lines from 1973. Gasoline prices had stabilized at a rate that, when adjusted for inflation, was virtually identical to pre-1973 prices. Since hikes in gasoline taxes had been modest, gasoline was still cheap in the United States. With every economic indicator and government policy showing that cheap gas was here to stay, Americans began returning to large cars with abandon.

The U.S. new-vehicle market climbed past fourteen million in 1978, and the demand for large cars was so strong that General Motors was thinking about converting one of its compact-car plants to production of full-size Oldsmobiles. Chrysler, which was in the process of downsizing its cars, worried that its latest New Yorker model would be too small. Ford was buried under such a blizzard of big-car orders that it was rationing cars with V-8 engines to its dealers!

All of this spelled big trouble for Toyota in the United States. After the delays in introducing new models, Toyota had focused its designers and production planners on turning out more fuel-efficient cars. The company's first front-wheel-drive car, the Tercel, was slated for intro-duction in the States with the 1980 model year. The Tercel was a subcompact economy car that had millions of dollars of development money tied up in it, and it would be hitting the market just as demand for those cars seemed to be disappearing.

Staff members of Toyota Motor Sales, U.S.A., tried to come up with a new strategy, but the development of any new models would take years. In the meantime, cars were piling up in dealer stocks, and some way had to be found to move them. Aggressive advertising and marketing campaigns had always served the company well, and that was the route it took again.

In suburban Miami, James Moran, Toyota's distributor for the south-eastern region, thought he knew what he had to do to move his cars. Nothing got sales moving faster than a sense of excitement, and Moran was going to create it with what he called Toyotathons. Backed by a massive advertising campaign, Moran had his dealers mimic old-time dance marathons by selling cars around the clock. "We are so desperate to move cars," the dealers proclaimed in their ads, "that we aren't going to close until we meet our sales quotas."

The dealers rented ambulances, parked them outside their busi-nesses, and turned on their flashing lights. These rescue vehicles stood ready to sweep away any salesperson who collapsed under the strain. There were cots in the showroom, and salesmen were forbidden to wear ties. Music blared on the sales floor, and every time someone sold a car, bells would ring and the customer's name was announced. People were frantically buying cars, and on Saturday afternoons customers would line up four deep waiting to get into showrooms.

The format worked so well for Moran and his dealers that they started holding sales at locations away from dealerships. They'd rent a big field or a mall parking lot and fill it with cars. Once they staged a boat-load sale right at the docks in Jacksonville, Florida. Moran bought every TV-commercial spot he could and showed footage of thousands of cars pouring onto the dock, waiting to be sold at special prices.

Sales increased tremendously, but everyone knew they could stage only so many Toyotathons. All of Toyota's production for the United States was locked into fuel-efficient cars for three or four years down the road. Toyota would still be able to move some cars in the States, but the expectation was that sales would continually erode.

Selling half a million cars a year in the United States was more than anyone had dared hope for when the American office had been established twenty-one years before. Now it looked as if 1977 would be a high point to be remembered fondly. It would take a miracle of the magnitude of the storms that had driven the Mongols from the coast of Japan seven centuries before to alter Toyota's U.S. plight.

That miracle took the form of the 1979 oil crisis. The Middle East was in turmoil again, and this time the United States was directly involved. The U.S. Embassy in Iran was under siege, and hostages were taken. There were massive anti-American demonstrations in the streets of Teheran, and President Carter was burned in effigy. It was the lead story on network news every evening for weeks and the central topic of everyday conversations. Television brought the second Middle East crisis home to Americans in the same way it had the Vietnam War.

Gasoline prices in the United States doubled within weeks, passing a dollar a gallon for the first time. Highly respected publications were predicting that, at the minimum, the price would rise to two dollars. This time, no one took the oil embargo lightly. Thermostats were turned down across the country, and high-intensity light bulbs were replaced with low-watt bulbs. Americans began driving to work in carpools. And if the carpool involved a new car, there was now a 60 percent chance it was a compact. Auto makers suddenly couldn't give away large cars.

The question of how so many Americans had come to drive big cars was a chicken-or-egg problem. Had the manufacturers created this market with their seductive advertising campaigns, or had they simply met consumer demand? American cars, like those of every nation, were superbly in tune with the psyche and geography of their native country. Top-of-the-line U.S. models were the ultimate "highway cruisers." They were born in the age when the interstate highway system was created and airplane travel was expensive. These cars allowed motorists to drive hundreds of miles across the open landscape in a product with a comfort level that resembled a living room on wheels.

Whatever the cause, the size of American cars grew like the corn in Kansas over the years. From 1967 to 1974, the Chevy Impala gained 6 inches in length and 556 pounds in weight, while its fuel mileage dropped from 13 to 9 miles to the gallon. The Ford LTD gained 6 inches and 931 pounds during the same time, with its mileage falling from 16 to 9 miles per gallon.

U.S. manufacturers had begun reducing the weight and improving the mileage of their cars in recent years. But it wasn't easy for large-car-oriented companies to shrink their products. When the market shifted to small cars, the advantage belonged to companies that were most experienced in building them.

American cars would never be the same after 1979. After having largely ignored or dismissed foreign cars for years, the Big Three would now have to learn from them. Toyota sold every car it could export to the United States in 1979, and the front-wheel-drive Tercel would hit the market in 1980. In terms of shifting the market in Toyota's favor, the second oil crisis was an incredible stroke of luck. But being able to sell more than 630,000 cars in 1979 and more than 705,000 in 1980 was far more than good fortune.

When the Motor & Equipment Manufacturers Association surveyed American households about their attitudes towards imported cars in the late 1970s, they found that the majority of those questioned believed imports had better fuel economy, engineering, and durability than their American counterparts. Even executives of the Big Three marveled openly about the high-quality "fit and finish" of Japanese cars and the way that every sensory input from the cars seemed to say: well made. But there was also more to the imports' massive new success than quality.

The custom of gift giving is a long and honored tradition in Japan. The gifts exchanged are often not extravagant, but they are given frequently and with great delight. As an extension of this practice, Japanese cars were loaded with thoughtful little features that people appreciated. They had trunk-lid release levers in the passenger compartment and adjustable seat backs. They had little tool kits in the trunk and spare fuses in the glove box. They were, in short, cars that gave people what they wanted, plus a little something extra, at a price they could afford.

This was no accident. Even when Toyota was selling only a relative handful of cars in the United States, the company was constantly researching every aspect of the U.S. market. An important part of total quality control was finding out what customers wanted, and Toyota took this aspect of its business very seriously. This, along with the constant improvements of *kaizen*, had allowed the company to achieve what Kiichiro Toyoda had set out to do in the late 1940s. The company was building small cars that were very good at being small. When the motorists of the world decided this was what they wanted, Toyota was waiting to give it to them.

American automobile manufacturers were dealt a harsh blow by the second oil crisis. Having repositioned themselves to meet the substantial pre-embargo demand for large cars, they were now locked into a market that had ceased to exist. It was estimated the Big Three would be writing off eight billion dollars in investments for large-car plants that were rendered prematurely obsolete. They wouldn't be able to get redesigned cars onto the market until 1984 at the earliest. In the intervening years, they could do little more than sit back and watch their sales plummet and their indebtedness soar.

Rampant inflation in the wake of the oil crisis had interest rates at 20 percent in 1980. Car sales were off so dramatically that 28 percent of the United Auto Workers' (UAW) membership was out of work. Chrysler asked the U.S. government for $1.5 billion in loan guarantees to stay afloat. Ford, GM, and American Motors were all losing money— GM's 1980 loss of $763 million was its first since 1921—at a time when they needed to invest huge sums in retooling. With combined 1980 losses of $4 billion, auto companies were cutting their dividends just as they were seeking large amounts of financing on the open market.

With the Big Three in serious financial trouble, and the sales of Japanese cars increasing, protectionist legislation against imports began to seem inevitable. The Department of the Treasury had already conducted an investigation into dumping—exporting cars at prices below those in other markets to increase market share and production volume. All dumping charges against foreign auto manufacturers were dropped two years later, but new measures surfaced on several other fronts.

The U.S. government increased the import duty on small trucks from 4 to 25 percent, and the UAW and Ford filed charges with the International Trade Commission (ITC). These suits claimed Japanese motor vehicle imports were causing widespread unemployment in the United States, as well as damaging the domestic auto industry. The ITC dismissed the suits, saying the problems of the American auto industry were not caused by imported cars but by the U.S. manufacturers' own sluggish response to the market shift to small cars.

Next, the UAW began applying strong pressure on Japanese manufacturers to build cars in the United States. In early 1981, Honda and Nissan responded by announcing plans to construct U.S. assembly plants. Eiji Toyoda, however, had serious reservations about following suit. Much of the company's success was dependent upon its highly efficient production system, and if that couldn't be replicated in a U.S. plant—and no one at Toyota thought it could be—then such a venture would be a catastrophe.

Forty-three years after Kiichiro Toyoda had first envisioned just-in-time production, Toyota had advanced the system to its theoretical end point for cars sold in Japan. The company didn't produce a component part until the car it would be used on was sold. Japanese Toyota dealers, who kept almost no inventory, were linked directly to the factory by computer.

When a dealer ordered a car, the factory put it into the production schedule, precipitating orders for the requisite components. As the car moved down the assembly line several days later, each component would reach the appropriate spot on the line just as the car moved into position. Plant inventories, including component parts and cars awaiting delivery, never exceeded four days' supply—the amount of time that elapsed between receiving an order and delivering a car.

Toyota's manufacturing flexibility allowed it to make a profit with sales as low as 64 percent of plant capacity, and its production efficiency produced cars with thirteen man-hours of labor, while the industry norm was nineteen to twenty-two hours. Yet all of this success ultimately hinged on one factor: the company's harmonious labor-management relations. During the previous decade, Toyota's annual output per worker had increased 86 percent.

Without the full cooperation of its workers, the Toyota production system would collapse. Now the company was being pressured to build cars in the United States, where harmonious labor relations were non-existent in the auto industry. Given America's adversarial labor relations, Eiji Toyoda was convinced that building cars in the U.S. would lower the quality of its products while increasing their cost.

The company's concerns about quality extended to U.S. component suppliers as well. Toyota's multitude of Japanese suppliers played a vital role in the company's total-quality-control system. Just as assembly workers were responsible for the quality of their work, so were Toyota's suppliers. These subcontractors were expected to employ the total-quality-control system in their plants and to coordinate their deliveries with the needs of the just-in-time production system. Since Toyota had taught its system to its suppliers, and since the majority of them were located close to Toyota City, it was easy for them to satisfy these requirements.

Toyota was able to achieve full cooperation from its suppliers because, as with its workers, Toyota maintained harmonious and long-term relations with them. While American manufacturers had subcontractors bid on orders, Toyota negotiated each year with the same suppliers. Since these suppliers didn't have to worry about being ousted by a lower bidder, they were willing to be highly cooperative.

Toyota brought its first-tier suppliers into the production process at the design stage, telling the contractor what requirements the company had for a certain part and then allowing the company to design components to meet those needs. If a supplier had financial or production problems, Toyota would send its people in to strengthen their methods. This system flowed throughout Toyota's network of three hundred suppliers, who were organized into two supplier associations.

Toyota's primary contractors—seat makers, for example—were responsible for assisting and monitoring the work of secondary subcontractors, who might supply springs for the seats. Likewise, the secondary subcontractors worked closely with the tertiary subcontractors, who might supply metal for the seat springs. This interlocking, mutual-assistance network, which had been established during the war, enabled Toyota to produce high-quality cars at competitive prices. The company was doubtful it could replicate this system in the United States, where business relationships were usually competitive.

Nonetheless, Toyota recognized its U.S. dealers would be in jeopardy if import restrictions were enacted. The company began investigating the possibility of U.S. production by commissioning three feasibility studies. These studies, carried out simultaneously by American and Japanese companies, offered differing opinions. The Japanese study found the company would have considerable difficulty establishing a U.S. plant that replicated the quality, productivity, and favorable labor relations that existed in Japan, while the American studies were cautiously optimistic.

Under these circumstances, Eiji Toyoda felt he couldn't take the enormous financial risk of building a U.S. assembly plant without first testing the waters. The only way to do that was through a joint venture with an American manufacturer, which would cost only half of the more than one billion dollars a new plant would require. Toyota's past joint-venture talks had been to acquire technological know-how. That was no longer the case. Toyota was now the master of production technology; what it had to learn was American industrial relations.

After its many discussions with Ford over the years, Toyota—and particularly Eiji Toyoda, who had studied there in the 1950s—felt the company had an established relationship with Ford. This was an important prerequisite for Toyota. As a family-led company that traced its roots to a provincial textile enterprise, Toyota was used to doing business with its neighbors. Even though the company had grown into an international conglomerate, Eiji still liked to feel its partners were friends of the family.

Toyota and Ford representatives began meeting in June of 1980, with Toyota proposing a joint venture to produce its compact Camry for the 1983 model year. Ford felt the Camry would conflict with its products, and there were also broad differences over the number of cars to be produced. Ford, looking for a new fuel-efficient car that would play a major part in its lineup, was insisting on an output of 500,000 to 600,000 cars at two factories. Toyota, which mainly wanted to test the feasibility of American production, proposed a plant for 250,000 cars, of which each company would sell half.

As the Ford talks continued, protectionist pressures continued to mount in the United States. A Department of Transportation report in January of 1981 found Japanese manufacturers had a $1,500-per-car cost advantage, half of which was due to "process and product technology which yield major productivity gains." U.S. manufacturers, the report said, would have to commit major resources to match these production efficiencies. It recommended negotiations be conducted with Japan to limit auto imports, while U.S. manufacturers began rebuilding.

Japanese auto makers argued vehemently against import restrictions, saying they were being punished for manufacturing desirable products efficiently. Nonetheless, the Japanese Ministry of International Trade and Industry agreed in May of 1981 to restrict exports for three years. The quota for the first year was 1.68 million cars, an 8 percent reduction from the previous year. In June the ministry notified Toyota that its U.S. exports would have to be reduced 9 percent, to 518,000 vehicles.

At the same time as Toyota's U.S. sales were cut, its talks with Ford were floundering. The companies had seemed to reach a compromise on building a Toyota minivan, even signing a letter of agreement on the deal. But then Ford questioned the market for the vehicle and backed out. Each side offered alternatives, but as time dragged on, it began to look hopeless. The two companies finally halted their talks in July.

As Toyota's talks with Ford were collapsing, General Motors was also facing a dilemma. With demand for compact cars at its peak, GM didn't have a viable small car on the market. Japanese cars were setting the price and quality standards in this category, and GM simply couldn't compete with them. Chevrolet had sold several million Chevettes, but the company was thought to be losing as much as eight hundred dollars on every sale. A new compact in preproduction for 1985 looked like more of the same. GM studies indicated it would be impossible to price the car competitively and earn a profit.

Roger Smith, GM's chairman, recognized something had to be done immediately. He couldn't allow the company to continue losing money on small cars, but neither could he abandon that segment. The fallout from GM customers, dealers, and investors would be incalculable. The company was planning to import small cars from Isuzu Motors and Suzuki Motors—affiliates GM had purchased a stake in after Japanese foreign investment laws were changed—but that wasn't really a solution either. These Japanese manufacturers had relatively low production, and GM would be importing subcompacts from them.

To make a profit in the much larger compact-car market, GM was going to have to obtain cars from a full-scale manufacturer like Toyota or Nissan, and the only way that was feasible was through a joint venture. Getting a joint venture past U.S. antitrust laws would be difficult enough, anything more involved would be impossible, and neither of the Japanese firms was open to outside investment in any case.

Since it was common knowledge in the auto industry that Toyota's talks with Ford were not going well, Roger Smith quietly put out the word that he would like to meet with someone from Toyota. He didn't specify the purpose of the discussions, but Smith had a firm grasp of GM's ultimate goal. If his corporation was going to regain its prosperity, it was going to have to learn how Toyota made such high-quality cars so inexpensively.

This was a humbling moment for the world's largest auto manufacturer. Only a few years before, Henry Ford II had canceled an almost-concluded agreement to buy engines from Honda when he learned of the deal. Ford said no car with his name on it would ever have a Japanese engine under the hood. For some people at GM, a joint-venture with Toyota would be even more unpalatable. It wasn't just engines GM was looking for. The colossus of Western auto manufacturing was going to ask Toyota—a company that had narrowly avoided bankruptcy thirty-one years before—to instruct it in the art of making cars.

14
THE CIRCLE COMPLETED

Seisi Kato, the chairman of Toyota Motor Sales Company, learned of GM's interest in talking with Toyota from a subordinate, who had met with a matchmaker between Japanese and American corporations. The matchmaker wasn't explicit about Roger Smith's intentions, so Kato was unclear about what would transpire in the meeting. GM was a massive and insular company, and Kato could only guess that Smith wanted to purchase components such as engines and transaxles from Toyota. GM wasn't buying any major components overseas, and Kato knew the company's small-car technology was lacking.

Kato's first job after graduating from college had been as an advertising clerk for GM of Japan. It wasn't an exalted position, but everything about it reflected the advantages of the Western world over the East. His salary was 50 percent higher than those of his classmates who had been lucky enough to find work in Depression-era Japan, and he had two days off a week, compared with the Japanese norm of one. He was a very happy young man, indeed, to land that position, and he moved into an expensive apartment, joined a tennis club, and savored a life of comfort that was as foreign to most Japanese in the 1930s as GM itself.

After he had been at GM a few years, Kato's friend and coworker, Shotaro Kamiya, left to go to work for the fledgling automotive department of Toyota Automatic Loom Works. Kamiya urged Kato to join him, but Kato resisted his friend's urgings. He finally agreed to at least visit the Toyoda plant to see what was going on. Accustomed as he was to the modern GM factory, where luxury cars were built on a smoothly flowing assembly line, the Toyoda operation could not have been more of a shock.

There was a great hurly-burly of disorder inside the dimly lit plant, and Kato was stunned by its primitiveness. Prototype vehicles were strewn about in disarray, as half a dozen models seemed to be under development at once. Welders' sparks flew as frames were constructed, and great bursts of steam poured from a foundry. The area was enveloped by an irregular din, as hundreds of men pounded hammers against metal.

Kato excused himself early that day, happy to escape the pandemonium. Nonetheless, something stuck with him when he returned to GM. It was a feeling of raw energy and purpose he sensed at the plant, something he had never experienced working for the Americans. He kept rolling the scene over excitedly in his mind, only to dismiss it each time with the realization of how reckless it would be to leave GM. Then a telegram arrived from Kamiya that pushed him over the edge. "Have some conviction," it read. "Join me!" Kato finally succumbed.

Seisi Kato remained with Toyota long after GM left Japan. He advanced through the ranks and eventually became chairman of its sales operation. Kato had fond memories of his years at GM. He had gotten his start in the business there, and even to an automobile man with a rival company, GM was still GM. Now he was going back.

Kato left Japan and traveled to the Meadowlands in East Rutherford, New Jersey, on December 20, 1981. Toyota was sponsoring a professional tennis tournament at the stadium, and it was Kato's job to award the trophy and a check to the winner. When the tournament ended, Kato made his presentation to tennis star Tracy Austin, and then he and his associates left to prepare for their appointment with Roger Smith the following day. The session would be held at the very pinnacle of international automotive prowess—the legendary fourteenth floor of the General Motors building in Detroit.

Kato began the meeting by telling Smith bluntly, "If GM is willing to buy engines and transaxles from Toyota, Toyota is willing to sell them." Rather than answering directly, however, Smith asked if he might bring an assistant into the meeting. When the man arrived and passed out his business cards, an important ritual in Japanese business meetings, everyone from Toyota was shocked. The new arrival was Jack Smith, no relation to Roger, GM's director of worldwide planning. Jack Smith's responsibilities included joint ventures.

The meeting proceeded in a halting and elliptical way, as both companies recognized the potential sensitivity of the subject. GM and Toyota were the first- and third-largest auto manufacturers in the world, and they held 50 percent of the U.S. market between them. When there was a hazy understanding that a cooperative venture was of interest to both parties, Seisi Kato returned to Japan to deliver a report.

Although the Toyota Motor Company and the Toyota Motor Sales Company were on the verge of being reunited as the Toyota Motor Corporation—with Kiichiro Toyoda's oldest son, Shoichiro, as president—the merger was not official yet. Therefore, manufacturing came under the purview of Eiji Toyoda, now chairman of Toyota Motor Company. A short time later, Eiji slipped quietly and expectantly into New York for a dinner meeting with Roger Smith.

Toyota was still under tremendous pressure to begin manufacturing in the United States, but Eiji saw the meeting with Smith as far more than a potential solution to an urgent problem. For most of the nearly five decades that Eiji had worked for Toyota, the company—the entire Japanese automobile industry—had stood in awe of General Motors. In the 1930s, when Eiji had spent part of a college summer test driving Kiichiro's first motorized bicycles, a single GM plant in Japan had been enough to intimidate every major Japanese corporation from entering the automobile business. Now, the chairmen of Toyota and GM were sitting down to dinner as colleagues.

Eiji had been mystified by the failure of the Ford talks, and he was anxious for the meeting with Smith to go well. Although speculation was rampant in the American press that Toyota had only gone through the motions with Ford, hoping to ward off U.S. import restrictions, that was not the case. Of all the American manufacturers, Toyota felt closest to Ford. Toyota had wanted a deal, and Eiji had been surprised and disappointed when the talks failed.

Eiji was delighted when Roger Smith proved to be charming and expansive during their meeting. The two men established an immediate rapport—one that would prove to be the single most important factor in ultimately making the deal work—and they formed the basis for an understanding that night. Toyota and GM would jointly produce a Corolla-class car at a closed GM plant in Fremont, California, where Toyota would implement their full production system.

The Fremont plant was an ideal location for Toyota, since it provided the most direct transportation route from Japan for parts. GM was happy to convert an unused facility into its contribution to the capitalization of the venture, and because the plant had been remodeled two years before, Toyota was glad to have such a modern facility.

Nonetheless, Eiji couldn't understand why GM had closed a plant that had just been refurbished.

In subsequent weeks, Eiji was to learn things about the UAW work force at Fremont that would confirm his worst apprehensions about American unions. There were eight hundred outstanding grievances and sixty contested firings at the plant when it closed, and it was reputed to have had the most undisciplined and uncooperative work force of any GM factory. Absenteeism had averaged 25 percent; there were problems with drugs, alcohol, and violence on the factory grounds; and confrontations between workers and management were commonplace. Were Toyota to rehire these people, Eiji was convinced, its carefully honed production system wouldn't have a chance.

Since Fremont was closed, however, the new company—called New United Motors Manufacturing, Inc. (NUMMI)—was under no obligation to rehire any of the more than five thousand laid-off workers. Given what Eiji knew about the workers, he reached a decision quickly. No former workers would be offered employment at the plant. The issue was considered moot, and Toyota went on to other matters—of which there were many.

The corporate cultures of GM and Toyota couldn't have been more dissimilar, and the negotiations to conclude the deal were long and arduous. Roger Smith and Eiji Toyoda may of been of like mind about the desirability of their enterprise, but many top people at each of their companies were not. Discussions got bogged down over fine points, and language problems complicated areas where there were existing agreements. At every major impasse, it was one of the two chairmen who got it back on track.

The two companies ultimately agreed that NUMMI would build a version of the Toyota Sprinter—a model of the Corolla not available in the United States—which would be sold to GM's Chevrolet division. Toyota would supply the engines and transaxles, with other parts being contracted from Toyota and GM divisions, as well as from outside subcontractors, on the basis of bids. Quality of workmanship, as well as price, would be considered in selecting suppliers.

Toyota would be paid a royalty for the design of its car and, under a cost-plus pricing arrangement, half the profits when NUMMI cars were sold to Chevrolet. To decrease the likelihood of antitrust action, the life of the new company would be limited to twelve years, with no more than 250,000 cars a year being built for GM. The company could, however, build a car exclusively for sale to Toyota, with the production of Chevy's car being shifted to Japan to free up production space at Fremont if necessary.

After a year of negotiations on these and other issues, Eiji Toyota and Roger Smith met in the cafeteria of the Fremont plant on February 17, 1983, to sign a memorandum of understanding. Each company would own 50 percent of the venture, with Toyota supplying $100 million and GM supplying $11 million in cash plus the Fremont plant, which was valued at $89 million. An additional $350 million would be raised to build a stamping plant and install equipment. Toyota would run the plant and designate the chief executive—Tatsuro Toyoda, Kiichiro's second son—who would be given an unusual degree of autonomy so the Toyota production system could be fully implemented.

Although many hurdles had been cleared at this point, two massive ones remained. In recognition of that, the letter of intent specified either party could withdraw from the deal until it was approved by the Federal Trade Commission (FTC). The agreement was predicated upon the creation of an effective labor-relations structure for the plant within 120 days of signing.

The labor-relations situation Toyota wanted to create at NUMMI was the antithesis of the one that had existed at Fremont in its final GM days. Mistrust between management and workers had been so great then that each group had regarded the other as the enemy, with communications occurring only in grievance and bargaining sessions. When management wanted workers to stop sitting on trash cans in break areas, they soldered nails on top of the cans. When the workers wanted telephone booths installed in the plant, they made it a contract demand—one specifying the booths have ventilation fans. Management installed the booths but then refused to supply electricity for the fans, saying the contract didn't specify *working* fans.

This hostility ultimately carried over onto the final battlefield: the assembly line. Mass-production workers were meant to be human robots, repeating the same simple tasks endlessly, with maximum production volume their only purpose. The bosses designed every aspect of the laborers' work and disciplined them when they failed to perform it satisfactorily. Workers reacted by demanding exquisitely detailed, finite job descriptions in their contracts and by not showing up for work when they could afford it. On a scale of one to ten, with one being the worst, Fremont workers said their relationship with GM was a one.

The Fremont plant had a massive repair area for defective cars at the end of the assembly line. Some cars arrived there because that was how the system worked—keep the line moving, let the inspectors filter out the flaws. But some cars were built faulty by retaliating workers, who saw this as their only way to even the score. Workers noticing production machinery working incorrectly would remain silent, convinced they'd be blamed for causing the problem. All the while, defective cars kept piling up.

Eiji Toyoda thought his company had avoided these travails when he signed the memorandum with Roger Smith in February of 1983. NUMMI was going to hire a new work force, and if the workers wanted to unionize after the plant was operational, that was fine. By then the Toyota production system would be instituted, having escaped sabotage by old attitudes.

Eiji planned to implement all the symbols Toyota used to epitomize cooperation between workers and management in Japan. There would be no reserved parking places at Fremont, and only one cafeteria. Managers would be encouraged to forswear coats and ties for the same uniforms workers wore. There would be no private offices, except for the president, and he would share. All white-collar personnel would work in a large open area, and production managers would have desks on the factory floor.

Perhaps most important, there would be only five levels of managers—instead of the seven in most American plants—with fewer managers at each level. Toyota believed workers knew more about assembling cars than managers did, and most of the responsibility for operating the plant would be in the workers' hands.

Instead of having rigid job classifications, workers would be organized into five- to ten-man teams. Each team member would be trained in every job the team performed and would rotate among them. In addition to installing parts, they would perform their own maintenance, quality inspections, and machine setups. They would be expected to solve problems on the floor as they came up, while constantly looking for ways to perform their jobs more efficiently. If defects were spotted during production, they would stop the assembly line until the root cause was corrected.

Any illusions Eiji had about the ease of implementing this radically different system in a closed GM plant lasted for only a few days. Because Toyota was Japan's largest industrial corporation and the number one exporter of automobiles to the United States, the decision to hire a new work force didn't go unnoticed. Trade friction between the U.S. and Japan was high. The UAW—with numerous unemployed members—was about to hold a convention and elect a new president, and the union would be negotiating national contracts with the Big Three the following year. Whatever happened at NUMMI was going to set a lot of precedents, and many people wanted to influence what they were going to be.

As political pressure built in the following weeks, it became apparent that NUMMI was going to have to deal with the UAW in some way. To avoid having GM's other UAW contracts complicate negotiations at NUMMI, Toyota volunteered to handle labor negotiations, and GM concurred. GM also had some vested interest in seeing laid-off Fremont workers rehired, as those with ten years of seniority were guaranteed 50 percent of their wages until retirement if they remained unemployed.

Toyota retained former U.S. Secretary of Labor William Usery to represent the company, and he met with the UAW leadership to explain Toyota's position. The company's main concern was the implementation of its production system, and the unconventional labor relationship it would require. Douglas Fraser, the outgoing union president, had been outspoken about forcing Japanese manufacturers to build cars in the United States, and he thought the union should cooperate. With the American automobile industry in decline, Fraser believed NUMMI was an important opportunity for the UAW to demonstrate its workers could compete with those in Japan.

Fraser's successor, Owen Bieber, was less enthusiastic. Since NUMMI hadn't committed to rehiring Fremont workers, he saw no reason for an incoming UAW president to bless the plan. Moreover, NUMMI wanted to dismantle work rules that had been won in collective bargaining, which could taint the national negotiations that were on the horizon.

Usery thought it was important for NUMMI to make some kind of pledge to the union before the UAW convention in May, and he traveled to Japan to meet with Eiji Toyoda. Eiji was adamant about not accepting a blanket rehiring of the Fremont workers, as he was convinced that it would doom NUMMI. After some discussions, a compromise was agreed upon: NUMMI agreed only to use Fremont workers as the "primary source" for recruitment. Usery announced this at a press conference, and the convention passed without NUMMI becoming an issue.

But as Usery attempted to continue his talks with the union in June, he reached an impasse. Owen Bieber, having succeeded Douglas Fraser, toughened his position. He refused to engage in any further discussion on work rules until the union was assured of recognition. Since NUMMI was considered a new venture, however, the company couldn't recognize the union—it hadn't hired any workers for the union to represent.

Under normal circumstances, workers in a new company vote on union representation after they are on the job, but Owen Bieber wouldn't talk about work rules under those conditions. Yet, the only way for NUMMI to recognize the union before it opened was to declare itself a successor to GM at the plant. That meant assuming GM's Fremont work force and their contract, including the provision that workers be recalled strictly according to seniority. This was completely unacceptable to Toyota, which was determined to hire workers selectively.

A compromise was found when Toyota's outside counsel suggested NUMMI commit to hiring 50 percent plus one of its workers from the Fremont work force. The lawyers theorized this would give the company "limited" successorship obligations—enough to recognize the UAW, but not so much as to inherit GM's contract. The lawyers acknowledged they were walking a fine line, but they felt the legal doctrine on successorship was hazy enough to permit this. Eiji Toyoda decided to tempt fate, hoping the good habits of the new workers would sufficiently dilute the bad habits of the old ones, and agreed to the plan.

With NUMMI's agreement on the work force in place, Usery resumed negotiations on the specific terms of the contract. Little progress was made, however, as the union continued to press for a full rehiring of the former workers and for concessions on other issues. Toyota wanted its work rules to be accepted carte blanche, while the UAW wanted to negotiate them point by point. The UAW worried about NUMMI concessions affecting their national contracts; Toyota was concerned the union would sue to have national contract provisions applied to the NUMMI contract retroactively.

It was late summer of 1983 by this time, and GM was moving

forward with renovations and construction at Fremont, as well as arranging financing for the plant. Production equipment had been ordered and was being prepared for shipment, but it seemed as though the factory that was being created would never have a work force. The 120-day period for establishing an effective labor relations structure for the plant had already been extended once, and now that extension was about to expire.

After a series of brainstorming sessions, everyone agreed an alternative had to be found to completing a full collective bargaining agreement before the plant opened. Until cars were being made, no one could accurately predict what the unique requirements of the Toyota production system would be at Fremont. Rather than continuing the fruitless negotiations on fine points, NUMMI and the UAW agreed to construct a letter of agreement on the principles of the venture.

The document would formalize each party's willingness to create an innovative labor relations structure, one that minimized traditional adversarial roles and emphasized mutual trust and good faith between workers and management. A full collective bargaining agreement would be executed after the plant was operating—and after the UAW's national contracts were signed.

In contrast to the four hundred pages of a normal UAW contract, the letter of agreement ran fifteen double-spaced pages. It committed NUMMI to hiring the majority of its workers from the Fremont work force and to recognizing the UAW as their bargaining agent. UAW seniority would not be honored, but workers would be paid prevailing UAW wages. The letter also promised two things American assembly workers weren't used to: long-term job security and a voice in plant operations.

Workers would be laid off only in times of severe economic duress, and then only after all NUMMI officers and managers had taken pay cuts and after all possible subcontract work had been brought in-house. Management would share information about the outlook for the plant with the workers, thus making them less vulnerable to surprise layoffs. In return for job security, workers had to give up the right to strike, accept severe penalties for excessive absenteeism, and agree to reduce the normal one hundred auto-plant job classifications to four.

Although NUMMI was only required to hire 50 percent plus one of its workers from the Fremont work force—few of whom had found better paying jobs—its negotiators let the union know informally that it would exceed the quota if the first people hired adapted well. As a show of good faith, the UAW agreed to revoke the charter of the old union local in Fremont, signifying that those who returned to the plant were employees of a new venture and members of a new local. A group of dissidents at the old local filed suit against the loss of their charter and against NUMMI's letter of intent, but both cases were dismissed.

NUMMI's labor problems were no sooner resolved than a crisis developed in the FTC investigation. The FTC had been looking into the high-profile case since spring of 1983, holding four months of hearings to examine the basic issues in the case. Those who favored the joint venture testified that, with Japanese manufacturing efficiency having virtually priced the Big Three out of the small car market, NUMMI would allow GM to learn how to produce cars more economically, thus lowering car prices for American consumers. Those opposed to the venture—most vocally, Chrysler chairman Lee Iacocca—insisted that any cooperation between Toyota and GM would drive other companies out of business and thus raise car prices for consumers through reduced competition.

Fifteen years earlier, NUMMI never would have won FTC approval. Any horizontal merger in a concentrated industry was challenged then, and the FTC was known in business circles as the "government's nanny." Those actions occurred, however, when the primary competition for American corporations was other domestic companies. With the coming of increased global competition, and the advent of Republican administrations, the FTC's criteria changed. The number of antitrust filings diminished as new administrations filled openings in the agency with their appointees.

Toyota's outside counsel—Arent, Fox, Kintner, Plotkin, and Kahn, a prominent Washington, D.C., firm whose partners included a former FTC chairman—had been confident from the beginning that, with time and production-volume limitations, NUMMI would win FTC approval. The events of the agency's investigation supported this view, until a major impasse developed in August. Toyota had supplied the FTC with more than twenty-five thousand documents for its review, deleting from them what the company believed was proprietary cost and pricing information. Now, the FTC was demanding that Toyota supply the deleted information, and Toyota refused to comply.

Toyota was unwilling to supply this information because the

company was certain its competitors and other government agencies would attempt to obtain the data and use it for their own purposes. Chrysler had been relentless in its opposition to the NUMMI joint venture and was likely to challenge a favorable FTC ruling in court. As part of such a suit, Chrysler could attempt to subpoena the documents Toyota had filed with the FTC. If this subpoena was granted, one of Toyota's chief competitors would be given access to the company's most confidential financial data.

As for government agencies, Japanese auto makers had already been burned by what they believed was an improper sharing of confidential information among bureaucrats. In 1975, Japanese auto manufacturers had been required to submit cost and pricing information to the U.S. government, data that was to be used only in a dumping investigation. Although the dumping charges were dismissed, the Internal Revenue Service soon began investigating the U.S. tax returns of Japanese auto makers, a sequence of events the manufacturers thought more than coincidental.

The stalemate over the data lasted for three months, and once again the entire joint venture was at stake. Construction continued at the Fremont plant, but everything else came to a standstill. The deadlock had been widely reported in the media, and that guaranteed the FTC would not alter its stand. Roger Smith called Toyota's outside counsel personally and urged them to find a compromise. After extended discussions, one was forged.

Toyota executives would fly in from Japan with the data in November, placing it in a depository in the offices of their outside counsel. The FTC would examine the information there, but would not take physical possession of it. Commission staff members were free to take notes on some matters but not on others. In return, Toyota agreed to waive the normal twenty-day time limit for reaching a decision on the case after the final documents were supplied.

On December 1, 1983, FTC staff members, having gone so far as to visit Toyota and GM plants to compare their production systems, recommended approval of the joint venture, saying its alleged anticompetitive effects were too uncertain to sustain a legal case. The only stipulations were a twelve-year life span and 250,000-vehicle annual production limit, and Toyota and GM were to restrict, and keep logs of, communications regarding product planning, pricing, and marketing.

Three weeks later, NUMMI was approved by the commissioners of the FTC by a three to two vote. The commissioners said that if GM could learn from Japanese producers how to build significantly lower-priced cars, and then implemented those lower-cost methods at its other plants, a more efficient, more competitive U.S. automobile industry would result. After a sixty-day public comment period, during which Chrysler filed a suit against the venture that it would later withdraw, the order took effect on April 11, 1984.

That evening, Eiji Toyoda and Roger Smith celebrated at a dinner held in Nagoya, outside Toyota City. After the meal and the speeches, the two chairmen exchanged symbolic gifts. GM's present to Eiji was sleek, modern, and high tech—a miniature of an ultramodern automobile sculpture that is installed outside the company's technical center. Toyota's offering was traditional and restrained—a delicate paper sculpture of a carp, the symbol of good fortune in Japan, that had been meticulous crafted by a native artist using ancestral techniques.

While the chairmen of Toyota and GM were celebrating in Japan, NUMMI's new labor-relations director, Bill Childs, was also making a ceremonial visit. Childs, who had followed in his father's footsteps as a union organizer before switching over to management, was on a mission that required immense tact. He was paying a courtesy call at Fremont's new UAW local, which for all intents and purposes was Fremont's old union local with a new charter, to find out if, after all the law suits and bad feelings, they couldn't be friends. With NUMMI's selective hiring policy, Childs couldn't promise anyone a job, so it would be quite a test of his charms.

Childs met with the members of the local's shop committee, who had been known for their obstreperousness under GM, and asked for their help. NUMMI was about to mail out applications, and Childs said he wanted to use the union's eligibility list rather than GM's. When the union said they'd supply one, Childs asked if they'd like to stuff some envelopes, since only a skeleton crew had been hired at NUMMI. The union people agreed again.

When the shop committee saw NUMMI's six-page applications, and the letters saying applicants would have to attend a four-day pre-employment workshops consisting of interviews, job simulations, and detailed discussions of the plant's philosophy and objectives, they weren't pleased. The word around the union hall was that Toyota worked its people to death, and now it looked like that was going to start before anyone was on the payroll.

Childs told the union people about the Toyota production system, and how much better they'd like it, as they sent out seven thousand applications. Nobody from the UAW really believed him. Still, some of them had been out of work for a long time, and many were middle-aged. Jobs with auto-industry wages were tough to find, so they went along with the talk, not taking it too seriously.

The first indication the union had that things might indeed be different was when Childs, without saying too much about it to higher management, made the members of the formerly militant shop committee the assembly operation's first employees. Then, as 3,500 applications were received, Childs asked the UAW to become a partner in the hiring process. Only 1,000 employees were needed for the start-up in October, with another 1,500 to be added when the plant went to two shifts in 1985, so there were a lot of decisions to be made.

Childs, other NUMMI managers, and UAW personnel examined the work histories of all former GM employees from Fremont who applied for jobs, seeking to reach a consensus on which would be good workers. People with records of habitual substance abuse or absenteeism were eliminated, but NUMMI bit the bullet on a lot of people it considered marginal. Bruce Lee, the director of the union's western district, had repeatedly shown good faith during NUMMI's preliminary talks with the UAW, and he argued forcefully for almost two hundred people he believed in. Everyone Lee spoke up for was hired.

Most of the early hires were people who would be training new employees and acting as team leaders once the assembly line started, and they were sent to Japan for training in the Toyota production system. NUMMI's managers held their collective breath as they dispatched diehard, opinionated, aggressive American union men—and women, blacks, and Hispanics—to homogeneous Toyota City, where one's company was considered to be almost family and everyone was respectful toward family members—particularly patriarchs.

The Americans went expecting the work pace on the assembly lines to be furious, but it proved to be steady rather than fast. Since a principle tenet of the Toyota system was the elimination of waste, there was no lost motion during assembly and little idle time. Workers were active fifty-six minutes an hour, rather than the American assembly plant norm of thirty-five. And the men on the assembly line were young, since Japan's diminished distinctions between blue- and white-collar workers made it easier for assembly workers to move on to other jobs in the company as they aged.

But the thing that struck the Americans most was how important the workers seemed to be to the company and to the assembly process. The plants weren't overgrown with robots and automation as they had expected. In fact, there were noticeably fewer robots than at the most modern U.S. plants. It was the workers who made the plants so efficient, and Toyota recognized that and respected it. Foremen weren't people who yelled at their workers as if they were children. Instead, foremen were called group leaders, and they listened to their workers and solicited their opinions.

As the Americans worked on the assembly line in Japan, they discovered that total quality control added an important element to the job satisfaction of production work. Rather than being just another cog in a machine, workers were required to think and to respond to the work they were doing. There was no getting around that the work was hard. But the Americans started feeling better about the work they did, and they came back to the United States enthusiastic about their new jobs.

To everyone's surprise, former Fremont workers were 90 percent of the work force when NUMMI started limited production in October. There was still a bit of tension in the air, as workers and management each let down their guard gradually. Problems developed, as everyone knew they would, but far fewer than expected. As production increased, new employees were added, with the proportion of former workers remaining high.

NUMMI workers responded particularly well to being given responsibilities that were unheard of at a U.S. plant. They were assigned to test the paint and steel that arrived, and when it was unsatisfactory, they discussed the problem with the suppliers. Often, this resulted in UAW personnel discussing production quality and techniques with workers from outside unions. When components proved difficult to install, engineers visited the workers to discuss design changes. Welders discovered how much more efficient it was for them to change their own welding tips, instead of having maintenance personnel do it, as was the practice at GM plants, because the welders were better judges of when the tips needed changing.

People were happy with their jobs, and NUMMI was pleased with the workers' performance, so rehiring former workers ceased being an issue. Former workers who weren't rehired had the right of appeal all the way to arbitration, and Dennis Cuneo, NUMMI's chief legal counsel, had expected to be involved in three to five hundred of those cases. Instead, because of mutual cooperation between the UAW and the company, there were only four.

Cuneo was pleased with the lack of legal work. As a former associate with Toyota's outside counsel, he had been involved with NUMMI almost since its inception. When the joint venture looked like it was going to be approved and Toyota had asked him to join NUMMI's board, he jumped at the chance. He was only thirty-three years old, but he was tired of shuffling papers and of never being sure just what it was he was accomplishing. The idea of building cars in an unprecedented international joint venture of companies and workers excited him tremendously.

Cuneo learned a good deal in his early days at NUMMI, as did everyone—including Toyota. The Fremont work force proved itself to be both skilled and adaptable. The workers learned new techniques quickly, and although production efficiency lagged slightly behind Japan, quality didn't. Defects averaged twelve per car during start-up, but dropped to one per car within a year. Worker absenteeism, which had averaged 25 percent under GM, hovered around 2 percent.

The Toyota production system had survived its trans-Pacific voyage. Within months, Eiji Toyoda began assembling a team to oversee the creation of a new plant in Kentucky. It would be the company's first independent American venture. Eiji was also anxiously awaiting a report from twenty of his top men who were currently in the United States on a special mission—studying the potential market for a Toyota luxury car.

15
PERCEPTIONS

The luxury-car project team that arrived in Los Angeles in May of 1985 was headed by Shoji Jimbo, its chief engineer, with the remaining nineteen members split between designers and engineers. Although there had been a lot of guarded discussion of the project in Japan over the previous two years, everyone knew this trip would have to yield the concept of the car they would create, and they were anxious. Toyota had never developed a car primarily for the American market, nor had it built a serious luxury sedan, and the opportunities for errors seemed infinite. In case the team needed a further reminder of how important this car was to Eiji Toyoda, the project had been dubbed "F-1" for "flagship."

John Koenig, Toyota's U.S. product-planning chief, and other Toyota officials from the California office had planned a one-month whirlwind tour of the most affluent areas of the country for the F-1 team, and they launched it by taking them to the best restaurants in L.A. The Americans wanted to be hospitable while also beginning their work of exposing the team to the lifestyles of luxury-car buyers. It was cushy duty, but these evenings always commenced with a decidedly unglamorous chore.

Rather than proceeding directly into the restaurant when they arrived, the group first convened in the parking lot. Expensive cars were as common as palm trees at upscale L.A. restaurants, and this was an important study opportunity. The point wasn't to examine the cars, however. It was to observe the behavior of the people who parked them.

The valets at chic restaurants are important arbitrators of automotive status in L.A. The parking spaces near the door, and those in prominent view of the street, are used to promote the restaurant by displaying the discriminating tastes of its clientele. Exotic sports cars and customized luxury vehicles are always the first to be wheeled into those berths. As they observed the selection process, the members of the F-1 team shook their heads in amazement. Otherwise respectable people in L.A. drove cars that would have branded them as members of the underworld in Japan!

One of the most familiar aphorisms of Japanese life is "The nail that sticks up gets hammered down." Japanese culture values humility and group identity, and it is expected those qualities will be reflected in all areas of public life. More than half the automobiles sold in Japan are painted white, a color that keeps a clean appearance and doesn't attract attention. Coming from this background, members of the F-1 team who had not visited the United States before had epiphanies, while standing in the parking lots of Los Angeles restaurants, about exactly how alien American culture was.

In the coming days, the team witnessed personalized cars being created when they visited a Cadillac dealership in suburban L.A. The dealer had a large facility on his grounds where new Cadillacs were modified in any of dozens of ways to distinguish them from all the other cars on the road. It was while walking around this dealership that the team gained another insight into the ways of some luxury-car buyers.

A brand new Cadillac rolled in on the back of a tow truck, its front end badly smashed. The general manager of the dealership, who had agreed to speak to the team about the luxury-car business, saw this as a good opportunity to provide instruction on the type of service luxury-car owners expected.

The owner of the car, the general manager said, had had an accident on his way home from picking up his new car. Although the car was heavily damaged, no one was hurt. The owner had exchanged paperwork with the other driver, then called his salesman at the dealership. The owner's instructions were simple. He wanted the dealership to "take care of the situation." The salesman looked out on his lot, saw a car that was similar to the one the man had purchased, and said that he would have it sent over to the man's home that afternoon.

An engineer from the F-1 team asked if the dealership always gave new vehicles to customers with cars in for repair. "Oh, no," the dealer said, "we aren't lending the car to the man. It's a replacement for his old car. We'll have his first car repaired, deal with the insurance company, then put it on the lot as a used car. We'll bill the customer for whatever the costs are. He doesn't care about the money. He just didn't want to be driving around in a car that has been damaged."

The team scoured Beverly Hills, Laguna Beach, Palos Verdes, and other wealthy areas in Southern California, touring people's homes, visiting exclusive shops, and stopping by country clubs. Every merchant who dealt with upscale shoppers told the team the same thing: superb service was a given in their businesses. Given the spotty history of customer satisfaction in the automotive service industry, the team recognized that their dealers would have to make extraordinary efforts in this area.

Then it was off to San Francisco, Denver, Chicago, New York, Miami, and Houston for more of the same. Everywhere they went, seeking to comprehend the needs of a defined market, the team found different kinds of wealth, and varying tastes. The United States was as divergent as Japan was consonant. Yet the whole idea of this project was to create a car based on what customers wanted, rather than what engineers thought they should have. How was the team going to build such an automobile when the lifestyles of affluent consumers digressed so markedly? The answer was found in focus groups.

In every city, the team gathered behind mirrored, one-way glass in a conference room, while a hired moderator posed a series of questions to people who owned, or wanted to own, luxury cars. The consumers, who did not know that Toyota was sponsoring the sessions, were asked what attributes made them feel a car was comfortable, luxurious, and prestigious. They were asked about the cars they owned, why they bought them, and what they might buy next. The Japanese engineers sometimes had trouble following when people talked too fast or used expressions they weren't familiar with, but a number of unassailable truths came through.

Domestic luxury-car owners tended to be older and slightly less educated than import buyers, and their automotive tastes had been set when Cadillacs and Lincolns were American icons of what upscale cars were supposed to be. This group, which Toyota had never considered a primary market, wanted a car with a smooth ride and lots of creature comforts. They also expressed a strong preference for buying domestic products.

The owners of German cars perceived their vehicles as being luxurious because of their engineering, but didn't find them especially comfortable. They had the sense, reinforced by the advertising for these cars, that they were supposed to suffer a bit for their hyperengineering, and many of them wished this weren't so. The F-1 team duly noted that their car should have engineering plus comfort.

Among owners of German cars, those with BMWs tended to be younger and earlier in their careers, and they wanted to make a statement with their vehicles. They said they would be hesitant about buying a new brand of luxury car until it was on the market a few years and had acquired a reputation as a prestige vehicle.

The Mercedes owners were more established. They had usually owned luxury cars before their current one, and they weren't as interested in having a car confer status on them. They were also more value oriented, and they expressed repeated concerns about high maintenance and repair costs which, when combined with the escalating price of the cars themselves, were making them hesitant about buying another Mercedes.

This information confirmed data the team received from psychologists and anthropologists who had been hired to study how people made decisions in the process of buying a luxury car. American buyers of expensive European cars, the social scientists reported, loved their extravagant cars and felt great about owning them. But every time they had to take them to a dealer's shop, it was painful. The owners felt they were being taken because of the high maintenance and repair costs. When infatuated owners of these cars had them repaired, the social scientists said, they suffered from "narcissistic injury."

This was delightful news to Shoji Jimbo, the chief engineer of the F-1 one team. He had thought all along that the Europeans had left themselves vulnerable on pricing. But one constant refrain from the focus group members underscored how difficult it would be for Toyota to seize on that market opportunity. When asked if they would buy a Japanese luxury car, many consumers said they couldn't even understand the concept of a Japanese luxury car. They thought the term was an oxymoron.

Luxury-car buyers, and especially women, said the Japanese made good-quality economy cars, but they didn't think Japanese cars were as safe as a luxury car should be. This belief was based on the Japanese having entered the American market with small cars, and on the vague notion that somehow the steel in Japanese cars wasn't quite as thick as the metal in those big German cars.

As chief engineer Jimbo heard this conviction repeated around the country, he was reminded of one of his first stops of the tour, a BMW dealership in California. The dealer had said he was familiar with Toyota's top-of-the-line Cressida, and he thought its engineering was equal to that in his BMWs. The problem, the man said, would be getting consumers to believe it. To succeed, Toyota would have to build an authentic luxury car and then get motorists to accept the *idea* of it.

The F-1 team found some encouragement in the sales figures of the hottest new entry in the luxury field, the Audi 5000. Audi had been only a minor player in the American market until 1983. The company introduced a new line of cars then and sold seventy-two thousand of them, doubling its U.S. sales in a single year. The model 5000-S accounted for two-thirds of those units, and it was being acclaimed as a ground-breaking luxury car. It was a sleek, with aerodynamic styling and great handling. *Car and Driver* magazine immediately named it one of the ten best cars in the world, and consumers in Toyota's focus groups said that, in the twenty-thousand-dollar price bracket, it was perceived as being a great value.

Audi had flourished by producing the right car at the right time, yet no one could assess how big a role the company's German heritage had played in consumer acceptance. Nonetheless, chief engineer Jimbo instructed his men to pay careful attention to the Audi 5000-S as they drove competing cars in the United States and again when they began their teardown inspections of these cars back home.

The team had already formed some basic concepts for their car, based upon their experiences in the United States. The engineers wanted a vehicle that had good performance and handling but also had a comfortable ride. They thought, and the people in the focus groups concurred, that the German cars were too stiff and starchy—too Teutonic. The American luxury cars, however, put too much emphasis on comfort, creating the sensation of sitting in a lounge chair instead of driving a car. They wanted to come in between these two extremes.

The designers wanted a car with fresh styling, but with all the talk of image and acceptability, they knew it would also have to echo styling cues from existing luxury cars. When people saw this new car being driven down the street, they would have to recognize it instantly as a luxury vehicle, even if they weren't able to specify the manufacturer.

The engineers returned to Japan in July to begin their work, while the designers moved into a house overlooking the Pacific in Laguna

Beach, a town filled with art galleries south of L.A. Over the next two months, the designers would do their first preliminary sketches and build their first one-fifth-scale clay models. Although no one talked about it, the pressure to produce had just increased markedly.

When chief engineer Jimbo returned to Japan, he inspected the first tangible fruits of the project, a test car for trying out components. The test car, called a mule, was a Cressida that had been enlarged to reflect the base specifications of the project car. Although the vehicle looked like the patched-together machine it was, its engine—a new, aluminum V-8—was what interested everyone most.

Work had started on the engine shortly after the feasibility study for the car was approved by Toyota's board in 1983. If the car was to be a display of Toyota's engineering prowess, its engine would be the most critical test and Jimbo wanted to give the engine team as much development time as possible. Everyone assumed the engine would be an offshoot of the high-performance four- and six-cylinder engines the company had developed a few years before, but that was not to be. Jimbo said the car had to have a new, extremely high-tech V-8.

Conventional wisdom was that "V" configuration engines—where the cylinders were mounted on offset banks—produced the smoothest operation. That was no longer true at Toyota. The engineers believed their "in-line" engines, with the cylinders in a single row, were inherently smoother and quieter—while also being cheaper to produce. Given this, the staff had assumed the luxury car would have a large, in-line, six-cylinder engine—as most of the European luxury cars did.

Jimbo had overruled them, saying a V8, while more difficult to tame and more expensive to build, was mandatory for the car's credentials. He knew Toyota would get only one shot at being judged a builder of prestigious cars, and he wasn't going to jeopardize it by cutting corners on the most important component. The engine of a car is like the sauce in classic French cooking—it separates the excellent from the merely good.

Toyota's first hurdle was to convince the automotive community it was building a great car. That would require innovative engineering, since Mercedes had made this a hallmark of the category. Word would leak out in the industry about various components of the car as it was in preproduction, and initial opinions would be formed. Then the company would have to convince automotive journalists, who would be the first outsiders to drive the car, that Toyota had accomplished what it had set out to do. If the company scrimped on something as elementary as the engine, all of the stories would make prominent mention of how disappointing it was, regardless of how superb the rest of the car was.

The engine Toyota created was indeed high-tech: all-aluminum construction, four overhead camshafts, and four valves per cylinder. The four-liter engine was designed to produce 250 horsepower, enough to power a nearly two-ton car to a cruising speed of 150 mph. While it was unlikely many motorists outside of Germany, where the autobahns have no speed limit, would ever drive the car that fast, it was imperative for the car's image to have that capability.

The European manufacturers had long ago established a basic tenet in the luxury car business: there must be a direct correlation between a vehicle's top cruising speed and its price. This belief was so firmly entrenched that luxury cars at the Frankfurt Auto Show, where the new Toyota would have to appear one day, were always displayed with their maximum cruising speeds posted adjacent to their prices.

As Toyota had learned in the late 1970s, there was some merit in using top cruising speed—as opposed to simply top speed—as a measure of a car's capabilities. Toyota introduced a high-powered car called the Soarer in Japan in 1979, thinking it had developed a true high-speed vehicle. With no suitable place to test the car at speed in Japan, one was sent to Germany for a trial on the autobahn. The car reached 100 mph easily enough, but beyond that its handling deteriorated so badly the test drivers had to back off. Even though the engine had ample power left, the rest of the car simply wasn't capable of utilizing it.

To ensure they had gotten the basic components of the car right this time, Toyota shipped the Cressida mule to Germany in May of 1986, after it had passed its initial testing in Japan. Under the auspices of its new chief engineer, Ichiro Suzuki, the car performed well in its speed tests, but flunked on another vital, but contradictory, measure. The fuel economy averaged only 20.5 mpg.

When Ichiro Suzuki, a body-structure specialist, became chief engineer of the F-1 project, after Shoji Jimbo joined Toyota's board, Suzuki and his team defined several new goals for the car. It would have a cruising speed of 150 mph, but it would also avoid the U.S. gas-guzzler tax, which meant average fuel economy of at least 22.5 mpg. Given the mule's performance in Germany, a 10 percent improvement in fuel economy was going to have to be found, without any loss in performance.

Knowing what Eiji's aspirations were for this car, Ichiro Suzuki recognized the fuel-economy-versus-performance incongruity was only the first of many such puzzles he would have to unravel. He termed this process *naokatsu*, or not making a single compromise. The car would have high performance yet good fuel economy, be elegantly styled yet aerodynamic, and quiet yet lightweight.

Suzuki intended to meet these criteria by employing source countermeasures. Just as *kaizen* and total quality control meant eliminating inefficiency and defects at their origins, source countermeasures meant eradicating unacceptable performance by eliminating design flaws. Fuel economy was governed by engine efficiency, vehicle weight, and body aerodynamics. If the fuel mileage was too low, the deficiencies in each of those three areas would have to be identified and removed.

Suzuki put the car on a weight-reduction plan, ordering that any design change that added more than a quarter of an ounce had to be approved by him. The engine group tore motors apart in search of any minor inefficiency that could be found, while the body group worked on the aerodynamics. When they couldn't make the body any slipperier, they went underneath it. They improved air flow under the car by flattening the floor pan and adding fairings to the bottom of the engine, muffler, and rear suspension. Ultimately, they achieved a coefficient of drag of .29, thought to be an industry record for a passenger sedan, and improved fuel economy to 23 mpg.

As the work progressed and the first hundreds of millions of dollars were being poured into the development of the ultimate Toyota, Eiji Toyoda reflected on what he had unleashed. It was August of 1986, and the second most important decision of the project, after initiating it in the first place, was at hand. The F-1 advance team had reported, after their research trip to the United States, that luxury-car buyers said they would feel uncomfortable purchasing so expensive a vehicle in a showroom where people were also buying trucks. If they shopped at clothing boutiques that served wine and hors d'oeuvres, they said, they didn't want to transact a luxury-car purchase in the middle of a Toyotathon.

The costs of starting a separate dealer network to sell the new car would be huge, and Toyota couldn't start a second channel in the United States with only one car. There would have to be two cars at the minimum, and if the second car weren't as well made as the first, it could destroy the whole project. Things were getting expensive and complicated, and the risk factor was going through the roof.

As Eiji weighed the decision, he thought about the fact that it was August. August had traditionally been a lucky month for the company. Toyota Motor Company had been incorporated in August; its first big plant, Motomachi, was opened in August; and its first cars were exported to the United States in August. All of this was fortuitous, and Eiji thought he understood about luck.

Kiichiro Toyoda had been the unlucky one. His greatest dream was to build passenger cars, but he was foiled at every turn. He agreed to build trucks to finance his cars, then had his factory taken over by the military. After the war, there was neither the money nor the materials to build cars, and he was forced to resign. When the company was finally assured of getting cars into production, he died suddenly.

Eiji believed he was the lucky Toyoda. He had been able to accomplish everything Kiichiro had set out to do. Toyota was an international conglomerate, the third largest auto manufacturer in the world. The company had gotten so big that Eiji had begun talking with Kiichiro's son, Shoichiro, about guarding against "large-corporation disease" setting in. Eiji was concerned Toyota would become so swollen and bureaucratic it would forget its roots and purpose. Thinking about these things, Eiji knew what he had to do—what Kiichiro would have done. A new dealer network would be created in the United States.

Most of the basic development work on the F-1 project was done in Japan. That was where the engineers, designers, and suppliers were, and it was where the car would be built. But now, three years into the project, and three years before the car was to go on sale, it was time to call on the special expertise of the people who knew the American market firsthand. So in October of 1986 key members of the American staff gathered in their suburban Los Angeles headquarters to perform an important but enjoyable task. They had been given the assignment of selecting the name for the new car.

The company had hired Lippincott & Margulies, a New York image consulting firm, to supply a list of potential names. From the huge list the company supplied, Toyota was allowed to select ten, which they would then own. People scanned the list, tossing out possibilities, while trying to imagine the impact these computer-derived words might have on the ears of potential buyers.

As the meeting progressed, the list gradually narrowed. Chaparel, Calibre, Vectre, and Verone all got some votes, as did Alexis. Alexis was the only name everyone could almost agree on, but it sounded more like a person than a car. With some additional discussion, this name was altered to Lexus. Everyone thought that would fit the car they had been imagining, even if they hadn't seen it. It was like naming a baby before birth—one which, by the time it came into the world, would have more than a billion dollars, and a lot of people's futures, riding on it.

The American staff on the project were enormously relieved when they saw the first full-scale clay model of the Lexus in Japan in February of 1987. Just as chief engineer Suzuki had promised, the car was sleek yet had presence, and it was modern with classic overtones. Since they had seen the first one-fifth scale models in Laguna Beach in 1985, eighteen additional models had been developed—and rejected—as the designers' work was subjected to top management critiques every two months. The result was a car the Americans knew they could sell.

As they studied the model and examined components being mocked up for the car, the Americans offered their own opinions. J. Davis Illingworth, the forty-four-year-old corporate manager of the project in the United States, was especially opposed to the touch-sensitive TV screen being considered to control the car's interior accessories. High-tech components were a big selling point in Japan, but Illingworth said the TV screen, which would work like an automatic-teller-machine screen to control the air-conditioning and other systems, was out of character for the car.

It addition to seeming gimmicky, Illingworth thought the screen was too complex. The goal was to make the interior as simple and clean as possible. He wanted large, readily identifiable knobs on all the controls so drivers would be able to work them quickly and with a minimum of attention.

Illingworth argued that previously Toyota had been known for vehicle quality, which really meant product reliability. With this car, he thought the company should emphasize perceptual quality, which came from the sensual feedbacks a driver got while operating the car. Everything about the car had to feel precise, particularly in the interior. He didn't think a TV screen would enhance that image, and Toyota agreed. The TV screen was scrapped.

The first running prototype of the Lexus arrived in California in August. The car had no identifying badges on it, and the body was not in final form, so staff members were able to drive it around Southern California without fear of giving anything away. The car was terrific to drive—silky smooth and incredibly quiet, but with strong performance.

Word had been filtering into Los Angeles for months about how Eiji Toyoda had been pushing the company's normally obsessive concern with quality to new heights. Four hundred and fifty prototypes— three times the normal number—were to be built and tested, at $250,000 per hand built edition. Testing would be conducted in Japan, the United States, Europe, Saudi Arabia, and Australia. Then after every prototype and every test, deficiencies would be found that would have to be eliminated at their source.

Old hands at the L.A. office were used to this kind of talk around the company. But at different points along the development path each of them came to understand that Eiji had been deadly serious when he had issued his challenge to build a car that was better than the best in the world. That recognition came for many when they drove the car for the first time. Even two years ahead of production, it was that good. But for John Koenig, it happened when he went to Japan to perform the prosaic task of inspecting paint.

Koenig, the U.S. product-planning chief who had longed for an upscale car to sell to his baby-boom peers, routinely traveled to Japan to scrutinize interior and exterior colors and trim when a new model was coming to the States. Normally, if twelve colors were to be offered, eight would already be in the product line and four would be new. Toyota, mindful of its frugal heritage, would have the four new colors painted on two prototypes, with the two colors on each car divided down the middle. However, for the thirteen Lexus colors under consideration, of which nine would be used, Koenig was presented with thirteen fully painted prototypes.

Koenig decided then that the Lexus was going to be a serious contender, even though its competition had multiplied in the three years since he had first made his pitch for the car in Japan. Honda had introduced its near-luxury Acura line in 1986, and Nissan had announced it would be competing head-to-head with Toyota with a new car called Infiniti.

* * *

Although he wasn't a currency broker, the yen-to-dollar exchange rate played heavily on Scott Gilbert's mind in early 1988. Gilbert was the account director for Lexus at Team One Advertising, a subsidiary that Toyota's ad agency, Saatchi & Saatchi, had spun off to launch the new line. A dollar had bought 260 yen during the early planning for the car in 1985. Since then, the exchange rate had been cut in half, adding a projected ten thousand dollars to the car's price.

It wouldn't have been easy getting people to buy a twenty-five-thousand-dollar unknown car. It wasn't like buying a can of soda. It was a big investment with a lot of risks. Would the car hold up? Would the dealer go out of business? With the price of the car now likely to be thirty-five thousand dollars, it became that much more difficult. Then there was the image problem.

Gilbert's realized his biggest challenge was going to be making it socially acceptable for people to buy this car, while making the purchase seem risk free. He knew Lexus could always sell cars to the small segment of the market composed of people who liked to try new things. But that was only ten thousand cars. He had to sell sixty to eighty thousand cars. That would require name recognition and credibility, built through an advertising campaign that ensured no Lexus owner would ever be asked, "What the hell is that thing?"

Gilbert was a young guy in his thirties, and, like most of the people working on the Lexus account, he had grown up in the sixties. Having come of age in that era back East, he thought of his generation as people who loved nothing so much as questioning authority, and he believed that insight gave him an edge in finding acceptance for the Lexus in a market segment dominated by two formidable competitors: Mercedes and BMW.

The target Lexus buyer was a forty-three-year-old male who earned over one hundred thousand dollars. Despite that hefty income, Gilbert thought there might be enough of the counterculture left in that guy to make him resent the competition's take-it-or-leave-it pricing and aloof image. During the sixties, people had occupied the offices of university presidents over that kind of attitude.

Gilbert had also gotten an important idea for shaping the antiauthoritarian campaign from Dave Illingworth, the Lexus U.S. corporate manager. One of the most fundamental principles of the Lexus project, he had said, was "underpromise and overdeliver." Gilbert thought underpromising and overdelivering was like buying *Rolling Stone* magazine to read about music and then finding lots of great general-interest articles in it. The magazine had sold a lot of subscriptions that way.

Gilbert thought these were solid concepts to plan a campaign around, but first he had to build some curiosity about this car. He had already taken the first steps in that direction, initiating a long, slow tease that would lead up to introduction day.

Team One had set up booths at the New York, Chicago, and Los Angeles auto shows, with displays showing only the new aluminum engine and a vague artist's rendition of the car. People entering the display were handed a card offering additional information about Lexus in exchange for their opinion of the project; their address, age, and income; and the brand name of their present car.

The fifteen thousand names this produced were combined with rented lists of owners of competing cars—Toyota had declared its list of Cressida owners off-limits—to create an eight-hundred-thousand-name mailing list. More evocative drawings of the car went out to these people, along with a reply card they could use to request additional information.

The sixty-five thousand people who responded to the mailing would receive a series of envelopes over the coming months. Each would reveal a bit more of the car, allowing recipients to feel the vehicle was developing before their eyes. The same package went to people who responded to ads in automotive magazines. In addition, the twenty-three thousand people who said they wanted to take a test drive and provided their telephone numbers would eventually receive videos of the car.

While Scott Gilbert was doing his best to expose people to impressionistic drawings of the flagship Lexus car, to be called the LS400, Chris Hostetter was equally determined to keep a final prototype of it hidden. The problem was, however, that Hostetter was caught in traffic in lower Manhattan, in broad daylight, with an LS400 that lacked only its badges. As people in all directions seemed to stare at the car, Hostetter's only defense was hundreds of dollars in cash in his pocket, which he hoped to use to buy the film of anyone he saw pointing a camera at it.

Hostetter, Toyota's U.S. car product-planning manager, was accompanying an entourage of Japanese engineers on a cross-country road test of the LS400. During their U.S. market research trip in 1985, the

F-1 team had driven competitors' cars through northern New Jersey. Finding the roads there filled with potholes, the team had decided to develop an optional air-suspension system for their car.

Now that the team had returned to the area with a prototype of such a car, they had insisted on testing it on the same roads. Unfortunately, the roads had been paved in the intervening years and now were quite smooth. Undaunted, the team headed into the most populous city in the United States to find the worst roads possible.

This was to be the final U.S. road test of the LS400 before production, and there was considerable disagreement between the American and Japanese team members on the fine tuning of the suspension. The Japanese were intent on tuning the car to have a soft American-car ride, while the Americans wanted to give it a more European feel. This debate continued as the team toured New York City, then headed south for Miami.

The LS400 was accompanied on the trip by a Mercedes and a BMW, which each engineer drove periodically for comparison purposes, and a van carrying technicians and spare parts. Every evening when the caravan stopped at an out-of-the-way motel, the better to avoid detection, the mechanics would climb under the LS400 at the back of the parking lot and install different calibration bushings, shocks, and stabilizer bars for the next day's testing.

The Americans finally won the day on the suspension by convincing the Japanese that most Lexus buyers would be coming from imported cars and that they would be used to that feel and want it. Although they didn't say it, the Americans also felt it was important to win this point because the automotive press was partial to European suspensions. The first press reviews of the car would set the tone for everything that followed, and they knew those notices would be very critical if the car had sloppy handling.

Chris Hostetter was pleased to win that battle and, with the trip a few days short of its conclusion, to have avoided any faux pas that would have revealed the identity of the car to outsiders. Then, at the end of a long day of driving, the caravan pulled into a North Carolina gas station for fuel. As Hostetter was filling the LS400, a wide-eyed man came over and asked who made the car Hostetter was driving.

"It's the new Mercedes," Hostetter said with a smile, only to be met by a blank stare. Hostetter then looked up from the gas pump to see his car being surrounded by a squad of Japanese engineers. Unnerved, Hostetter quickly began talking to the engineers in German, while preparing to make a hasty exit.

With the earliest phase of the marketing program under way, and the prototypes in final testing, everyone connected with Lexus was paying careful attention to the fortunes of Honda's new Acura line. Honda had done Toyota a favor by introducing its upscale cars in March of 1986. Acura's initial success demonstrated—up to a point—U.S. consumer acceptance of more expensive vehicles from an established Japanese manufacturer. What prevented Lexus officials from prematurely assuming their own success, however, were the notable differences between their new product line and Honda's.

There were two Acura models: the Integra, a small, twelve-thousand-dollar sporty car with a four-cylinder engine, and the Legend, a mid-sized, twenty-thousand-dollar low-level luxury car with a six-cylinder engine. Both of these vehicles had front-wheel drive, and they were logical moves upmarket from Honda's Accord.

By advancing only one step above its existing cars, Honda had expanded its product line to accommodate loyal Honda owners as their finances improved and they wanted to buy more expensive cars. This was confirmed when more than half the Acuras sold were the lower-priced Integra model, and the more expensive Legend didn't attract traditional luxury-car buyers.

The Lexus line would include the mid-sized ES250, which would compete with the Legend in the twenty-thousand-dollar price range, and the large LS400, which would be priced between the thirty-thousand-dollar American luxury cars and the forty-thousand-dollar-and-up European cars.

Lexus would be leapfrogging Honda, going two steps upmarket and into territory where many Toyota owners might not be able to follow. The company was projecting that its lower-priced ES250 would account for only 30 to 40 percent of its sales.

Given these discrepancies, Scott Gilbert, of the Lexus ad agency, wasn't certain what conclusions he could draw from Honda's success. But having learned how important image was in the luxury market from his research, Gilbert was almost certain Honda had made a mistake in deciding to link its name so closely to the Acura. Although Acura had its own sales channel, the car's parentage was prominently mentioned in its advertising. The car was marketed as "Acura, a new luxury line from the American Honda Company."

While Gilbert thought this coupling might have given some initial credibility to Acura, he also suspected Honda's advertising message would be interpreted as "If you want to buy a good Honda, buy an Acura." If that were true, Honda would be cannibalizing the reputation of its existing cars to prop up its new line.

When syndicated image studies—consumer research conducted by independent companies and sold to manufacturers—showed that, indeed, consumers had lowered their opinions of Honda's Accord in the wake of the Acura introduction, Gilbert decided he needed to do some additional research in a hurry. It was late spring of 1988, and he was scheduled to make a presentation on the Lexus advertising campaign in Toyota City in June.

Gilbert convened a series of focus groups in Los Angeles, Chicago, New York, and Dallas, including in them only people who had purchased a car comparable to the ES250 and the LS400 within the past two years. He wanted to find out if the Acura advertising, which had damaged the Accord, had actually benefited the Acura line. He also wanted to know what consumers thought about a similar Toyota-Lexus link. The results he got were unequivocal.

In city after city, when the focus-group members were asked "Is there currently a Japanese luxury vehicle?" their near-unanimous response was "no." When asked to list the names of luxury cars they knew of, few people mentioned Acura. Gilbert concluded that even though the Legend was only marginally a luxury car to begin with, its image may actually have been diminished by the Honda association.

When, after being told Toyota planned to introduce a luxury car, the consumers were asked if the new car should be associated with Toyota, the vast majority of the respondents felt it would be a mistake. Toyota's image, they said, was as a maker of economical, reliable cars, and that association would dilute the image of the luxury car.

What the consumers in the focus groups didn't say, but syndicated image studies did, was that Toyota's image was being further skewed by the voluntary restraint agreement between the U.S. and Japanese governments, which was regulating Toyota's U.S. exports. Toyota was restricted to selling 631,659 cars in the United States in 1986, but it could sell as many trucks as it wanted, since trucks had a 25-percent duty tacked onto them at the port. Toyota had sold 381,861 trucks in 1986, for a three-to-two car-truck product ratio.

But since trucks were the only line with the opportunity for growth, two-thirds of the company's advertising money was being spent promoting them. Even the company's top U.S. executives were driving trucks as their company cars. Cars may have accounted for 60 percent of sales, but the image that was being promoted was one that had haunted the company throughout its early history: Toyota for trucks.

As Scott Gilbert reviewed this situation, he realized there was really only one solution. He would have to go to Japan and tell the top management at Toyota that the company name would not be able to appear anywhere in the U.S. advertising campaign for the best car Toyota had ever built.

There was one factor, however, that made Gilbert's task less awkward. He would be traveling with Eiji Toyoda's son, Tetsuro. Tetsuro had been working in California as the coordinator between the Japanese and American staffs on the Lexus project for several years. Unlike his father, Tetsuro was a businessman rather than an engineer, and he appreciated how vital image was to the Lexus. Tetsuro had lobbied to have a tool kit included in the trunk of the car, even though few owners would use it, because of the positive impression it made. He had also been a strong advocate in the successful effort to have Nakamichi create its first original-equipment automobile sound system for the Lexus.

When Gilbert arrived in Japan, he got a concentrated exposure to the company's seriousness about the Lexus, which others on the project had been getting piecemeal over the years. Gilbert met with each of the twenty-four engineering groups involved in creating the car, and they had a common message for him. Whatever components they were building, they said, would be better than the current international benchmark.

As Gilbert listened to the engineers talking about building the world's fastest, quietest, and most powerful air-conditioner, or the world's most perfectly balanced drive shaft, he sensed both the technology and the level of commitment that was going into the car. This realization would eventually be expressed as the car's advertising slogan: "The relentless pursuit of perfection."

Gilbert made presentations on the advertising plans to a series of key managers and department heads, all of whom had read his advance report on what he would be saying. The report had explained in great detail his reasoning for not wanting to use the Toyota name in the advertising. Nonetheless, Gilbert's throat was dry when he and Tetsuro finally went in to meet with Eiji Toyoda and Kiichiro's son Shoichiro, who was now the president of the company.

Tetsuro took the lead, giving an overview of developments in the United States, and then adding that because it could hurt Lexus, and possibly the Toyota line as well, the two names wouldn't be used together in the advertising. In addition to being a safer approach, he said, there could be some long-term benefits. If Lexus was allowed to succeed on its own, it could enhance the image of Toyota in the coming years.

Gilbert stared intently as Eiji, who didn't keep him in suspense. Eiji said he understood the workings of the marketplace, and that the company always had to do what was in its best long-term interest. Eiji gave his blessing, and Gilbert breathed a sigh of relief.

With the Lexus introduction less than a year away, opening night jitters were starting to build among the U.S. staff as they began a final component of their program, the training of dealer personnel. Twelve hundred dealers had applied for the fewer than one hundred inaugural Lexus stores, and this flood of prospects allowed the company to be both selective and demanding.

The automobile business had changed radically since Toyota had first exported to the United States. There were fewer manufacturers then, with steady market growth, so companies could stake out a niche and do business. In the intervening years, the increased number of models available and slower economic growth had spawned fierce competition. Product quality and pricing gaps dwindled, and a certain familiarity crept into styling. With cars harder to distinguish from each other, many people in the automotive industry thought word of mouth about dealers had become the deciding factor in car sales.

This notion had fostered a burgeoning business in the polling of consumers' opinions about their cars and the dealers they bought them from. Toyota capitalized on that by looking at customer satisfaction scores first when examining Lexus applications. Every Lexus customer would be leaving another manufacturer, and the company would have to retain 70 percent of those owners to be successful. The company thought its dealers were the key to that.

Lexus couldn't ask its dealers to call on customers in their homes, as was the custom in Japan, but the company did want them to cultivate long-term relationships. To encourage such relationships, there would be no absentee ownership of dealerships unless the attending general manager held at least 25-percent equity in the operation. The dealers would also have to invest three to five million dollars in a facility that met exacting specifications and be solvent enough to survive three to five years without a profit.

To forge links between customers and the parent company, Lexus would install a satellite communications system between its dealers and corporate headquarters. Dealers would be able to obtain the service history of any car in an instant, while the company could monitor customer satisfaction and service problems in the field. When dealers' service records were entered into the system, the data would be studied in California, before being forwarded to Japan so engineers could heed how their cars were performing in the field.

As dealer personnel began arriving for the first of what would eventually be eight-six days of training days per dealership, they were told succinctly how Lexus expected its customers to be treated: as if they were guests in the private home of a dealer. People who could afford to spend thirty-five thousand dollars on an automobile had accomplished certain things in life, and that was to be reflected in their handling. The company would support the dealers with a comprehensive warranty, a roadside assistance plan, a toll-free customer line to company headquarters, and anything else it would take to keep owners happy.

Although customer service was to be emphasized, it wasn't going to be mentioned prominently in Lexus advertising. Consultants from enterprises such as the Ritz-Carlton hotels had warned the company it was one thing to provide excellent service and another to brag about it. Doing so, they said, would invite complaints. Consumers would take it as a challenge and be tempted to contrive grievances, just to demonstrate how discerning they were. In addition, when ads extolling the commitment of Lexus dealers were tested, they were judged to have little credibility.

Instead, Scott Gilbert was directing the second phase of the advertising campaign toward helping consumers understand the technology of the new car. He was trying to convince them Lexus had the right performance, safety, and convenience credentials to be a bona fide luxury car. This approach would also provide a secondary benefit. If the initial purchasers were asked why they had bought an unproven product, they would have the data at hand to defend their judgment.

This process had begun with long-lead press conferences for writers from automotive magazines, or "buff books." These writers had gotten their first look at the car in the fall of 1988. While they weren't permitted to drive the car then or publish pictures, they could look it over and also examine a special engine that was mounted on a display stand. When various buttons were pushed, sections of the engine would swing back to display the high-tech goodies that were hidden inside.

With production about to begin in Japan in May of 1989, a contingent of nine writers was flown to Germany for a daring acid test. They were provided with four LS400s, plus a Mercedes, a BMW, an Audi, and a Jaguar, and turned loose on the autobahn. They were given three days to do their comparative testing, and asked only to withhold their verdicts from print until the car was about to be introduced.

One immediate benefit Lexus derived from this work with the press was an insight gained from a press-conference demonstration. To document the extraordinary smoothness designed into the engine, the company secured a car with its wheels off the ground, placed a glass brimming with water on top of the engine, and then accelerated the engine to top speed. When the water didn't even ripple, and the glass failed to move, the normally cynical journalists broke into spontaneous applause.

Scott Gilbert recognized then that if he could show people the fine detailing that went into the car, they might feel okay about buying it. This would result in an ad in which the announcer explained how diligently Lexus had worked to perfect the car. With the accompaniment of corresponding sounds, he would talk about eliminating road, wind, and gear noise until all that was left was the beautiful sound of the stereo. And the water-glass demonstration had proven too successful not to repeat. It would be restaged on television with champagne glasses.

Even with all these efforts, the image issue still kept Lexus people awake at nights. An intense campaign was begun in the final months before introduction to expose the car and its name in the environs of luxury-car buyers. Lexus sponsored a two-thousand-person black-tie dinner for the opening of "Phantom of the Opera" in Los Angeles, as well as the U.S. Polo Association Open Championship. There were charity golf tournaments and sponsorships of operas, orchestras, and ballets.

Sometimes an LS400 would be present at the events, and other times there would be just a little glossy black gift bag with a small present inside. The company was careful to be subtle and tactful. The point was not to make an immediate sale. That would happen when the dealers opened in a few months. The objective was to enable people who didn't spend their weekends cruising car dealerships to feel it was appropriate for them to make that trip.

Car sales were in a slump all through the summer of 1989, and with the yen still trading at under 150 to the dollar, the LS400 was set to go on sale on September 1 with a base price of thirty-five thousand dollars. The base car was well equipped, but with a leather interior, premium sound system, and a few other goodies, it topped out at forty-three thousand dollars. Dave Illingworth, now general manager of Lexus, was worried about those numbers.

The mark had also been strong against the dollar, and the efficiency of European manufacturers hadn't improved, so the LS400 was ten thousand dollars to twenty-five thousand dollars under its competition. Nonetheless, the car market in the United States is notoriously fickle, and despite all the market research, no one could say with finality that Americans would pay that kind of money for a Japanese car. To keep from scaring anyone off, Illingworth ordered that dealers were not to have a single car in their inventories with a price over forty thousand dollars on introduction day.

Illingworth was frantic with last-minute tasks and trying not to think about reviews, but he knew the first notices about the car would be momentous. When they came in early August, they seemed divinely inspired. Virtually without exception, the automotive writers said the LS400 was faster, quieter, and more comfortable than the world's best—the significantly more expensive Mercedes-Benz and BMW. The LS400 was, they said, a truly remarkable car, and a tremendous value to boot. Illingworth dispatched an urgent message to his dealers: Forget September 1; start selling cars immediately.

The Lexus TV campaign broke on August 21 on Monday Night Football, supplemented by a print blitz in buff books, news weeklies, business and lifestyle magazines, and newspapers. The company could have saved money by advertising only in zoned editions of these publications that circulated in the well-defined neighborhoods where luxury-car buyers lived, but that was deemed shortsighted. Lexus never forgot its obligation to protect its first buyers from social ostracism. The advertising blanket ensured that when the East Coast sophisticate called his grandmother in the Midwest to brag about his great new car, she would be able to say, "Oh, yes. I just read about that."

Sales were brisk from the first day, but the dealers held to their company-extracted pledge not to add surcharges to the list price of the cars when stocks got low. The company had made it clear that nobody associated with Lexus was ever to lose sight of the long-term consequences of their actions.

The only question that remained was the identity of Lexus buyers. The luxury-car market wasn't huge, and the company had to win over Mercedes and BMW owners to create volume. The early research confirmed that was happening. A quarter of the initial purchasers of the LS400 were CEOs or presidents of companies, and the average purchaser's income was $225,000. When people who could have afforded more expensive cars bought the Lexus, the Lexus staff thought everything was going to be okay. When those people passed over the base models to place orders for the forty-three-thousand-dollar editions that had been withheld from production, they were positive.

The buyers said they were amazed the car could be simultaneously quiet and tremendously responsive. While driving at speed, you had to look at the tachometer to see if the engine was running. The European manufacturers castigated Lexus for this, when asked for their comments on the LS400. It was imperative, they said, for the driver to feel and hear the engine. That's what the engineers said, but a lot of customers had stopped listening to their dictates.

EPILOGUE

Richard Chitty's life had been comparatively tranquil during the Lexus launch. As the corporate manager of parts, service, and customer satisfaction, his job had mostly entailed spreading the Lexus creed: treat the customer right. Dealer personnel had been trained exhaustively, the parts bins in the service departments were full, and he had authorization to fly factory mechanics out to assist any dealer who couldn't remedy the isolated glitch that was bound to occur in a car or two. Chitty expected his worries to come further down the road, as cars piled up miles and components wore out.

The LS400 was the most thoroughly tested car Toyota had ever produced. Eiji Toyoda had spent six years making sure of that. No expense was spared as prototypes were shipped all over the globe during a 2.7-million-mile proving program. New production equipment was designed to meet rigorous standards in the factory, and extra quality-inspection steps were added to the assembly line. With this kind of backing, Richard Chitty thought he had a dream job. That changed when a customer relations worker came charging into his office in late November of 1989.

A call had just come in on the Lexus customer-service line from a dealer near San Diego. During a test drive of an LS400 on the San Diego Freeway, a customer had engaged the car's cruise control. When the driver hit the brakes as the car neared an exit ramp, the cruise control hadn't kicked off as it was designed to do. Instead, the engine kept running at highway speed until the dealer reached over and manually disengaged the system.

The first thing Richard Chitty thought about was the Audi. The Audi 5000-S had been the darling of the automotive world when the F-1 team was conducting focus groups in the United States in 1985.

Then, in February of 1986, the *New York Times* ran an article on unintended acceleration in automobiles. The article said that unintended acceleration, in which cars accelerate without drivers' consciously stepping on the gas, was a little understood phenomenon. It was often blamed for accidents, but no one had ever found mechanical defects in the cars in question. The article noted that the cars of most major manufacturers had been investigated for this complaint at one time or another, including Audi.

A Long Island woman who believed her Audi had been involved in two accidents because of this condition, read the article and began calling consumer groups to tell her story. Ultimately her complaint reached New York Attorney General Robert Abrams, who had received other such complaints about the Audi 5000-S. Within weeks, Abrams and other consumer advocates concluded the Audi was more vulnerable to this phenomenon than other cars, and they called for Audi to recall all the 5000-model cars it had sold over the previous decade.

In the following months, the Audi unintended-acceleration issue snowballed amid frequent news stories—and strenuous denials from Audi that there was anything wrong with its cars. In November, the TV program *60 Minutes* ran a report on Audi featuring the tragic story of an Ohio woman who had killed her six-year-old son when her Audi rammed the boy in their garage. The distraught woman said it was a case of unintended acceleration, and her claim was supported by an engineer who rigged an Audi to produce unintended acceleration on camera.

Audi of America vigorously defended its cars, insisting it was driver error—people pushing the gas pedal instead of the brake—that was causing these incidents, but that only seemed to make things worse. Many people judged Audi arrogant and insensitive in making their point, and that only seemed to cause consumer advocates to push the issue harder.

Audi finally agreed to recall 250,000 cars in January of 1987, but the matter had taken on a life of its own by then. The sales of all Audi models plummeted, as did the resale value of Audi cars already on the road. The company took a multitude of steps in the coming months—guaranteeing resale values, offering discounts of up to five thousand dollars on new cars, and running massive ad campaigns addressing the issue—but nothing could undo all the damage.

In June of 1988, Audi was fully exonerated in a civil case brought by the Ohio woman whose son had been killed, and by early 1989 the governments of the United States, Japan, and Canada had certified that it was driver error, not a defective car, that was the cause of unintended Audi acceleration. Articles were printed in respected publications calling the Audi affair a witch hunt, and the company was vindicated. But it was a Pyrrhic victory. Audi had been decimated in the United States. Its 1985 sales of 74,061 had fallen 69 percent, to 22,943, by 1988.

When Richard Chitty remembered what had happened to Audi, he concluded that the stuck cruise control in San Diego could put the entire Lexus division at risk, three months after it had launched its first car. Chitty sent men to San Diego to remove the cruise control system in question and express it to Japan, while others contacted dealers to ask if they had had any similar reports. There were no other instances of this problem, but people from headquarters were able to duplicate the failure in testing.

Chitty had five days to notify the National Highway Traffic Safety Administration of the problem and of the action the company planned to take. In that time, engineers in Japan would have to identify what had caused the component to fail, how many cars the component was installed on, and what was going to be done to fix it. Replacement parts would have to be produced immediately, service procedures written, and shipments arranged.

As this was unfolding, two other isolated incidents occurred. A car in Texas suffered a deformed bulb in the rear-center taillight, apparently from heat building up under the lens, and a clamp came loose on a wire from the alternator to the battery on another car, causing it to lose electrical power.

Eiji Toyoda was distressed when he heard these reports, but this was not the time to assess blame. He ordered that immediate action be taken. The engineers were not to waste time investigating which cars had defective components. All three parts were to be replaced on every car that had been produced. The campaign was to be carried out in record time, and the American office was to ensure that no customer suffered any inconvenience as a result of the recall.

The entire Lexus field staff gathered at their California headquarters on Friday, December 1, for an all-day training session. Each person was assigned four or five dealers to contact in person before the end of business on Monday. They were to tell the dealer what was going to happen, how company was going to handle it, and what they should do.

Richard Chitty reminded his staff that they had been preaching customer service to their dealers for a year, and that this was the acid test of the company's commitment. The dealers would have everything they needed—the parts and the instructions—before any cars arrived at their shops. Since 8,500 cars had been sold, all the parts couldn't be produced overnight, so there would be daily shipments from Japan, which would be allocated to coincide with each dealer's daily appointment schedule.

In return, the company wanted the dealers to be in personal contact with every one of their customers *before* the official recall letters arrived at their homes on Wednesday of the following week. The dealers would also be asked to go to extraordinary lengths to make the repair process painless for their customers.

At three o'clock on Friday afternoon, company officials notified the National Highway Traffic Safety Administration they were issuing a recall. Dealers began calling their customers on Monday, explaining what was about to happen, and asking them not to use the cruise control on their cars until after the repairs were completed. Loaner cars would be available to those who brought their cars in, and the dealers would make house calls when their customers couldn't deliver their cars. Cars that were brought in would be washed and filled with gas before they were returned. As this was unfolding, Dave Illingworth, the Lexus general manager, was composing a letter of apology that would be sent to each customer.

There were only eight people in the Lexus customer relations department at the time, and they cleared their schedules in anticipation of a flood of calls on their toll-free customer telephone lines as the recall campaign began. Three calls related to the campaign were received during the first week, with the total reaching twelve in the weeks to come. The company compiled a 95-percent completion rate on the campaign—against an industry average of 50 to 60 percent. The cars that weren't returned were in the hands of competing manufacturers for teardown or had been shipped out of the country.

Ironically, in the aftermath of the recall, Lexus set a new record for the smallest number of initial car defects in a syndicated consumer survey. Lexus owners reported an average of less than one defect per car. In 1990, its first full year, Lexus sold 63,534 cars in the United States,

112 fewer than BMW and 14,841 fewer than Mercedes. Almost half the trade-ins at Lexus dealers were European luxury cars. The Nissan Infiniti never proved to be a threat, reaching only half of Lexus's sales.

Eiji Toyoda had accomplished his greatest aspiration. He had taken Kiichiro's quest to the highest echelon. Toyota now produced cars that were recognized as being among the world's best. It was an accomplishment that called for celebration and reflection, but, at seventy-seven, Eiji had no time for that.

While Toyota had been absorbed in bringing the Lexus to America, the Japanese government had greatly reduced the tax on large cars in Japan. Lexus, with all its production committed to the United States, couldn't respond immediately. In that period of lapsed vigilance during 1990, BMW and Mercedes sold seventy thousand cars between them in Japan.

The Japanese were acquiring a taste for expensive Western cars, and Eiji would have to get his best product into the domestic market quickly to join the fray. The West was still changing Japan, 137 years after Commodore Perry's arrival.

But Eiji took great satisfaction in another change he had observed. For years, the slogan of Mercedes-Benz had been "The best or nothing." After the Lexus was introduced, the company revised its slogan to "The best for the customer." The West might still be changing Japan, but the descendants of a farming family from the village of Yamaguchi were also changing the West.

INDEX

256